Consent of the Damned

UNIVERSITY PRESS OF FLORIDA

Florida A&M University, Tallahassee
Florida Atlantic University, Boca Raton
Florida Gulf Coast University, Ft. Myers
Florida International University, Miami
Florida State University, Tallahassee
New College of Florida, Sarasota
University of Central Florida, Orlando
University of Florida, Gainesville
University of North Florida, Jacksonville
University of South Florida, Tampa
University of West Florida, Pensacola

Consent
of the
Damned

Ordinary Argentinians in the Dirty War

David M. K. Sheinin

University Press of Florida
Gainesville
Tallahassee
Tampa
Boca Raton
Pensacola
Orlando
Miami
Jacksonville
Ft. Myers
Sarasota

This book may be available in an electronic edition.

First cloth printing, 2012
First paperback printing, 2013

Library of Congress Cataloging-in-Publication Data
Sheinin, David.
Consent of the damned : ordinary Argentinians in the dirty war / David M. K. Sheinin.
p. cm.
Includes bibliographical references and index.
ISBN 978-0-8130-4239-8 (cloth: alk. paper)
ISBN 978-0-8130-4961-8 (pbk.)
    1. Argentina—Politics and government—20th century. 2. Political persecution—
Argentina—History—20th century. 3. National socialism—Moral and ethical aspects—
Argentina. 4. Political violence—Argentina—History—20th century. 5. Human rights—
Argentina—History—20th century. 6. Argentina—Military policy—20th century. I.
Title.
F2849.2.S49 2012
982.06—dc23   2012031671

University Press of Florida
15 Northwest 15th Street
Gainesville, FL 32611-2079
http://www.upf.com

For Mariana Laura Gomez
La que supo volar.

Contents

Acknowledgments

I am grateful to librarians and archivists at Memorial Library (University of Wisconsin), Robarts Library (University of Toronto), the Library of Congress (United States), the Library of Congress (Argentina), the National Archives and Records Administration (United States), the Library of the Museum of the City (Buenos Aires), the National Library (Buenos Aires), and facilities at the Ministries of Defense, Foreign Relations, and the Interior in Argentina. I thank the Social Sciences and Humanities Research Council of Canada, the Tinker Foundation, and Trent University as well as the History Department and Latin American, Caribbean, and Iberian Studies Program at the University of Wisconsin–Madison. Colleagues in the Tel Aviv University Latin America Seminar, the Truman Institute and the Liwerant Center (The Hebrew University), and the Toronto Latin American Research Group made extensive critical comments on versions of these chapters that improved the volume tremendously.

Raanan Rein and Jeff Lesser have set generous context to my work by scholarly example and *menschlichkeit*. I am a better historian for the adventures that Daniel de Anchorena and I have shared. Francisco A. Scarano, Thomas G. Paterson, Peter Blanchard, Lester D. Langley, and Carlos Alberto Mayo are my mentors past and present; without them I'd be floundering. Dale T. Graden is the historian whose lead I follow and Harry Shuber is the teacher I would like to be. I am thankful for the encouragement and high skill of Amy Gorelick, Kate Babbitt, and the expert team of professionals at the University Press of Florida. Sergio Victor Palma taught me most of what I know about race in Argentina (and tried to teach me a proper uppercut). I could not have written this book without the generous assistance and immeasurable friendship of Carmen Rebagliatti, Javier Lafont, and Min. Carlos Dellepiane. I thank Jorge Troisi Melean, Steve Stern, Florencia Mallon, Gillian McGillivray, Geneviève Dorais, Claudio Lafont, George MacDougall, Robert W. Wright, Timothy J. Stapleton, Ivana Elbl, Antonio Cazorla Sánchez, Ingrid Bolivar, Michael Donoghue, Gerardo Bompadre, Derek Lipman, Ricardo Cardona, Simon Piña, Nicolás Hidalgo, Eric Swanson, Leo Senkman, Mario Sznajder, and Kris Ruggiero. María Gomez, Santiago Vega, Alejandro Miranda, Ricardo Piña, Miriam Merlo, and Julian Gonzalez have made me part of their family. Rose Sheinin, Gabi Sheinin, Daniela Sheinin, Mica Sheinin, Jack Shuber, and Eleanor Shuber have kept me on in theirs. Mariana Laura Gomez is still teaching me how to fly.

Introduction

How Unpopular Was the Argentine Dictatorship?

Argentines have not yet begun to contemplate with rigor a set of questions that many around the globe have begun to debate openly and sometimes ferociously. Dictatorship implies violent control from above, but is there a popular component to authoritarian rule? If so, can that support or acceptance be measured?[1] As in France through much of the late twentieth century, in Argentina myths of a democracy-dictatorship binary persist. The belief that democracy is morally good, dictatorship is unabashedly evil, and there can be no middle ground precludes posing or resolving questions related to the possible gray zone of partial support for or partial acceptance of a dictatorship by the Argentine people or even nonconfrontational communication between Argentines and the dictatorship. It has set rigid terms for political discourse and memory making and has created a dominant ideology of the past that isolates those who do not share a common memory of the evils of the dictatorship by labeling them as careless or ignorant (or worse). For Argentine novelist Luisa Valenzuela, there are no ambiguities: There are those who support dictatorship and those who oppose it. There is "the razor's edge we are treading" and "the chasms yawning on either side." There is memory and there is "oblivion at all costs."[2]

While no poll results or other survey database show how Argentines dealt with the military government from 1976 to 1983,[3] a patchwork of evidence suggests that they reacted with the same range of responses as the French did to the Vichy government and the Germans to Nazi rule.[4] Argentines knew the March 1976 coup d'état was coming. Alarmed by economic turmoil and political unrest, many prominent Argentines urged the military to assume command of the government and applauded military rule when it arrived. On the eve of the coup, a giant of Argentine democracy, Radical Party leader Ricardo Balbín, urged the head of the armed forces, General Jorge Rafael Videla, to move quickly to end the chaos. Many believe that writer Jorge Luis Borges lost whatever opportunity he might have had to win the Nobel Prize for Literature when he stated publicly after the coup d'état that now "we are governed by gentlemen." Journalist Jacobo Timerman, who later became the most famous victim of dictatorship terror, also praised the new military regime in the aftermath of the coup.[5]

Argentine commentators have routinely found these responses and the positive reaction of the Catholic Church hierarchy in Argentina to military rule to be aberrant and unrepresentative of what Argentines believed. But were they? The military was adept at assuming multiple political identities and at times concealed its thuggish features. February 1977, for example, marked the hundredth anniversary of the birth of General Enrique Mosconi, the father of Yacimientos Petrolíferos Fiscales (the state oil company) and a venerated defender of state intervention in the economy. While the military government was in the process of dismantling what it could of Mosconi's legacy and the state's role in the economy, the generals recognized the positive popular perception of Mosconi. The dictatorship was front and center in celebrating the anniversary in a range of public ceremonies and in lauding the ongoing relevance of Mosconi's politics.[6]

There was no uniform reaction in support of or in opposition to a dictatorship with multiple public identities, just as there is no correct or incorrect memory of state terror. In post-1945 France, the ranks of the Resistance suddenly swelled as many "joined" after the fact. French President François Mitterand (1981–1995) famously drew on the fact that he had fought in the Resistance; he was more circumspect about the seeming contradiction of having also worked for the wartime Vichy regime. In the context of the strongly pro-democracy political and cultural climate that existed in Argentina after 1983, it is easy to understand why many Argentines who had not staked out a clearly anti-military position or who, like Mitterand, had adopted more than one political identity, either kept quiet or tweaked their dictatorship-era selves to deemphasize ties to state terror.

The questionable rigidity of the democracy-dictatorship binary is nowhere more evident than in the construction of a human rights edifice in Argentina. Before 1970, human rights meant little to most Argentines. Although the idea now unifies a variety of protections that are widely understood, at that time human rights was largely absent from public discourse beyond the world of international diplomacy and some narrow portions of the law. Until the emergence of Amnesty International as a powerful global voice in the aftermath of the 1973 coup d'état in Chile, what Argentines would come to understand as "human rights" existed as a disparate combination of ideas, politics, and law. There were legislative and constitutional guarantees against torture, kidnapping, illicit detention, and more in the context of authoritarian rule. But while those provisions emerged in a framework of state-sponsored violence, they came before the public knew about the mass killings that would mark state terror after March 1976 and they were not part of a conception of human rights that could tie Argentina to the nascent international human rights movement. Instead, human rights activists categorized Argentina with dictatorships around the world.

If Argentina's dictatorship of the late 1970s came to define the abuse of human rights, the persistence of the democracy-dictatorship binary as a conceptual given after the fall of military rule in 1983 has led to an unusual stiffness in that definition. Constituencies in many countries that emerged from dictatorships in the 1980s began with a dictatorship-influenced conception of human rights abuses but then evolved over time in their understanding of rights.[7] In Argentina, though, a dominant ideology of human rights problems that had been formed in the era of dictatorship remained entrenched with unusual force and in a way that continues to reference the military dictatorship of the late 1970s in the first instance. The administration of President Raúl Alfonsín came to power in late 1983 thanks, in large measure, to his record as an anti-dictatorship lawyer and a pro–human rights hero during the dark days of military rule. Alfonsín swept into power promising an end to human rights abuses. Very quickly, though, caught up in the realpolitik of late Cold War international relations and the strictures of economic instability in Argentina, the new democracy found itself limited in what it could achieve.

Through the end of his term in 1989, Alfonsín centered much of his foreign policy on nuclear arms reductions, the threat that Soviet and American nuclear one-upmanship posed to humanity, and the inherent dangers nuclear weapons posed to human rights. Two years after Alfonsín's term ended, though, Foreign Minister Guido di Tella introduced a cynicism about human rights that guided postdictatorship democracy in the 1980s and continued into the 1990s. Behind closed doors, he sneered at those who championed the issues that directed foreign relations connected to human rights. By the mid-1980s, the Soviet Union was buying more than 20 percent of Argentine exports, an equation that had come into force during military rule and that took precedence over both moralities and human rights in Argentine foreign policy making. Di Tella wrote of the absurd ease with which Argentina was able to participate in this market, noting that "selling cereals to Russia is like selling oranges to Paraguay."[8] "Thanks to Lenin," he continued, referring to Russia's weakened agricultural economy, "we'll be able to do it for a long time to come." Di Tella did not want anything to compromise that business advantage. "The more we ignore unpleasant aspects [of] Soviet politics the better," he wrote.[9] Little had changed from the late 1970s, when the Soviet Union and the Argentine military had each ignored the human rights violations of the other in their search for improved commercial ties.

This cynicism about human rights in postdictatorship Argentine government policy was the product of a society that could not put the legacy of dictatorship to rest. As late as 1999, the great anti-authoritarian rocker Charly García wanted to commemorate *los vuelos*, the infamous military flights that dropped drugged prisoners into the Río de la Plata, by having helicopters drop sacks that simulated human remains into the River Plate during a concert. However, under the full glare of the media, the nation's preeminent human rights organization, the Madres de Plaza de Mayo, made it clear to García that his performance art would be unseemly and unacceptable.[10] More than fifteen years after the fall of the military, human rights were still being framed through *los vuelos* and other dictatorship-era touchstones. At the same time, a majority of ongoing human rights violations against working people—like those of the infamously violent *bonaerense* (the Buenos Aires provincial police)—had little immediate bearing on the legacy of mass murder.[11] At the time, some wondered how it was possible that García, an iconic anti-dictatorship cultural figure, could be censored in the name of "protecting" an ambiguous sanctity related to memory and human rights.

This book sets out to explain the construction and persistence of an Argentine human rights regime after 1976 in three stages. First, human rights and the abuse of human rights in Argentina came to be understood after 1975 both there and around the world for reasons outlined in Amnesty International's growing campaign against the dictatorship. This campaign equated the dictatorship with ferocious state terror. But how Argentines came to understand the issue of human rights depended on a relationship between them and the dictatorship that was more complex than the dictatorship-democracy binary. Stated otherwise, "human rights" did not appear out of the blue in late-1970s Argentina. While many Argentines suffered directly from the consequences of military violence, some remember the military government as a necessary evil or as a savior. For example, in keeping with military narratives of the 1976 coup d'état as salvation from a violent political left, neighbors still visit a small memorial in Rosario to leave flowers in memory of nine police officers killed in September 1976 by leftist Montonero guerrillas outside the Rosario Central soccer stadium.[12]

Many Argentines experienced state terror indirectly, if at all. Boxer Sergio Victor Palma told me that his response to the 1976 coup d'état was "Hallelujah." At the time, Palma, who was 20, was making a living carting enormous rolls of cloth on his shoulders in the commercial El Once neighborhood of Buenos Aires. Like many working people, Palma hoped desperately that military rule would end his precarious financial situation and the Weimar Republic–like inflation that gripped Argentina. Other working Argentines, like boxing world champion Juan Martín "Látigo" Coggi, saw little change in their lives with the arrival of the dictatorship. Coggi's only contact with authoritarian rule was incidental and distant. One Friday night in 1976, for example, Coggi was fighting in the street in the working-class town of Brandsen for cash before an audience of about 300 when somebody shouted that a Ford Falcon was coming. Everyone scattered. When I asked him why, Coggi answered that "some assholes went by in a Ford Falcon." Everybody knew that Falcons were what military task force units drove. What happened after that? "Nothing," Coggi replied. "We came back and started the fight again."[13]

A second stage of the book explains the emergence of human rights as an idea or set of ideas stressing the role of the military itself in narrative building and myth making—the chilling human rights–based justification for state terror that quickly became fodder for human rights groups. As human rights organizations chronicled emerging data on abuses after March 1976, the military began a process of legitimizing its own human rights gray zone between dictatorship and democracy. It did so by appealing directly and indirectly to a public that, if not openly supportive of dictatorship, tended in its majority to be ambivalent in many regards and in some cases sympathetic to the military's objectives of modernization, the creation of wealth, and the suppression of a violent political left. The military also drew on a long-popular fascination with violence in Argentine society to legitimize and normalize state terror. Many have credited police and military officers in the mid-1970s, for example, with having first used the gruesomely anonymous term "disappeared"[14] for those whose family members suspected had been illicitly detained or killed by the military or by the paramilitary right. In fact, Argentines would have recognized that term from popular gossip magazines such as *Ahora* and other sources that date as far back as the 1950s. In 1962, after an anonymous assassin killed sixteen-year-old Norma Mirta Penjerek, police couched their initial response for a rapt public in language designed to raise doubts about whether a crime had even been committed. Before Penjerek's body was found one morning in Lavallol, the police offered the hypothesis that many adolescent women were "disappearing" in Buenos Aires to live "the easy life" (prostitution).[15]

Beginning in March 1976, the military structured an elaborate defense of its actions that presented a narrative of soldiers defending order and human rights in Argentina in the face of an onslaught by leftist terrorists (which the military called the "Dirty War"). As ludicrous as this rationale became in the face of the government's horrifying human rights record, the narrative initially resonated with many Argentines who were anxious for economic and political stability and hoped for a quick return to democracy. But Argentina was also able to convince a majority of its international trade and diplomatic partners of its pro–human rights narrative. At the United Nations and in other international venues and in bilateral relations, the Argentine military staved off the sort of critique related to human rights that had entered the public and private language of foreign policy makers in the United States, Canada, and western European countries. The dictatorship suffered only minimal damage economically and diplomatically from fallout related to human rights abuses. In fact, by many measures, including levels of commerce and membership on important international bodies, Argentina's foreign relations improved notably during the dictatorship.

The positive human rights legacy of the dictatorship in the arena of foreign relations leads to a third stage of analysis in this volume. In late 1983 and early 1984, there was no more important factor in the transition from dictatorship to democracy than human rights. Many Argentines looked to Raúl Alfonsín to guide the nation into a new era where dictatorship and state terror would be consigned to the past. The Alfonsín administration charted a public pro–human rights course that linked the president's Radical Party to a vision of an Argentina free of human rights abuses. At the same time, throughout the 1980s, the new democracy faced some of the same domestic and international economic pressures the dictatorship had confronted. Weakened by the shaky economy, the new government often quietly confirmed and even defended the military's international record on human rights. This suggests that in some regards, the transition from dictatorship to democracy in Argentina was not the firm break with the past that the Alfonsín administration tried to argue—and many Argentines believed—it was.

1

Dictatorship, Media, and Message

There is no denying that democratic rule in Argentina after 1983 marked a break with authoritarian rule. Just over half of the voters chose Raúl Alfonsín's Radical Civic Union party in an election that fielded over fifteen candidates. The election demonstrated that democratic institutions in Argentina had a strength that military rule could never muster. Even so, President Raúl Alfonsín found it difficult to shake or resolve the stain caused by the dictatorship's abuse of human rights. The military came to power because it made fanciful promises that Argentina would no longer be the underdeveloped, economically troubled nation of the past. Under military tutelage and a prompt return to democracy, it would become a country that participated fully in an international system that would increase material consumption in a capitalist economy. The "new" Argentina, the military said, would quickly produce victories over poverty, political instability, and economic uncertainty.[1]

The dictatorship offered a violent ideological and cultural break from what many officers viewed as perpetually debilitating elements of Argentine identity. The prime villain, so the military narrative went, was *peronismo*. During his first two terms as president (1946–1955), Juan Perón and his wife, Evita, had spearheaded dramatic social change by promoting the strength of trade unions, legislating benefits that included guaranteed paid vacations and rights for single mothers, and attacking some wealthy Argentines and their institutions, albeit in a haphazard way. At the same time, a Peronist cultural revolution took place that led to the advancement of working people of color from Argentina's interior provinces in a variety of ways and in many sectors of society.[2]

Argentines have most closely identified with two key issues vis-à-vis the dictatorship: the country's internal war on civilians and radical changes in economic policies that helped undermine *peronista* social, political, and economic legacies. Military leaders sought a return to what they imagined as a lost Argentine identity founded on social discipline, hard work, and sharp class and gender hierarchies that placed women, for example, in subservient, domestic roles. Their foil was Perón, whom they blamed for social turmoil and much of Argentina's ills. The dictatorship that came into power after March 1976 was not the first to react with alarm to Peronist Argentina. Indeed, military views were not an isolated response to social change. Journalist Graciela Mochkofsky has written about how the white middle class had rejected what Perón represented fourteen years before the 1976 coup d'état. For example, in 1962, Jacobo Timerman launched his news magazine *Primera Plana*, which attracted a broad readership that was eager for European- and American-style modernization and anxious to show themselves "finally free of Evita, blacks (*cabecitas negras*), and vulgar Peronism."[3] The military went much further: It associated Peronism with a decadent national identity. In their efforts to break down barriers to the free flow of capital and goods across the nation's borders, high-ranking officers reviled Peronist protectionist economic nationalism. They fought the trappings of the Peronist social welfare state and the power of organized labor. More chillingly, they associated myriad changes in the 1960s with Peronism, from the rise of the revolutionary left to avant-garde art and literature to the independence that birth control brought women to an ambiguously defined "moral decline."[4]

Print and other media sources reveal middle-class, urban sensibilities, prejudices, and ideals regarding *peronista* identities. They also provide direct and indirect representations of the military government's social, political, and cultural objectives. Under military rule, print media, television, and film helped set standards of cultural ideals about beauty, sport celebrity, and humor. The dominant historical memories in Argentina, which were reconstructed after 1983 and the return to democracy, emphasize a near-universal resistance to all that the military dictatorship represented, including human rights violations, conservative Catholicism, and the dominant ideology of rigid morality. In the imagination and memory of the middle class of the 1980s and 1990s, the history of the dictatorship has broken free of the "chronological boundaries of 1976–83." Instead, this group has constructed a history of that period that emphasizes the Argentine people's "unfinished projects and their permanent resistance [to oppression]."[5] It is true that many middle-class Argentines opposed the dictatorship and resisted oppression and that many more lamented the accompanying shift to the right politically and socially, the assault on *peronista* societal norms, and the grotesque state terror. At the same time, during the almost eight years of military rule, many middle-class Argentines subscribed to the politics and culture of the military's "new" Argentina.[6]

Some were collaborators. Many of those who cooperated with the regime were professionals who participated fully in the terror apparatus, including physicians, priests, military officers, and parents who welcomed stolen children into their homes as "adopted." Many more had qualms about the military's policies and actions, but for reasons that included exhaustion and fear that the political and economic turmoil that preceded the dictatorship would return, said nothing and even participated at one level or another in the dictatorship's projects of reform, modernization, and a return to order. On two unusual occasions in particular, the normally tacit support of urban middle-class Argentines for the military's goals regarding stability and progress exploded into open and enthusiastic public backing. The first was the Argentine victory at the 1978 FIFA World Cup, when thousands of Argentines poured into city streets to celebrate their nation's triumph at an athletic event the military had organized to showcase a "modern" Argentina. The second was the Malvinas War of 1982, when middle-class Argentines—many of whom deeply regretted their euphoric support for military rule in retrospect—strongly backed their government's attack on the British-held islands.[7]

Middle-class complacency about or support for the dictatorship was conditioned in part by the media and by military propaganda. Diana Taylor has argued that the military regime used images, performance, the manipulation of information, and strong communication skills to entrench, normalize, and conceal its rule of terror.[8] The military government and its media allies cast Argentine identity as intertwined with a national project to counter "foreign propaganda" and with the need for Argentines to stand together in opposition to criticism from overseas. This combative assertion of national identity was most famously expressed in the military's "Somos Derechos y Humanos" campaign, which urged Argentines to be proud of their national morality and challenged the accusations of Amnesty International and other foreign assertions that Argentina was violating human rights.

The government and its allies used dozens of media messages to project military rule as normal and progressive and to tie the objectives of the dictatorship to "Argentine" identities, moralities, and dreams. In 1977, for example, the Argentine Advertising Council (Consejo Publicitario Argentino) launched a series of advertisements that used the slogan "Me? I'm Argentine." One advertisement told Argentines not to sit on the sidelines politically and to support their government, claiming that "a negative attitude affects us all negatively."[9] Just as Argentine military leaders had in the past,[10] the 1970s military won control of some print and media using censorship, directives, and outright seizures. The navy seized the state-owned Channel 13 television station after the coup d'état. News broadcasts on this and other government stations became vehicles for propaganda from the dictatorship, relentlessly bombarding the nation with official positions that bore no reference to the rampant state-sponsored terror. Through late 1976, the press offered extensive coverage of the military's "good news" story of a supposed restoration of order and a purported end to political violence in the aftermath of the March coup d'état. In December, for example, the popular social magazine *Siete Dias* published a typical puff piece on Tucumán, the focus of the military's war on a very modest and highly exaggerated guerrilla presence through late 1976. In part as a challenge to some leftist media that through the mid-1970s had promoted violent revolution in Argentina,[11] the magazine cheerily reported that the province had finally been able to "recover its rhythm" thanks to the two-year military operation against the subversives.[12]

According to journalist Pablo Sirvén, while military units unleashed the greatest massacre in contemporary Argentina, "TV was filled with models wanting to be journalists; soccer became the number one news item; reports on travel and other frivolities effectively numbed the sensibilities of TV viewers; and a proliferation of light situation comedies ended any possibility of thoughtful programming that might otherwise have reflected even minimally on what was really happening."[13]

At the same time, there was strong opposition to military rule, as there had been in the past. Ten years earlier, at the time of the coup led by Juan Carlos Onganía in March 1966, the satirical magazine *Tía Vicenta* had had a circulation of 500,000. Onganía closed the magazine down quickly, concerned over its stinging indictment of leading political figures. The magazine *Humor*, which was founded in 1978, was less biting in the satirical barbs it took at leading military and political figures of the dictatorship of that decade. It was able to survive the *proceso* because it aimed only modest jabs at the generals. But the magazine's role was complex. While one might argue that *Humor* was a publication that criticized the generals, one might also reason that its modest condemnations helped lend legitimacy to the regime by suggesting that a certain freedom of the media existed and that the generals were not beyond rebuke.[14]

There was less complexity or subtlety in popular gossip magazines. *Para Tí*, *Gente*, *Siete Dias*, and *Radiolandia*, among others, lauded the military takeover and the values the generals espoused, including a traditional family structure, an erasure of *peronista* working-class politics, a restoration of order, and an idealization of foreign consumer cultures. Through sycophantic editorials and upbeat stories on the new regime, these and other publications affirmed military values and dismissed accusations of human rights violations. The variety of the stories they included and the values those stories represented also indirectly affirmed military values. These magazines were targeted at and represented the values of an urban middle class that had been made anxious over the preceding thirty years by the rise of *peronismo* and the growth of working-class strength—and by two decades of political violence and economic turmoil. These Argentines were not necessarily supporters of the dictatorship and were, for the most part, opposed to the gross human rights violations that the generals perpetrated. But the military's messages of the hope of rapid modernization appealed to them, as did the promise of prosperity and a rapid return to democracy—all values that were affirmed by the most widely read magazines of the day.[15]

Popular magazines advanced military cultural, political, and social agendas, including the campaign against so-called subversion and what the generals argued was the moral attack on Argentina by the revolutionary left. Agencies set in place to control the media, including the Dirección General de Publicaciones and the Secretaría de Información Pública, maintained lists of magazines, newspapers, and publishers that the dictatorship used or planned to use to advance its ideas and positions. Conspicuously absent from the military's lists of complicit media was the powerful Editorial Atlántida, which published some of the most important magazines of that and other eras—including *El Gráfico*, *Para Tí*, and *Gente*. This was not because Atlántida did not toe the military line; in fact, it was a stalwart supporter of military rule.[16]

Perhaps the closest collaboration between a publication and the dictatorship was that linking Atlantida's children's magazine *Billiken* and the commander in chief of the armed forces. In 1979, in recognition of the magazine's depiction of military ideals of family and morality, the government made the sixtieth anniversary of the publication an occasion to highlight its own public campaign for "The Child, the School, and the Armed Forces," in conjunction with a celebration of the 400th anniversary of the city of Buenos Aires. One of many areas where *Billiken* reinforced military ideals was with regard to the generals' obsession with political, cultural, and clinical "hygiene." *Billiken* authors wrote frequently about beautifully groomed adults and children, clean clothing, and vaccination. It used what journalist Paula Guitelman has called "war metaphors" in its rhetoric about the war on tooth decay, an "attack" on the common cold, and the "struggle" against rabies. *Billiken* also highlighted conservative ideas about race, the promotion of whiteness, and gender ideologies that established clear divisions between male and female roles in the family and in society in ways that were both subtle and overt.[17]

Gossip and entertainment magazines such as sports magazines appealed to middle-class readers in the decades leading up to and through the 1976 coup d'état. The former (such as *Gente* and *Siete Días*) targeted women readers with stories about Hollywood, ideals of beauty, and images of the good life. Sports magazines (such as *El Gráfico*, *Goles*, and *KO Mundial*) focused on the sons, brothers, and fathers of these women and featured messages that emphasized masculinity and Argentine national identities.[18]

Many in the media shifted right in their editorial policies after the military came to power in March 1976. Reflecting what might have ranged from middle-class relief over the coup d'état to complicity with the dictatorship's modernization ideals, media support for the dictatorship was explicit, even though references to military objectives were sometimes oblique and metaphoric. An article in *Siete Dias* in late 1976, for example, featured the deteriorating political situation in Rhodesia. It indirectly defended the *proceso* emphasis on order and political progress through eliminating dangerous subversion. "Rhodesia: la inocencia condenada a muerte" featured a full-page photograph of a white Rhodesian child holding an automatic rifle with the help of her father. The article explained Rhodesia's crisis in the same dramatic Cold War context that lay at the root of the military's explanation for its own brutal reaction to "communist" subversion. It implemented a South Asian metaphor that appealed to Argentine military leaders who blamed weak American politicians for the "loss" of Vietnam. Rhodesia, according to the article, was on the verge of becoming a "new Vietnam." While white leaders were working judiciously to create a multiracial government, "irresponsible" black subversives were trying to destabilize the nation and bring chaos.[19]

More important than the media's overt support for the regime was its indirect emphasis on the ideological priorities of the dictatorship. The media supported the military's radical redirection of the economy through breaking down economic barriers to foreign imports and investments with its emphasis on Argentina as technologically and economically modern. A December 1976 article in *Siete Dias* introduced Argentines to the new jumbo jet (Boeing 747) that the national airline, Aerolineas Argentinas, had purchased.[20] Magazines and newspapers were filled with advertisements for products from overseas that emphasized foreign, mostly American, ideals of youth, wealth, and beauty. A 1976 ad for Levi's jeans featured the word "Wanted!" and an American western theme.[21] When the media mentioned danger or violence, they did not identify the most significant threat of the period—the military's internal war. Magazines stressed instead the military's version of a subversive threat from leftists and more oblique or foreign sources of violence, such as the presence of *pirañas* in Argentina's rivers, the menace of the Son of Sam murders in New York City, and the racialized sexual predilections of Ugandan dictator Idi Amin.[22] A magazine review of the "best of" 1976 included the American television series *Kojak* (best drama series), Werner Herzog's *Aguirre: The Wrath of God* (best foreign film), and the author Saul Bellow (1976 winner of the Nobel Prize for Literature). But the media offered no hint that Argentina had descended into a period of extreme violence.[23]

The dramatic rise of comedians Alberto Olmedo and Jorge Porcel is perhaps the most prominent example of how popular culture reflected military ideologies. Even as the military imposed widespread censorship and took control of the bodies that regulated popular culture such as the Instituto Nacional de Cinematografía, the films of Porcel and Olmedo thrived. These films depended on a raw objectification of women. Actresses Susana Giménez and Moria Casán often played opposite Olmedo and Porcel in roles that portrayed them as highly sexualized and consumed with a lust for money. This humor, in films such as *Con mi mujer no puedo* (1977) and *Mi mujer no es mi Señora* (1978), reinforced the economic and financial views of the dictatorship, which exalted money as a mediator of human relations and sanctified the family by presenting "prohibited," alternative sexual possibilities only outside the context of marriage and family.[24] This genre of titillating comedy, which indirectly juxtaposed funny bad behavior with the correct and proper conduct approved of by the dictatorship, accounted for fully one-quarter of all films made during the *proceso*.

In keeping with the military's propaganda that the coup d'état had restored normalcy and put Argentina back on a path toward democracy, modernization, and progress, middle-class Argentines keenly followed the activities of movie stars and other celebrities who seemed oblivious to the crisis. A *Radiolandia 2000* report on beach life in Punta del Este, Uruguay, in the summer of 1978–1979 found "beautiful women, a European climate, and sophistication." Young people were listening to John Paul Young's "Love Is in the Air," the Rolling Stones' "Miss You," and Eric Clapton's "Cocaine." Susana Giménez was in Uruguay, as were Alberto Olmedo and tango musician Astor Piazzolla. Even when radio personality Magdalena Ruiz Guiñazú, a persecuted opponent of the dictatorship, was mentioned, there was no reference to politics. The story on her focused on the chalet she had just purchased in Punta del Este.[25] Under the dictatorship there was an intensified and voyeuristic celebration in the media of what the middle class viewed as the good life.[26]

In deemphasizing political conflict and in the campaign to suggest normalcy in all regards, the media joined military leaders in portraying Buenos Aires as contrasting starkly with the images Amnesty International and other foreign critics presented of a city rife with violence. There were remarkable and convoluted denials of torture, executions, and kidnappings. In 1979, for example, in an interview about problems the Argentine justice system faced, Federal Judge Evaristo Santa Maria managed to entirely ignore the violence facing the nation and the breakdown in justice. He spoke of the need for more judges, a larger budget for the nation's courts, and better salaries for those on the bench.[27] At the same time, the media presented an exaggerated nostalgia for Buenos Aires traditions and institutions that suggested peaceful continuity in everyday life. Admiral Emilio Massera, a member of the first *proceso junta*, a psychopath who personally oversaw torture sessions in clandestine detention centers and a well-known fan of tango music, spent many evenings listening to his favorite singer, Edmundo Rivera, at the city's most famous tango spot, El Viejo Almacen. In January 1979, *Radiolandia 2000* reinforced the military's idea of a city in peace. It featured a long article on a nostalgic tango culture that celebrated Massera's favorites—Rivero and El Viejo Almacen—while stressing the club's old San Telmo neighborhood and the need to preserve this important cultural institution.[28]

In solidarity with the generals, the media tended to quickly reject foreign and domestic critics of military rule, as it did in April 1980, when human rights lawyer and future president Raúl Alfonsín called for a return to democracy and free elections. In response, the popular magazine *Gente* reprinted a very brief foreign report on Alfonsín's remarks in conjunction with a much longer retort from right-wing journalist Renée Sallas, who parroted the military line that generals also wanted democracy, only without irresponsible haste that might return Argentina to the political chaos of the period before 1976.[29]

Many among Argentina's urban middle class ignored or were simply unaware of the violence the nation's military rulers had perpetrated during the previous dictatorship. Many Argentines filtered their concern about violence through apolitical representations of violence in popular culture. One long-standing concern of many Argentines was the "violence" associated with highway driving in Argentina. In the late 1970s, as it had for two decades, the Argentine media produced images and descriptions of horrific car crashes on the nation's highways. Words such as "suicide" and "killing" that were used to describe highway accidents expressed a fear of violence. And while fast drivers were described as emulators of Juan Manuel Fangio—the great 1950s Argentine Formula 1 driver—the ongoing linkages of highway disaster with violence helped position a new sports hero, Carlos Reutemann, as a graceful and exceptional new Argentine ideal.[30]

The emergence of Guillermo Vilas (tennis) and Carlos Reutemann (Formula 1 racing) as dictatorship-era sports heroes occurred in two important contexts. They contrasted sharply with national sports figures linked to *peronista* cultures that the military disparaged. Prominent among these were world champion boxers Victor Galíndez and Carlos Monzón. Perón had taken a personal interest in promoting boxing, a sport that sometimes rivaled the popularity of soccer in the 1970s. The most celebrated boxing champions often identified themselves as Peronist, but more important, they reflected Perón's narrative of working-class struggle in their hardscrabble climbs to the top. Like Monzón, the prototypical Argentine boxer was black, tough, from the interior of the country, and had overcome extreme poverty and other hardships. Like Galíndez, boxing heroes combined raw power with a good heart and the ability to triumph over sinister elite interests.[31]

Reutemann and Vilas also marked a middle-class celebration of leisure and celebrity in a manner that did not suggest a hint of crisis in Argentina. In one important regard, Argentina's most accomplished race car driver, Juan Manuel Fangio, who had emerged as a world champion and a sports hero during the dictatorship of the late 1950s, had played a role similar to those of Vilas and Reutemann in the 1970s.[32] Fangio's period of greatest popularity came after a coup d'état, just as Reutemann's rise to popularity did in 1976. Media portrayals of Reutemann dovetailed with the dictatorship's discourses on modernization, the dangers of *peronista* working-class ideals, and the need to achieve prosperity by bringing Argentine goals of success and modernization into line with those of wealthy nations.[33]

Vilas's rise was equally striking after the March 1976 coup d'état. Although his success was largely due to his ability and dedication, it was also tied to how the media shaped his image in the context of dictatorship-era ideologies and norms. Vilas had won a Masters tennis tournament in 1974 in Melbourne, Australia.[34] But 1977 marked his emergence as a superstar in his sport. His first moment of dramatic triumph came in his April 1977 victory over U.S. player Dick Stockton in a Davis Cup match played in Buenos Aires.[35] De facto president Jorge Rafael Videla, who was not a prominent sports fanatic, showed up at the match to introduce the players to an unprecedented crowd of 7,000. After the match he warmly saluted Vilas on his victory. Military order was tied to Vilas's triumph not only in Videla's presence at the match but also in the protection the police provided for the tennis star in the face of what *Siete Dias* called the crowd's "delirium." In media portrayals of the event, the public's nontraditional behavior at the tennis match reinforced notions of an Argentina at peace; fans were enjoying themselves in a relaxed manner. "We've never seen anything like it," gushed U.S. journalists Bud Collins and Walter Bingham in response to the outpouring of support for Vilas. Vilas and his Davis Cup teammates reflected another positive character trait for Argentines. As the Argentine media described the contest, while the U.S. players were individualistic to their self-detriment, the Argentines had worked as a team; Vilas would not discuss his own triumphs until the team had defeated the Americans for the number-one spot in the Americas.[36]

In June, Vilas won the French Open and subsequently reached the number-one ranking in the world (a position no other Argentine man has reclaimed to date). That came in his September victory at the U.S. Open in Forest Hills, New York, over the dynamic American Jimmy Connors—a victory made all the more compelling by a 6–0 win in the final set of the match. From the moment of this triumph, the Argentine media cast him as a hero.[37] Two hours after winning Forest Hills, Vilas led a group of friends to dinner at an Argentine restaurant in Queens, La Vuelta de Martín Fierro. Shortly before the meal ended hours later, Vilas took a microphone to thank his supporters, particularly those who had backed him as an also-ran. "Do you remember," he asked those present, as though it had been more than a few days before, "when they all said that I always reached the finals but never won? Well, they gave me a hard time. They said that all I was good for was coming in second, that I was like River Plate, or [Carlos] Reutemann . . . or like [perennial Radical Party presidential candidate Ricardo] Balbín."[38] Highly skilled, gritty, individualistic, with a strong drive to win, and sentimental to boot, Vilas was casting himself as the archetypical Argentine sports hero.

A year later, Reutemann was also lionized in the media when he erased his image as a perennial also-ran. Reutemann's equivalent of Vilas's Forest Hills victory came in April 1978 at the West Coast Grand Prix in Long Beach, California. In beating the world's best driver, Niki Lauda, Reutemann demonstrated the heroic traits of courage, tenacity, patience, and high intelligence.[39] For philosopher Jorge Luis García Venturini, Reutemann's victory marked a key triumph for the moral values linked to sport, qualities the military dictatorship emphasized. According to both García Venturini and the dictatorship, these qualities stood in contrast to world trends toward disorder, emotionalism, and sloth—enemies of Argentine progress and the hallmarks of the so-called subversives who had been defeated in 1976.[40]

As early as January 1977, at the Buenos Aires Grand Prix, the Argentine media tied Reutemann's rising star to the dictatorship. According to the rabidly pro-dictatorship *Gente*, the race, which was attended by 42,000 spectators, was characterized by Niki Lauda's inability to finish, Jody Scheckter's victory, and Reutemann's brilliance in placing third. The Argentine racer's success on Argentine soil illustrated how the military regime wished the nation to be seen—and how middle-class Argentines saw their country.[41] The media portrayed Reutemann's skills and image as evidence of Argentine normalcy not only because of the fantastic success of the race but also because of the joyous celebrations at the postrace parties, the beautiful women present at those parties, and the power of the cars. Such portrayals depended on an image of Argentina as a "democratic" nation that by all appearances functioned like France, Great Britain, Italy, or any other country where a Grand Prix race might take place. The military's only intrusion into the action was perfectly timed. It came as the winner reached the podium. In imagery similar to that surrounding Guillermo Vilas's 1977 Davis Cup victory in Buenos Aires, the media showed soldiers "protecting" the winner, Jody Scheckter, from the imaginary subversive enemies that the military insisted were a threat to Argentine society and democracy. The media image of Argentine soldiers suggested that they were protectors of democratic values and society, a far cry from their true roles as torturers and executioners of thousands of Argentine men, women, and children. Reutemann and Vilas became cultural vehicles through which the military could project propaganda that depicted social normalcy.

At times, the media represented Reutemann and Vilas as contrasting starkly with heroes in "baser," more working-class sports such as boxing or soccer.[42] Their dignity, exceptional intelligence, and high morality were not only traits the military claimed for itself and its model citizens, they also stood in contrast to the kind of conduct that had to be defeated and might well be present in other sports. For media talking head García Venturini, subversion and terrorism in Argentina and around the world was the consequence of the vague mix of factors—an increase in irrational thought, nihilism, spiritualism, witchcraft cults, and the celebration of working-class soccer stars. These were all elements that the military claimed constituted basic traits of those who opposed the dictatorship. Where Reutemann's Long Beach victory marked a genuine moral triumph for Argentina, the nation's sporting culture—which focused on soccer and, according to some proponents of military rule, manifested most dangerously in fanaticism—represented a dangerous challenge to the military's modernizing project.[43]

Like Reutemann, Vilas lent credibility to the dictatorship by accepting and reflecting the standards of normalcy the military imposed on a brutalized nation. Other celebrities participated in this tragic farce. In an absurd denial by omission of the dictatorship's violence against women, for example, esteemed authors Silvina Bullrich and Marta Lynch wrote indignant public letters to the Ayatollah Khomeini decrying the treatment of women under the Iranian revolution.[44] They said nothing of the incarceration and torture of pregnant women in their own country. When de facto president Jorge Rafael Videla invited Vilas to meet with him before he participated in the Forest Hills tournament, the tennis star was in awe. "I had never spoken with the president," gushed Vilas to *Siete Dias*. "You can imagine that when I received the call I was surprised, and very pleasantly. I'm sure he's busy with many things and, while I know that tennis is now important in Argentina, I never expected that he would be able to spend a full half hour with me. It was a great honor, particularly when he told me that he would like to have attended my matches at Forest Hills, but that previous obligations had made that impossible."[45] The imagery paired a respectful Vilas and a dutifully statesmanlike Videla.

The dictatorship regularly accused foreign enemies, including communists, Amnesty International activists, the Jimmy Carter administration, and French socialists of an assortment of international conspiracies against Argentines. When Vilas was not invited to the Masters tournament in 1978—the last in the annual Grand Prix series—many in the media saw yet another conspiracy against Argentina, this time orchestrated by ambiguously identified international tennis powers.[46] By 1980, Vilas was an important face of Argentina abroad and an idealized figure for Argentines. He exemplified the military's promise of an Argentina that was able to transcend the chaos of the recent past and the traditional *peronista* politics that grated against military sensibilities for a number of reasons, including the fact that they were an ongoing reminder that a majority of Argentines were poor and unjustly so. Vilas and Reutemann were idols for middle-class urban Argentines who sympathized with the military's distaste for *peronismo* and who joined the media in imagining both men as transcendent figures who represented Argentina's potential for greatness.

The sometimes-contradictory image of Vilas reflected the depth and complexity of middle-class fantasies of how the tennis star demonstrated the best of what was Argentine. Vilas was often portrayed in the media as accessible, a typical Argentine who enjoyed a good steak and a *mate* while on the road. Even his losses—which set him apart, in the end, from Björn Borg or Jimmy Connors, the best players in the world—were cast in a positive *arielista* light. Unlike the unemotional Swede Borg, Vilas made it abundantly clear that he did not wish to play like a "machine" in order to win at all costs.[47] His fans loved that "human" quality of their champion. At the same time, Vilas was regularly cast as one of the international smart set, one of the beautiful people. In April 1980, for example, he was photographed with Princess Grace of Monaco after he had played a match at the Monte Carlo Open. Here the tennis star was no simple, *mate*-swilling Argentine. He symbolized a fantasy of middle-class Argentines, promoted by the fiction that Argentina was a modern international nation and that ordinary Argentines could aspire to a glamorous high life. Two years later, Vilas was linked romantically to Princess Caroline of Monaco. This likely did more for his popular image in Argentina than any victory on the court.[48]

At times, the media parroted the dictatorship's disparagement of working-class culture. In 1979, when Vilas represented his country in a Davis Cup match in Buenos Aires against Chile, crowds shouted and applauded the errors of the Chilean players. At one point, rowdy fans went much further than they had at the 1977 Davis Cup matches. Some grabbed Vilas and began to rip his clothes off. The magazine *Gente* recoiled at what its editors regarded as an ugly intrusion into the game of tennis by a public far more violent than anything Argentines had seen the previous year at the World Cup of soccer. *Gente* explained the actions of the crowd as a pathology, tying the hooliganism not only to an assault on the dignity of an upper-class pastime but also to barbaric behavior conditioned by a 48 percent illiteracy rate in Argentina—a fact that conflicted with the military's portrayal of an ordered modern society where the rule of law should prevail. *Gente* ranted that the Davis Cup incident had undone all of the hard work undertaken at the time of the World Cup to improve Argentina's image abroad and was yet another illustration of "the person who harasses a woman alone on the street, who votes irresponsibly, who has no respect for a red light . . . all this, we repeat, is semi-illiteracy."[49] The military continued to criticize the conduct and morality of members of the public who did not exemplify its narrowly defined ideals. Some military leaders went so far as to claim that women who dressed in pants could reasonably be suspected of "subversive" activities.[50] Media vitriol toward working-class Argentines and what they had represented politically before 1976 coincided with the dictatorship's assault on *peronismo* and the ways it had promoted the interests of working Argentines. The military also constructed Vilas as a cultural figure who represented the opposite of Argentine working-class cultures and exemplified military ideals.

While there was very little reliable information on how these two athletes lived their lives outside the public eye, Reutemann's superstar image was even more morally impeccable than that of Vilas. In keeping with the military's promotion of traditional family values and gender roles—and its denigration of women who worked outside the home—Reutemann's public image was that of the ideal Argentine family man. He was married to a beautiful blond wife, Mimicha, and had two striking young children, Mariana and Cora Inés. Reutemann was portrayed as a dedicated father who struggled to balance the pressures of being Ferrari's top driver with the demands of fatherhood and the responsibilities of a good husband.[51] Even when the Reutemanns separated in 1979, a decision that was at odds with the military's dominant ideology of family above all else, the media skirted the issue to enhance the carefully constructed image of the moral family man. A *Gente* article cast Reutemann's separation in the context of the demands of his Formula 1 career, a framework in which the marriages of other drivers, including James Hunt, Clay Regazzoni, and Hans Stuck, had fallen apart because of work-related stress.[52]

The media images of Reutemann as white and good looking emphasized the nation's European heritage over a more ambiguous *criollo* mix of indigenous and European ancestries. Reutemann also embodied self-discipline; he neither smoked nor drank alcohol. There were no scandals or skeletons in his closet. He had only one goal, to become a champion Formula 1 driver. At the same time, the media focused on what seemed to be Reutemann's superhuman qualities. When asked in late 1977 whether he feared driving in the rain, Reutemann answered that he did not. "Fear is an essential human emotion," journalist Martín Calvo told Reutemann. "How is it possible you don't believe in fear, that you don't feel it?" "For you," Reutemann replied, "fear might well be an essential emotion. For me it would be absurd to admit to feeling fear." Reutemann went on to say that when he had an accident in a race in Sweden, there was no time to feel any emotion at all.[53]

Unlike Reutemann, Vilas was not a family man. Tongues wagged in the popular media when he vacationed with Princess Caroline of Monaco in Tahiti in 1982. The media had toned down Vilas's playboy image after the coup d'état. After March 1976, it was more inclined to cast Vilas in a way that matched military ideals of a quietly dignified sports hero. While it was clear to all that Vilas was not married, was something of a sex symbol nationally and internationally, and kept the company of different women, after the coup the details of his social life were rarely splashed across the pages of popular magazines or newspapers, as had been the case before 1976. In the sort of article it would simply not print after the coup, *Gente* ran a cover story a month before the military takeover on the love affair between Vilas and model Mirta Teresa Massa. Extensive details about the comings and goings of the lovebirds were interspersed with suggestive telephoto lens shots of the couple.[54] The coup brought a new morality to the print media and a reinvention of the Vilas image as more staid. There would be no more paparazzi-style photos of the tennis star.

In early 1978, the Argentine media celebrated Ferrari's decision to make Reutemann their number-one driver, which reinforced the links between Reutemann's looks, his success, and his class. *Radiolandia 2000* pointed out that Reutemann was positioned to take on his chief nemesis, Austrian driver Niki Lauda. The popular magazine published a photograph of Lauda that showed the burns he had over most of his face as a result of a car accident, an image that contrasted clearly with Reutemann's movie-star appearance.[55] Both Vilas and Reutemann socialized with international figures who afforded them prestige and cachet. Those connections paralleled the military government's aspirations to be accepted in the international community and the middle-class consumer culture of the dictatorship era that increasingly prized the trappings of what was perceived as the international good life.

In November 1978, *Gente* reported on the friendship between Reutemann and U.S. actor Paul Newman, a racing aficionado. Newman was scripted as the opposite of the squeaky-clean Reutemann. The American seemed more rough around the edges. The magazine reported that Newman had told Reutemann that he admired his rigor, his professionalism, and his abstinence from alcohol. According to the magazine, Newman respected the fact that Reutemann "[didn't] eat French fries, that [he did] a thousand laps of the track a day, and that [he] [came] out fresh as a daisy." The media's portrayal of Reutemann as a clean-living Argentine bon vivant was enhanced by Newman's star status and at the same time was contrasted with Newman's modest bad side. "Honestly," Newman confided to Reutemann, whom Argentines would never have confused with a gambler, "I'm a big poker player. One night I bet Lee Marvin that I could outplay him for the number of hours he'd like. He accepted and I ended up beating him over forty-five and a half hours."[56]

If Argentines of the 1970s understood the moral significance in the difference between how Newman and Reutemann lived their lives, by the early 1980s such lines were no longer as clearly drawn. The shine had begun to wear off the military-era culture of order, consumerism, and traditional morality. At the same time, the media attention to Vilas and Reutemann also began to shift. There was no precise end point to dictatorship cultures. Much of what the dictatorship created socially, institutionally, and culturally persisted long after the fall of the generals at the end of 1983. The humor of Olmedo and Porcel did not begin to wane until the late 1980s, for example.[57] But as early as 1981, the media began to portray the unease of the middle class with an increasing distaste for military moralities and an open dissatisfaction with the ongoing economic troubles in Argentina that the dictatorship had promised to resolve. For the first time since the coup d'état, the media began to reflect on political themes. In February 1981, five years after the famous actress Irma Roy had lost her television job for political reasons, *Radiolandia 2000* reported sympathetically on her inability to find work. One year later, the magazine *Revista 10* did a very similar exposé on the actor Mario Luciani, who had also been out of work since the coup d'état. Neither magazine would have contemplated even this indirect a criticism of the military regime three years earlier.

In the aftermath of the Malvinas War of 1982, the media illustrated growing middle-class hostility to the regime by no longer presenting the government in exclusively glowing terms and by offering critical views of the regime. In September 1982, the magazine *Gente* led with an exposé of high-level and massive government corruption in conjunction with the 1978 FIFA World Cup in Buenos Aires.[58] Moreover, after 1980, the luster of both Reutemann and Vilas began to fade as Argentines in many walks of life began to challenge the authority of the generals. Argentines explored new interests politically and culturally, presaging the explosive incursion of foreign information, ideas, and arts after 1983. While Reutemann and Formula 1 remained at the top of the Argentine racing world, for example, there was a dramatic increase in media attention to (and fan support for) competing events in motocross, Formula 2, Formula 3, and stock-car racing.[59]

A September 1981 article in *Radiolandia 2000* speculated without any real evidence that Reutemann might retire. In contrast to heroic portrayals in earlier articles, Reutemann was now presented as a driver who had reached his peak. Photographs showed him as stern and tired, without his trademark smile.[60] The images the media transmitted of both athletes and the ways the public perceived them changed in tandem with the growing doubts many Argentines began to have about the military regime. Just as intolerance for military rule and what it represented politically, culturally, and socially built slowly, there was no abrupt transformation in the public image of the two athletes. In 1979 and 1980, for example, Vilas's authority as both a tennis player and an Argentine of international stature allowed him to predict a remarkable 60 percent possibility of success for the Argentine Davis Cup team in the upcoming international competition that year. Vilas's reputation for success and professionalism lent credibility to his forecast for another national triumph. That authority no longer existed by the end of military rule four years later.[61]

In 1980, the media still portrayed Carlos Reutemann much as it did the nation itself under the dictatorship—as staid, solid, successful, and progressing professionally according to plan. If Reutemann had a "weakness," a feature that kept him second place on the international circuit, it was one that made him even more popular with the public. Argentine fans found endearing that Reutemann approached his sport with his "heart" rather than his head.[62] "Every day I'm more content," Reutemann told journalists in 1980. Like Vilas, he had matured as a champion in the public imagination and spoke with the confidence and generosity appropriate to his high status about his fellow race car drivers, his busy schedule, and the technology behind the latest Ford, Renault, and BMW racing cars on the circuit.[63]

In 1981, the media began to chip away at the images of the two athletes, much as it did at the images of the previously untouchable military rulers. While both men remained popular and continued to perform well on their respective international circuits, the media highlighted chinks in their armor as never before. For example, articles began to emphasize the eccentricities of Vilas's new coach and advisor Ion Tiriac; at the time, the Romanian helped cultivate an image of himself in the press as fiery and unpredictable. To Argentine fans of Vilas, he seemed a "Transylvanian" wild man with a hot temper.[64] As many middle-class Argentines became more worried about the contradictions between dictatorship politics and "progress," the sudden new media portrayal of Tiriac's "bad boy" image made Vilas a similarly contradictory figure. As he was portrayed in the Argentine press, Tiriac seemed the mirror image of both his dignified charge and the genteel ambiance of the tennis world.

Reutemann's success also came to be tempered by doubt and uncertainties. In May 1981, Reutemann won the Belgian Grand Prix. But the smiling, handsome face that had graced the pages of newspapers and magazines after past victories was gone. El Gráfico ran a photograph of Reutemann seated and slumped over. His face was covered by his hands alongside the caption, "I can't feel happy." The familiar victory narrative that stressed the courageous driver who raced at high speeds and outthought his opponents was now tempered by a darker Reutemann who was troubled by the violence of his sport—in this case the regularity of crashes on the course, but more pointedly his own responsibility for the death of a mechanic who had been crushed by Reutemann's car during a practice pit stop. "What will you do now?" asked Reutemann's friend Rafael Grajales after the race. "Nothing, nothing," answered a shaken Reutemann. "I'm going home; I want to relax and forget about all of this."[65] The race car driver still represented the dictatorship in the imagination of the Argentine middle class, only now that image was confused, even dark.

The fall of the dictatorship in 1983 coincided with the end of an era in Argentine sport and in how the government communicated through popular media. The shift was not immediate, but the media and the public no longer celebrated sporting heroes as they had in the past. In the 1980s and 1990s, sports notables did not dominate the covers of popular magazines in the way that Vilas and Reutemann had done. In part, this change can be tied to the globalization of sport. The 1980s, for example, marked the emergence of powerfully wealthy sport franchises, such as the Manchester United soccer team in England and fight promoter Don King's boxing superstars in the United States. Many of Argentina's best athletes went to work and live in Europe or the United States. They distanced themselves physically and culturally from Argentine fans and narratives that tied them to national identity.

The last of the media sports superstars, Diego Maradona, illustrated this transformation tragically in a popular narrative that saw his dramatic rise and a triumphant move to Europe, only to be followed by a career that ended with drug addiction, health problems, and disorientation. For many Argentines, these were all symptoms of the loss of an essentially Argentine identity, first through his move away from family and community to the big city and then through a second move to Europe. While the San Antonio Spurs' Manu Ginóbili, the highest-paid Argentine athlete in history, is a superstar in Argentina, his cultural importance is far less than was that of Maradona, Reutemann, or Vilas in their day. Ginóbili lives in Texas, and when he visits Argentina the stays are brief, often incognito, and replete with bodyguards that keep away countrymen who might do him harm. There are no photographs of the quiet Ginóbili celebrating a victory with friends in an Argentine restaurant in the United States or sipping on a *mate*.

The shift in the ties between sport and political culture can be linked to other changes in Argentina after the fall of dictatorial rule. As censorship and other limitations on the movement of information, ideals, music, and art fell away—a change impelled in part by technological advances that included the arrival of cable television in 1982—Argentines became more focused on international sport and less interested in national sports and sports heroes. As a result of these trends, popular Argentine sports figures do not embody the larger-than-life narratives the media created for Reutemann or Vilas. Today's sports figures are more glamorous because of their distance from Argentina, and in the popular imagination they are less imbued with Argentine identity traits—in short, they are less Argentine.

In an Argentina under democratic rule, there has been no successor to Reutemann, no driver who has raced for the top position in Formula 1 driving. While interest in the sport remained strong in the two decades that followed the dictatorship, fans tended to be of the generation of men who had followed Carlos Reutemann's rise and watched the sport on television in neighborhood bars on Sunday mornings. Gabriela Sabatini followed Vilas as a tennis icon in Argentina. But while she captured the attention of the media and the public for both her tennis prowess and her beauty, Sabatini was an unlikely sports hero and underlined the changes that had taken place in the intersections of Argentine sport and popular culture. She was a woman, an incongruity in a country that had never celebrated a woman's triumphs as equal to those of a Reutemann or a Vilas. This, as much as anything else, was an indication of the democratization of popular culture and rights after the end of the dictatorship.[66]

In addition, Sabatini shattered the family and social values of the military era (if there was anything left of them). A strong woman, she had a muscular physique and hit the ball with powerful baseline strokes, "like those of a man." Her image contrasted sharply with the women who had appeared in popular magazines at the height of Reutemann's and Vilas's popularity—Reutemann's wife and Vilas's romantic partners, among others. Unlike those women, Sabatini remained independent in all regards. The romantic and family narratives that had categorized and enhanced the reputations of Reutemann and Vilas—the family man and the playboy, respectively—had no relevance to Sabatini. That she could never be tied to a fiancé or husband and that her lesbian identity eventually crept out as an open secret—one that the media, respectfully and to their credit, never reported in a degrading manner—did not much matter to the public.[67]

The rise of Guillermo Vilas and Carlos Reutemann as sports heroes and media darlings illustrates how middle-class, urban Argentines bought into a dictatorship-era fantasy of normalcy, modernization, and an Argentina on track to "overcome" its chaotic past. It also exposes the falseness of a binary that posits only two dictatorship-era identities—either for or against the dictatorship. There were gray zones where Argentines might, for example, be appalled at state-sponsored terror but at the same time dream about the sort of life that Vilas led on the tennis tour in Monaco and might associate that sort of life with the military's promise of stability, order, and better earning power. Torture and killing did not always condition the views and actions of Argentines. Memories are sometimes contradictory. An Argentine who lived through the dictatorship told historian Emmanuel Kahan that a military curfew obliged him to be in his home by 10 p.m. every night. Some minutes later, in the same conversation, he happily reminisced about parties during the dictatorship that kept him out until the wee hours of the morning. When Kahan asked him about the contradiction of late-night parties and an official curfew, he was met with a blank stare.[68]

While many Argentines wish for and remember a dictatorship era in which every Argentine struggled against the military's violations of human rights and in which the military government found itself isolated in an international community of outraged nation-states, the reality is as foggy and complicated as the memory of Kahan's interview subject. Many fought the human rights abuses of the dictatorship, but many more reacted to news of a disappearance with the well-known dictum "*por algo será*" ("there must have been a good reason"). While a handful of countries held Argentina accountable for human rights abuses, many more discounted human rights as a problem in international relations.

2

"A Correct, Hermeneutic Reading"

Fantasies of a Constitutional Coup and the Promotion of Indigenous Rights

In his 1980 novel *Respiración artificial*, Argentine writer Ricardo Piglia imagined a protagonist who mysteriously disappears. Readers understand that this disappearance comes in the context of a dictatorship, though Piglia makes no mention of military rule. There is no discussion of a coup, of dictatorship, or of massive state-sponsored terror. We know of the context because Piglia gives us dates; the disappearance happens weeks after the March 1976 coup d'état. That's all we ever know for certain. Piglia's narrative becomes a horrific fantasy of what Argentina's military rulers concocted as an elaborate denial of state-sponsored terror and an equally convoluted defense of the dictatorship as in favor of human rights. Disappearance is mysterious. Piglia unmasks the military fantasy of Argentina as peaceful under dictatorship—like Sweden or the

Argentina of Carlos Reutemann—where the explanation for a "disappearance" might lead to all sorts of conclusions.[1]

In this vein, Piglia also probed how contortions of logic become normalcy. A central character in his novel finds that "*Mein Kampf* was a sort of perfect complement or apocryphal sequel to the *Discourse on Method*."[2] Piglia is taken with time as a continuum and how the present might alter the future. After a reading of Edgar Allan Poe's short stories published in the *Baltimore Sun*, an exiled Argentine in Piglia's novel imagines "some isolated, almost trivial, letters exchanged by future Argentines. Letters that seem to have gotten lost in time. Little by little the Hero begins to understand. He tries, using almost invisible signals, to decipher what is going to happen."[3] In the story, an imagined oddity becomes reality as present, past, and future become blurred.

After the coup d'état in March 1976, various branches of government immediately set about this exercise in blurring reality, anticipating the firestorm of international protest that would come. With neither irony nor humor, the dictatorship drew on an Argentine Supreme Court opinion that the coup had marked a "correct, hermeneutic reading"[4] of the 1853 Argentine Constitution and a body of law that had ensued. This pseudo-legal validation for the coup quickly became a nightmarish version of strict constitutional constructionism. The military advanced the tautology that there was no human rights problem because human rights were enshrined in the Constitution and in law. Thus, reports of torture, clandestine detention, and disappearances at the hands of the government were impossible because the law prohibited such actions. As blunt a tool as this argument was, Argentine leaders anticipated correctly that this very simple logic would be adopted by the same media sources that would lionize Guillermo Vilas and Carlos Reutemann and would appeal to their primary overseas audience—poor and Soviet-bloc nations with which Argentina hoped to maintain strong ties. With the exception of the United States, Canada, and Western Europe, national governments and business partners around the globe had little difficulty swallowing the fabrication and maintaining good relations with the dictatorship.[5]

In a telling irony, the junta experienced little pressure from Communist states on the issue of human rights. This was somewhat surprising, given the context of Cold War politics and the conviction of some Argentine military ideologues that the Soviets were behind Argentina's revolutionary left and the growing international "conspiracy" to invent a human rights problem there. Shortly after the coup, for example, the Cuban government secretly assured the Argentine military that although it had intervened in the domestic politics of some countries in the Americas, it had and would have nothing to do with Argentine insurgents. Cuban authorities understood that such links would jeopardize friendly relations with Argentina that Cuba valued (in the field of nuclear medicine, for example) and told the Argentines as much. While they opposed the Argentine coup d'état, they considered it a "necessary change" because "bandits" (meaning the previous Peronist government) had taken over in Argentina, inspiring chaos.[6]

There has been extensive discussion in the aftermath of the dictatorship about "how much" Argentines inside and outside of government knew about the rampant human rights abuses under state-sponsored terror between 1976 and the fall of military rule in late 1983. Some clearly knew a great deal while others knew relatively little. One employee of the National Atomic Energy Commission stated years later that during the dictatorship he had had no idea that the navy was operating the most notorious clandestine detention center in the nation—the Escuela Mecánica de la Armada (ESMA)—directly across the street from where he worked every day. At the same time, this opponent of the dictatorship did suspect (as did many of his colleagues) that the military was using a small apartment along another side of the commission's headquarters as a torture center. That apartment has never been identified as such by any of those searching for answers to state terror in the aftermath of the dictatorship. Others recall that the military regularly assassinated people in Parque Centenario, located in the geographical center of Buenos Aires, but again, there is no official record of those assassinations among the records of state terror painstakingly produced after the fall of military rule in 1983.[7]

What seems clear in many cases is that the notion explored in the Oscar-winning film *La historia oficial* (1985) of a strict binary separating those who "knew" from those who did not know about the atrocities is as fanciful as the notion that many Argentines did not share the military's fantasy of a modern, new Argentina. Inside and outside government, there was a range of awareness of the torture, kidnapping, and assassination of thousands. At an official level, the government was prepared to function on parallel tracks on the question of human rights. First, thousands were involved in the rampant human rights violations. For example, we know that those in charge of clandestine detention centers in Argentina made a point of forcing all military and police personnel present to participate in the violence perpetrated as a means of making everybody present complicit. The military argued that these violent measures were necessary to eliminate a threat to national security.

This chapter concerns a second tactic the military government used in its elaboration and exercise of human rights policy: The new regime immediately attempted to show that it was a defender of human rights. This involved demonstrating that Argentina continued to adhere to a set of constitutional norms and legal precedents that made human rights abuses anathema. This was an exercise in manipulation and obfuscation that used the legal system and national penitentiary system as a mask for clandestine detention, torture, and execution. Whether or not every national and provincial government official "knew" about what some (including the military itself) called the Dirty War, many believed in the new Argentine military rulers and thousands of sympathizers imagined, which included ideas about how to build a new society that would protect civil and human rights.

Many Argentines believed themselves to be part of a process in which a new Argentina would establish progressive norms about protecting human rights. This would lead to the end of political chaos, "primitive" living conditions that had been exacerbated by economic and political uncertainty over the previous half-century, and poverty. One key population the military was concerned with in the project of ordering Argentine life toward the modern was indigenous Argentines, the group that was perhaps farthest in social, economic, and cultural terms from the ideals imagined through Vilas and Reutemann. Not only did the military government see no contradiction between protecting the human rights of indigenous Argentines and a modernization policy that might draw them away from their traditional lifestyles, they saw each as a necessity for the advancement of the other. The fact that some Argentines could find a way to ignore state terror while at the same time identifying themselves as promoters of the human rights of indigenous Argentines as they freed them of their "primitive" past was one symptom of the violence of authoritarian rule after March 1976.[8]

The Argentine military's defense of its position on human rights began with the 1853 Constitution as a key protection of individual rights and liberties. The military claimed that it had come to power to defend these rights. Article 14 of the Constitution explicitly protected the right to work, to enter and leave the republic at will, to free speech without censorship, and to the free practice of religious faith. Constitutional provisions extended to both citizens and permanent residents. There was more. In 1948, Argentina had subscribed to the United Nations Declaration on the Rights of Man and signed the Inter-American Declaration on the Rights and Responsibilities of Man. Federal Decree 7672 (1963) made the United Nations Convention against Discrimination in Education (1960) law. Law 17.677 (1968) adopted the International Labour Organization's prohibition on discrimination in the workplace (1958). Law 21.338 (1976) distinguished between homicide and the more serious crime of racially or religiously motivated homicide. The military claimed for itself the practical legacy of this body of law; the dictatorship reasoned that because of these laws, Argentina could not be anything other than a defender of human rights.[9]

Coupled with the fantasy of strict legal constructionism was the idea that the new government was ushering in a national revival. In the military's recounting of the events that led to March 1976, the coup was a response to a grotesque vacuum in political power characterized by disorder, corruption, a murkily defined subversion, and economic crisis. The government that had taken the country to the verge of chaos had been incapacitated and paralyzed. The state, Argentina's generals maintained, had lost its ability to maintain order and internal security in the face of escalating and indiscriminate violence perpetrated by a range of leftist groups. The objectives of the mandate of the Proceso de Reorganización Nacional—the military's term for its governance project—were to reorganize the institutions of the nation, revive "essential values," and eradicate subversion.[10]

This narrative identified 1970 as a watershed. That year had marked the beginning of a "generalized and coordinated" aggression against national institutions in Argentina. The military blamed three revolutionary groups in particular for the descent into chaos—the Montoneros guerrillas, the Fuerzas Armadas Revolucionarias (FAR), and the Ejército Revolucionario del Pueblo (ERP). As they had at the time of the 1955 coup d'état a generation before, the armed forces blamed Peronists for disorder and violence because they identified key guerrilla groups with Peronism. But the military was also targeting the democratic Peronist government that had been elected in March 1973 after seven years of military rule.

Although the government of President Héctor Cámpora had no ties with the guerrilla left, Peronist or otherwise, military officers resented that Cámpora had freed political prisoners under a general amnesty law—or, according to the 1976 junta, had immediately freed terrorist delinquents. The military's justification for its own quasi-judicial use of violence depended on its vilification of democratically elected leaders as individuals who were unable to implement the rule of law.[11]

In a gruesome irony, the military narrative of societal breakdown before 1976 drew heavily on the notion of democratically elected government in Argentina as contradictory—as defending civil and human rights in principle but as unable to protect those rights because its institutions were too corrupt. The military identified the return of former president Juan Perón from exile and his September 1973 election to the presidency (which many considered to be a reopening of democracy in Argentina) as largely responsible for a deterioration in democratic rule. "Even though Perón reached government through elections," the Argentine Ministry of Foreign Relations maintained, "not only did terrorism not decline, but on the contrary, its exponents increased their activity."[12] Between March 1973 and October 1974, the military identified forty-four assassinations carried out by terrorists. Military apologists for the coup d'état claimed in retrospect that irresponsible democratic rule, not military intervention, had paved the way for the worst sorts of human rights violations in 1970s Argentina. The military argued that in a climate of terror that pervaded Argentine society during these months, terrorist kidnappings and other violence from the revolutionary left were largely unreported because of fear of reprisals.[13]

In this military narrative of the coup as national salvation, the period after 1974 was even more destructive. When Juan Perón died on 1 July 1974 and his wife—the vice-president—rose to the presidency, the result was disastrous. With jarring misogyny that saw a direct connection between women who sought independence from traditional domestic roles and moral breakdown, the dictatorship exaggerated the ineptitude and weakness of Isabel Perón as president.[14] The terrorists took advantage of her political weakness to sow still greater political chaos and to intensify their psychological and paramilitary actions, as the military referred to them. The notion of small left-wing guerrilla groups developing tactics of psychological warfare was a key justification for the coup and the human rights violations that followed. In the military's narrative of events, after

June 1974, the extraordinary and uncommon measures the military took (actions that reasonable observers might call human rights abuses) had to be assessed in the context of a war against an uncontrollable and ever-stronger guerrilla movement that risked creating a second Cuba in the hemisphere. This scenario dovetailed with the civilization-threatening scenario in Rhodesia in December 1976, as *Siete Dias* portrayed events there.

The use of the term "paramilitary" to characterize the revolutionary left was one of the earliest tactics of the military regime. The military's version of the chronology leading up to March 1976 ignored the role of right-wing organizations such as the violent paramilitary group Alianza Argentina Anticomunista in social and political breakdown and the military's own ties to such groups. Instead, military leaders explained that in light of escalating leftist violence, the 1976 coup and its vicious aftermath was a logical endpoint in a process that had begun with the decision of Isabel Perón's administration early in 1975 to order the armed forces into the field. The goal of the military's "Operación Independencia" had been to reestablish government authority in the southwest of Tucumán, where guerrillas controlled several enclaves. In its scenario of a descent into chaos, the military claimed that by mid-1975, order no longer existed in Argentina.[15]

The military's defense of the coup d'état and the dictatorship that followed relied on an exaggerated description of a terrorist menace that was increasing in strength. By 1975, assassinations by terrorists were at times selective, at times indiscriminate. In the military's version of the coup, by the time it assumed control of the government in March 1976, it was almost too late. According to the military's version of this history, the generals did not launch an internal war; instead, the country had already sunk into war. It is true that the Montoneros had explosives and weapons factories. They also had some $70 million obtained from unnamed foreign donors—which the military viewed as an international communist threat to Argentina—and from their criminal activities within the country. They had houses, land, all manner of vehicles, and a host of shell companies they had set up to conceal their activities. Under these circumstances, "the armed forces were forced to step up their war on armed subversion to eliminate terrorism and to guarantee public order."[16]

The military reasoned that foreigners were simply unable to understand that the nation's military rulers were defenders, not violators, of human rights. Democracy had failed the nation. The terrorists who had been prosecuted and imprisoned before 1976 had not been reformed by the penal system. Freed by Cámpora and by Juan Perón in a "demagogic amnesty," many had redoubled their subversive activities in an attempt to undermine national institutions and take control of the country. In light of this new generalized aggression, "Argentine society was forced to defend itself using the force necessary to repel" the menace.[17]

For the military, the protection of human rights could only be accomplished by the state when what officers called "mutual respect" existed among individuals, a condition that had been destroyed by the proliferation of terrorism. Moreover, the protection of human rights was predicated on a state's ability, "based on its historic destiny," to overcome ambiguously defined political crises whose resolution could only be achieved with a prolonged period of military government (whose proposed length was never clear). For Argentina, the rise of terrorism was an example of such a crisis. The military coup d'état, then, was a defense of human rights.[18]

While military authorities insisted that a terrorist menace remained strong, they recognized all the same that there had been a weakening of terrorist activity after the coup. In fact, media images of protected tennis stars and race car drivers proved the military's efficacy in ending the subversive menace. Part of that triumph, they claimed, was the flight of terrorist leaders and other leftists from the country. That flight narrative allowed the military to represent the subversive danger as alive and well outside the country. The military claimed that such exiles were supporting the subversives who remained inside Argentina. It also provided military and police with an oft-used excuse for "disappearances": Authorities frequently suggested that disappeared people might well have left the country along with other subversives.[19]

The Argentine government correctly anticipated foreign criticism for human rights abuses, and that condemnation came quickly. Argentina came to international attention as never before, and the dictatorship became the focus of angry opposition around the world. In many nations, refugees from Argentina, Chile, and other countries joined forces with a range of grassroots left and center-left political groups, governments, and international human rights organizations in a growing condemnation of the dictatorship. The left-wing guerrilla movements, some of which had been decimated by the military in the mid-1970s, mounted campaigns against the Argentine military around the world. In April 1978 in London, the Montoneros released a statement in English calling for the defeat of the dictatorship.[20] Popular Latin American folk singers reached a large audience beyond Spanish-speaking communities for the first time as they appeared in support of the victims of Argentine state terror. At one of dozens of such events throughout North America and Europe, Uruguayan artist Daniel Viglietti sang at the Columbia University Teachers College Auditorium on 26 March 1978 at an event sponsored by the Columbia University Committee for Human Rights in Chile. One day earlier, Roy Brown (Puerto Rico) and Martín Ruiz (Argentina) had sung in a "tribute to the Argentine resistance" at William O'Shea Junior High School in New York.[21]

On 24 March 1978, a group from Boston joined a protest at the Argentine consulate in New York to mark the two-year anniversary of the 1976 coup d'état. Sponsors of the Boston group included the Chilean Refugee Committee, the Argentine Coalition of Boston, the Puerto Rican Solidarity Committee, and the Boston Committee to End Sterilization Abuse. Organizers cited the restoration of human and civil rights in Argentina as their key objectives. The groups criticized the "the systematic violation" by the Argentine military "of all internationally recognized human rights."[22]

When the dictatorship determined to use the FIFA World Cup, which was scheduled for Argentina in 1978, as a showcase for the nation's modernity and efficiency, dozens of organizations around the world warned people of the ruse. On 1 March 1978, the British Broadcasting Corporation television program *Tonight* alerted viewers to the discomfort of many Argentines about the upcoming World Cup and their sense that the championship would serve as a tool to conceal the nation's human rights record.[23] The Argentine Support Movement in London denounced the disappearances and the millions spent on the World Cup, demanded the release of all political prisoners, and urged Britons to contact their members of Parliament in support of commercial sanctions against Argentina for human rights violations.[24]

The most effective protests came from Amnesty International, which made its name as the leading international human rights organization largely through its unrelenting criticisms of the Argentine and Chilean dictatorships in the 1970s. In a 1978 pamphlet, Amnesty International USA asked, "If you lived in Argentina, would you like to be a lawyer?"

The question was answered through the case of Mireya Rojo, legal advisor to the Metalworkers Union in Villa Constitución. Three years after being detained in August 1975, Rojo weighed only eighty pounds, had tuberculosis, and had yet to be tried on any charges. The same question was asked and answered for a dozen professions, including priest, journalist, and physician. The impact outside Argentina was powerful and without precedent. Amnesty personalized and humanized Argentine human rights abuses for middle-class North Americans and Europeans by presenting the cases of normal professionals with active family lives.[25] Amnesty's commentary was generally more lucid and better researched than those of other human rights groups. Though incomplete, its list of secret prison camps in Argentina, for example, was accurate. More important, despite Argentine military denials, Amnesty insisted that in 1978, there had been no decrease in the level of human rights abuses, torture, and assassinations in Argentina.

Consistently, the Argentine military's response to these mounting protests was a combination of fear, frenzy, and paranoia and a conviction that the dictatorship would be able to counter the attacks effectively. Diplomats, officers, and bureaucrats did everything they could to characterize protests against human rights violations as part of an international communist conspiracy tied to an ill-defined terrorist threat in Argentina. For the military, any criticism of human rights violations in Argentina was "Marxist" inspired. For example, according to the military, such sources of supposed subversion in Belgium included the Brussels daily *Le Soir*, a host of sports magazines and television programs, and even children's publications. In 1978, the Argentine ambassador in Belgium, Carlos A. Delia, who had instructions from the Ministry of Foreign Relations to monitor and to counter criticisms of the Argentine government's violations of human rights, described a Brussels newspaper as under the sway of international Marxist propaganda: "With growing force, the Marxist anti-Argentine propaganda has made of Brussels one of [international communism's] leading bastions."[26]

Like Argentine diplomats in dozens of countries, Delia blamed "anti-Argentine" propaganda in the media for a daily onslaught of letters, phone calls, and telegrams sent to the embassy to demand the liberty of political prisoners. Delia highlighted the impact that the trickster, leftist guerrilla, and self-described Central Intelligence Agency operative Rodolfo Galimberti had made in the Belgian media.[27] Delia's reports also reflected the military's ideology about the left. There was no political nuance. In describing mounting opposition to the dictatorship within the European Parliament, Delia divided the European polity in two—the left (socialists, some Christian Democrats, and communists), which opposed the Argentine military, and the "moderates" (liberals, Gaullists, conservatives, and some Christian Democrats). Moreover, he equated the diatribes against Argentina in the European Parliament with that body's mandate to save the continent from its "decadence"—its slide from civilization toward communist barbarism. One of the actions Delia took to counter the "Marxist" attacks was to organize a group of what he described as mostly young, "independent journalists," who, he argued implausibly, appreciated the Argentine government's defense of western civilization and understood the danger of a communist menace.[28]

The mandate of Argentine diplomats to gather information about and to counter enemies of the dictatorship was only one part of the Argentine counterattack. A handful of ministries and agencies of the government set about to undermine the integrity of members of the international media who criticized the regime. In May 1978, Argentina's secret police, the Secretaria de Inteligencia de Estado (SIDE), reported on the purported links between the Inter Press Service (IPS), based in Rome, and the Montoneros. Among the (unproven) clues to the IPS's "subversive" tendencies was the funding it had supposedly received from Chile's Christian Democrat president, Eduardo Frei, in 1970; the fact that it had employed Argentine leftist journalists, including Juan Gelman, José María Pasquini Durán, and Juan Manuel Francia; and its purported ties to rebel groups in Mozambique. SIDE's denunciation of IPS journalists was blatantly anti-Semitic. The IPS's correspondent in Geneva, Isabelle Vichniac, came under suspicion because "her husband was one of the most conspicuous directors of Jewish Zionism in Geneva: he's considered the director of the Zionist offensive in the region." Here and elsewhere, the military used the term "Zionism" to denote a so-called Jewish attack on Argentine anti-Semitism. A number of journalists were labeled as dangerous simply because they had worked for Jacobo Timerman's *Opinión* newspaper.[29]

The military denounced as false Amnesty International's accusations that there were some 6,000 political prisoners in Argentina. It countered the claims of the Association of Exiled Argentine Lawyers (France) that the coup was unconstitutional. It reviled the statement by the International

Commission of Jurists for Human Rights that there were thousands of detainees in Argentina. Insisting that its actions were justified by what it called the exceptional violence that had gripped the nation because terrorist attacks had become part of everyday life, the military cited Articles 14 through 18 of the 1853 Constitution, which protected civil rights. It also pointed to constitutional provisions for restricting those same rights in the event of "internal upheaval." According to Article 23, a state of siege could be declared in the event of internal upheaval or a foreign attack that could endanger the functioning of the Constitution.[30] The military government reasoned that Article 67, paragraph 26, of the Constitution established the right and responsibility of Congress to declare a state of siege, while Article 86, paragraph 19, authorized the president to exercise exceptional powers conferred by Article 23. This became the central argument for the March 1976 coup d'état. Military authorities reasoned that the coup had to be considered a constitutionally mandated response to internal disorder. By this twisted logic, the coup was not a capricious assertion of military power.

Another basis for military authority could be found in the history of the state of siege in Argentina—thirty-two instances since 1862, including the most recent case (6 November 1974) by the government that preceded the coup and was in place when the current dictatorship took over. That the nation was being governed by constitutional terms of a state of siege before, during, and after the 1976 coup (as the military claimed) lent further credence to the legitimacy of the coup. The government argued that this application of the Constitution in defense of society was a response to an unprecedented emergency, even though individual rights were violated. This assertion depended on the military's case that the terrorist threat was tied to an international communist conspiracy: "For more than a century the country had never found itself involved in an international conflagration; as a consequence, it had never suffered a foreign attack or internal chaos equivalent to the current threat from terrorist subversion."[31] Citing the Argentine Supreme Court's opinion that the coup was a "correct, hermeneutic" reading of the Constitution, the military also referred to international legal provisions that allowed for the suspension of individual guarantees in situations of extreme danger for the nation. These include Article 27 of the American Convention on Human Rights of the Inter-American Commission on Human Rights,

Article 15 of the European Convention for the Protection of Human Rights and Fundamental Freedoms, and Article 14 of the UN's International Covenant on Civil and Political Rights.

The foundational document for the dictatorship was the military's declaration of a "Process of National Reorganization" on 24 March 1976. The military maintained that this declaration defended human and civil rights and set limits on the authority of the new government that kept the nation in strict conformity with constitutional and international law. The preamble to the declaration reaffirmed Argentina's commitment to constitutional guarantees of civil rights and explicitly referred to Argentina's status as a refuge for the oppressed, a nation that welcomed "all men who wish to inhabit Argentine soil."

At the same time, there was a profound contradiction in military reasoning. The dictatorship asserted, for example, that in defense of civil rights, the power to arrest or transfer people under the state of siege was the exclusive prerogative of the president of the nation. That authority could not be delegated elsewhere. Moreover, the state of siege did not relieve the judiciary from exercising "a reasonable control of arrests," by which judges could assess arrests in relation to the extent of the crisis and constitutional defenses, among other factors. Yet from the beginning of the dictatorship until its end, military authorities gave no diplomatic, judicial, or political credence to the claim that the dictatorship had created two parallel systems of detention and punishment. Military government statements on incarceration related exclusively to formal processes of arrest and detention and ignored or denied the existence of an extralegal process of detentions, disappearances, executions, and torture. Thus, the military refused to acknowledge the bulk of human rights violations that took place between 1976 and 1983.[32]

The military's insistence that there were no disappearances under military rule—or that they could be explained away simply and with no reference to state terror—led to absurd justifications and legalistic wrangling with foreign critics. In response to Amnesty International and others who attacked the absence of habeas corpus provisions for illegal detentions, the Argentine government recited a set of legal norms protecting such rights, including Article 18 of the Constitution, that were not applied in practice. Argentine authorities also suggested that the government was charting new ground in the protection of human rights. Referring to prisoners arrested at the discretion of executive authority, for example, the government noted that Law 21.650 (1977) offered those who were detained a new option—the choice to go into exile. By the terms of this legislation, the president could deny a request to be allowed to go into exile only when the detained party might pose a danger to the peace and security of the nation. Moreover, if a request for exile was denied, the arrested party might appeal the decision six months later. This suggestion of order and liberal judicial thinking ignored entirely that the vast majority of those who were detained had no access to the legal system and thus no ability to appeal anything.[33]

Military authorities kept extensive data on those who were under detention and used those numbers to refute accusations of widespread disappearances and executions. By mid-1976, 8,575 people had been detained after 6 November 1974. The military claimed in 1979 that 5,729 had been released from captivity, 245 were under supervised release, 10 were under house arrest, 819 were (mysteriously) exercising alternatives to incarceration by the terms of Article 23 of the Constitution and Laws 21.449 and 21.650, and 222 had been expelled from the country. At the end of 1979, this ostensibly left only 1,550 political prisoners. This account indicated that more prisoners had been released than the number that was currently detained, and it ignored altogether executions and disappearances.[34]

Military authorities supported their defense-of-regime argument by pointing to how they had solved the problem of the breakdown of order promoted by the proliferation of terrorist organizations after 1970. These organizations included the Junta de Coordinación Revolucionaria, the Frente Nacional de Liberación, the Tendencia Revolucionaria Peronista, Juventud Guevarista, the Movimiento Peronista Auténtico, and the Partido Obrero Trotskista. The military argued that the country had been in a state of virtual civil war for years prior to the 1976 coup and that the new regime had restored peace to Argentina and was guaranteeing freedoms that had been nonexistent before the coup. People traveled freely to and from all parts of the country, authorities claimed, noting that in 1979 alone, two million people had traveled across Argentine borders. Authorities boasted that since the coup, Argentina had hosted hundreds of international congresses, meetings, and seminars and other gatherings. The military singled out two triumphs in particular: the FIFA World Cup and the XII International Cancer Congress, both of which were held in Buenos Aires in 1978. According to the military, in both cases and in spite of efforts by Argentine "terrorists," these events were great successes that were marked by the enthusiastic support of participants, journalists, foreign visitors, and above all, the Argentine people.[35]

While authorities sometimes determined suspects for detention and disappearance through identifying books in their private libraries, the government countered accusations of censorship by turning to Article 14 of the Constitution, which ostensibly protected freedom of the press. However, Comunicado 19 from the governing Junta de Comandantes made it a crime to promote terror, and the junta saw no contradiction between the sweeping powers of the communiqué to limit free speech and the constitutional right to freedom of the press. Ostensibly, the communiqué was meant, like so many of the military government's positions, to counter subversion and terror while supposedly promoting civil rights.

When Amnesty International and other groups condemned the Argentine government for detaining lawyers as alleged terrorists, military leaders responded with two strategies that typified their moral and legal self-justification. First, they framed the problem as part of a formal judicial process, as though there were no disappearances or illegal detention centers. Second, they simply denied the accusations and discredited the accusers and the evidence they presented. The military characterized Amnesty International as both ignorant and dangerous because its denunciations deceived readers "through the use of emotional language directed at winning converts to a 'noble cause.'"[36]

The military lied brazenly in its claim that the national judiciary was strong and independent—much more independent, in fact, than it had been before the coup. The government made its case by referring to constitutional protections of an independent judiciary and through the example of the Jacobo Timerman case. When Timerman emerged as the most famous example of how human rights were being denied in Argentina, the government position was that Timerman had been reasonably detained and that his case showed that judicial normalcy and fairness reigned—precisely the opposite of what the international community argued.

Timerman, the director of the newspaper *La Opinión*, was arrested and brought before the Second War Council (a military tribunal) for his ostensible links to a "financial group associated with terrorist subversion." The council absolved Timerman of that crime on 13 October 1977.

The military pointed to his continued detention as part of a fair judicial system even as the international community vehemently protested his detention as a human rights violation. Article 23 of the Constitution, which provided for a range of measures that could be put into place during the state of siege, supposedly was the basis for Timerman's ongoing incarceration. The military argued that the length of his imprisonment corresponded exactly to the time it took the judicial system to consider, with reasonable alacrity, Timerman's two requests for a writ of habeas corpus. The Supreme Court denied the first on 21 July 1978. A second request was granted on 17 September 1979, at which time the prisoner was released and allowed to leave the country. According to the government, the Court's decision balanced the norms of a state of siege with constitutional provisions that had never been abrogated. In other words, Timerman's arrest and his detention and release demonstrated a respect for human rights. According to the military, the Supreme Court had acted as a defender of the Constitution.[37]

But the Argentine government responded to the most serious accusations of torture, disappearances, and assassinations by simply denying their existence. When any foreign group referred to clandestine detention camps, for example, the military responded by pointing to the constitutionally designated judicial and penitentiary systems. The army repeatedly said that criticisms that the Argentine armed forces were running clandestine detention centers were false. Its argument always turned to a review of the terms by which formal penal processes operated, including the system of provincial prisons and the Federal Penitentiary Service, each of which was only marginally connected to most of the human rights abuses that were occurring. The government pointed out that the International Committee of the Red Cross had regular access to provincial and federal prisons; the organization visited thirty-two prisons in 1978 alone. In 1979, the Inter-American Commission on Human Rights (CIDH) visited Argentina and interviewed prisoners at the Villa Devoto, Caseros, Resistencia, Rawson, and Unidad 9 de La Plata federal and provincial jails and at (constitutionally sanctioned) military detention centers at Magdalena and Córdoba.[38]

Not only did the generals present an image of normalcy, but they also argued that Argentina was breaking new ground in protecting human rights. In 1979, the military inaugurated a new federal prison in Buenos

Aires. Construction had begun in 1960 on the 25-story monstrosity. The military described the Caseros prison as one of the most modern penal institutions in the world—"the Argentine prison system in the vanguard in the Americas"—and said it was designed to use progressive methods to reform prisoners so they could quickly reenter society. The government also argued that subversives benefited from the penal system's orientation toward "reeducation and re-socialization." It responded to demands for information about the disappeared with statements about presidential Decree 780 (1979), which regulated the supposedly progressive treatment of "subversive delinquents" in the penal system.[39]

Law 14.467 (1979) introduced more progressive language in describing the work of the penal system. It stressed "the social adaptation of each prisoner through curative, educational, and therapeutic work . . . in conjunction with relevant international principles, especially those outlined in the [United Nations'] *Standard Minimum Rules for the Treatment of Prisoners*."[40] On paper Argentina adhered to requirements related to the physical and mental health of inmates, including providing prisoners with access to libraries and recreational and cultural activities.[41]

For the military, prison discipline was an ordered system of gradual sanctions that were gauged by the transgressions of individual prisoners. "Special prisoners" (political detainees) were assured that they would have a prison regimen that included recreation, access to educational materials and books, and spiritual assistance—all of which were provided for in Decree 780 (1979). Military authorities heatedly denied accusations of torture in Argentina, pointing to Article 144 of the Argentine Penal Code, which made torture punishable by one to five years in prison. The junta denied outright the thousands of accusations of kidnappings and disappearances by foreign activists, governments, and journalists, although it said that it took all reports of such crimes seriously. It noted that the "disappearance" of people from their place of residence was common in many parts of the world in the wake of severe upheaval. In Argentina, military officials reasoned, there were several likely reasons for the so-called disappearances. First, some may have been the result of armed conflict between terrorist groups and the military. There were purportedly large numbers of unidentified deaths because of the way the left-wing terrorists prosecuted their war. Terrorists carried no identification. Months or years sometimes passed between a disappearance and the denunciation of a disappearance by family members because they knew of the political activities of the individuals in question and did not wish to give them up. Sometimes a "disappeared" person had simply not been in contact with family members.[42]

The military had many other explanations for why "subversives" had disappeared. Some terrorists had been assassinated by their own organizations as deserters or as traitors. Many communiqués from guerrilla groups that announced such sentences identified the executed member only by his nom de guerre. Some who were wounded in firefights with the military and then carried off by their comrades died later and were buried in unknown graves. Some of those who had disappeared were terrorist deserters in hiding. In some cases, people on the list of those who had disappeared had suddenly appeared before the authorities to confess their membership in a terrorist group and to provide evidence against such organizations. Such "young people" received reduced sentences. For their security and for the security of their families, their names were never published. What the military never admitted was that the armed forces routinely leaked disinformation after its members had kidnapped a supposed opponent of the regime that suggested that the Montoneros or another leftist group was responsible for the disappearance.[43]

The regime insisted that humanitarian reasons were at the heart of some decisions about how it handled information about disappearances. At times, the military claimed, denunciations of disappearances were part of a terrorist scheme: Many reports of disappeared persons came from subversive organizations hoping to find deserters. The military claimed to be keeping secret many names of those in hiding from the terrorists—another "explanation" for disappearances. It also said that capricious terrorists might suddenly decide to go underground without warning friends, co-workers, or family members. In November 1979, after a brutal terrorist attack in Buenos Aires in which a well-known executive died, the government argued that a number of those detained by police turned out to have been previously identified as "disappeared."[44]

The military also took credit for helping families resolve a range of problems relating to disappearances. Law 22.068 (1979) permitted a judge to declare a disappeared person deceased if there was compelling evidence. The dictatorship cited humanitarian concern for families that hoped to put the financial and civil affairs of disappeared relatives in order. The law was unnecessary, though. Such protections about the presumption of death already existed in the Argentine Civil Code and were in keeping with similar legislation in other nations.[45]

The junta aggressively denied accusations from foreign organizations that the Argentine military had destroyed the labor movement. The military insisted that the March 1976 coup d'état was justified by Argentina's return to a peaceful representative democracy. In the context of a profound, subversive-induced crisis, the military regime had resolved to transform the structure of organized labor to safeguard workers' rights, including the right to organize. In the inverted logic of the dictatorship, the military had intervened in union activities and denied workers basic human rights as a way of strengthening democracy. Authorities glossed over the military's intervention in syndical activity and its execution of union leaders, including the execution of Oscar Smith, the general secretary of the Light and Power Workers Union in Buenos Aires.[46] The military claimed absurdly that unions were able to function without restriction. Here as elsewhere, military officials coded much of their language. In oblique reference to the elimination of so-called subversives from positions of union leadership, for example, the military insisted that a new syndical structure assured real democracy for all workers.

Other coded language stressed the military's putative commitment to collective bargaining agreements; its fostering of dialogue between employers and workers not governed by collective agreements; and the use of "salary flexibility" (meaning low wages) to "maintain a good real wage" and low unemployment rates. There were unintentionally grim references to the state of siege. Unstated economic and social conditions meant that the legally protected right to assembly had to be curtailed, the military claimed. Still more ominously, the supposed chaos within unions before 1976 and the resulting economic paralysis meant that the dictatorship had to take measures to assure minimally healthy levels of productivity in Argentina. But it did not say that such measures included the elimination of fundamental democratic rights, including the right to strike, as well as the assassination and imprisonment of labor leaders who were hostile to the regime. Still, the military insisted, there was give and take in the post-coup workplace that illustrated a strong democratic apparatus and a protection of basic rights. It pointed out that despite the fact that strikes were prohibited, for example, the dictatorship did not always stringently apply restrictions on radical labor activity. A number of strikes, protests, workplace absences, and cases of working to rule had taken place with not a hint of repression. However, the government never gave any examples of such tolerance.[47]

The military government also insisted that workplace discrimination because of sex, race, nationality, religion, or political ideals was not allowed in the new Argentina. It noted that the workday was limited to eight hours and that workers had statutory holidays and mandatory vacation periods, plus paid days for accident or sickness. Argentina was ostensibly a leader in the protection of women's rights. Employers could not employ women in painful, unhealthy, or dangerous work. Women were entitled to two hours of rest at midday and 90 days of maternity leave, and pregnancy and maternity leave were not grounds for dismissal. Each of these claims failed to distinguish between laws that were on the books and actual practices in the workplace.

The military particularly prided itself on having advanced human rights for indigenous peoples. Historical narratives in Argentina have long denied the existence of indigenous peoples in Argentina, claiming that such groups had been destroyed in wars of conquest that took place through the end of the nineteenth century. Many Argentines accepted this construction of their nation and saw Argentina as a melting pot of white European immigrants. A succession of Argentine governments adopted policies to isolate and destroy indigenous Argentines even as dominant historical narratives denied their existence. Non-indigenous Argentines clung to the illusion of a nation free of indigenous peoples and felt disdain for native peoples. That disdain opened the door for decades of government mistreatment. In 1924, for example, police in the Chaco National Territory killed 500 Toba and Mocovi people who were protesting poor living conditions. In 1947, when thousands of Pilagá people began following a charismatic priest and healer, federal troops responded to panic among local landowners by killing some 800 to 2,000 of them. While they contended with these and other episodes of extreme violence, indigenous Argentines lived in abject poverty outside mainstream Argentine society.[48]

After March 1976, while Argentine authorities made certain to trumpet the government's "progress" on indigenous rights as an example of the regime's support for human rights, military authorities also believed that they could succeed where other governments had failed and could "modernize" indigenous peoples by removing them from their traditional communities. Indigenous Argentines (who accounted for 2–3 percent of the population) remained mired in grinding poverty. Data on infant mortality, malnutrition, and a range of diseases that were absent in other communities suggested a horrific crisis for indigenous Argentines. Tuberculosis and venereal disease were endemic in indigenous communities across the republic and were mostly untreated. This accounted in significant measure for high morbidity rates. In Chubut, government statistics showed that the combination of harsh weather, malnutrition, and poor medical attention had led to widespread blindness among indigenous peoples. When the military came to power, all provinces reported high levels of alcoholism among indigenous peoples. The federal government was aware that some storeowners in rural areas encouraged alcoholism (and its disorienting effects) so they could take advantage of indigenous Argentines who were selling wood, iguana skins, wool, or traditional crafts.[49]

As part of a larger approach to society that combined a rapid shift to free market economics with a vision of modernity, Argentine authorities moved to improve conditions for indigenous peoples after the coup, suggesting that such interventions were a new level of defense of human rights in Argentina. In the late 1970s and early 1980s, the national director for social assistance organized a series of meetings that brought together representatives from the ministries of defense, foreign relations, labor, health, and education and officials from several provinces that had higher concentrations of indigenous people. The objective of the meetings was to end poverty among indigenous peoples, integrate them into the "national life," and lay the groundwork for presenting the results of such efforts to the international community as a triumph of human rights in Argentina.[50]

Military authorities identified new levels of government responsibility for maintaining and advancing indigenous rights. A 1978 presidential decree (2336/78) made the National Superintendence of Frontiers (in the Ministry of Defense) responsible for indigenous reservations, government land distribution to indigenous peoples, housing construction, and the promotion of social and cultural activities, from sporting events to traditional music and arts festivals. Military officials imagined a "national model" into which indigenous peoples would fit. This meant that indigenous people would cease to live indigenous lives. The government would direct individuals and communities into activities that would stream-line their rapid emergence as productive citizens. The plan highlighted a commodification of indigenous identity: Indigenous economies around the country would be tied together to market souvenirs and other prod-ucts in a way that promoted a constructed "national" indigenous identity that could prove to be lucrative for participants and their communities.[51]

Tribal leaders reacted negatively. They warned of tribal breakdown and of potential antagonisms between indigenous peoples and nonin-digenous peoples who lived nearby. Indigenous leaders feared that reli-gious syncretism would alter traditional belief structures. They were also deeply concerned that the new policies would lead to a *mestizaje* of indig-enous culture and a melding of indigenous and non-indigenous practices that would have the effect of devastating indigenous identities. The cen-tral project of the military government was the government-supported national marketing of "traditional" crafts as a form of Argentine cultural enrichment and as a point of contact with other Latin American (in this case, indigenous) cultures. The government would promote indigenous identity in the narrow context of small business development and ad-vancement through hard work, but this effort would have no relevance to indigenous languages, belief systems, or spirituality. The centerpieces of the project would be the creation of a market in Buenos Aires to sell indigenous crafts and a national census of those engaged in traditional crafts production. Despite the complaints of indigenous Argentines that such a project was not in their best interests, military authorities believed that the project would promote the independence and well-being of in-digenous peoples and stabilize family and community structures in in-digenous communities.[52]

Dictatorship authorities saw themselves as addressing a long-standing neglect of indigenous peoples. They imagined their government correct-ing earlier inadequacies in government policies that had not found a way to help indigenous peoples break free of state subsidies. They recognized the scandalous conditions in which aboriginal peoples lived. Authori-ties transferred indigenous peoples in extreme crisis to so-called *villas de emergencia* (emergency villages), where food and water could be dis-tributed more effectively. The government claimed that publicly funded school cafeterias were a key tool for preventing so-called mental defi-ciency and malnutrition among children aged five and under. For many indigenous children, this meal was the only one of the day. However, schools were often nonexistent in rural communities.

Like previous governments, the dictatorship did not distinguish among the various indigenous ethnic groups. But it felt comfortable in its claim that a "primitive" indigenous culture was inherently limiting to the advancement of indigenous peoples. It argued that poor Spanish language skills created adaptation problems for children in rural schools and highlighted "nomadic" lifestyles as detrimental to school work. At the same time, there was confusion over whether indigenous identity or rural identity was the cause of problems. Like previous governments, the dictatorship dismissed racism as the root of the federal government's neglect of indigenous people, instead claiming that the policies of previous governments toward indigenous people amounted to abandonment.[53]

The military government drew on legal precedents and constitutional provisions as it constructed a program for improving the lives of indigenous Argentines. It based its project in part on Law 14.932/59 (1959), which protected indigenous populations and sought to integrate them into the national mainstream and made Argentina party to Convention 107 (Indigenous and Tribal Peoples Convention) of the International Labour Organization. The government also drew upon Law 17.722/68 (1968), which made Argentina an adherent to the International Convention on the Elimination of Racial Discrimination. Argentine authorities tied their goals to larger anti-racism projects of the dictatorship era. Law 17.693/78 (1978) created a National Conciliation Commission to fight discrimination in teaching and classroom. Military authorities saw their approach to indigenous Argentines as a way to counter backward, racist influences in Argentine culture. For example, bureaucrats in a number of government ministries found that some priests who were working with indigenous peoples were disregarding Catholic Church directives by continuing to evangelize in a way that prevented indigenous peoples from participating in traditional dance and song rituals. At the same time, the dictatorship took no action to counter that evangelization.[54]

As part of a series of meetings designed to advance indigenous rights, dozens of national government, provincial government, and indigenous community delegates came together in Buenos Aires in November 1982. In response to ongoing reports that indigenous peoples were being denied their basic rights, including being turned away from health clinics in the province of Misiones, the Ministry of Social Action made impassioned pleas for the rights of indigenous Argentines: "*La Nación ha olvidado casi a las poblaciones indígenas. No se han integrado a nuestra sociedad de origen europeo. Son marginales, condenados al atraaso, la miseria y la enfermedad*" (The nation has all but forgotten indigenous populations. They have not integrated themselves into our European society. They are marginal, condemned to backwardness, misery, and illness).[55]

As the dictatorship moved toward implementing its project after 1980, it identified the National Directorate of Social Assistance as the coordinating agency but promoted a decentralized approach whereby provincial governments that were better able to assess the starting point for the economic advancement of indigenous communities would implement the plan. With the assistance of government anthropologists, the dictatorship divided indigenous communities into *monoculturalista* (monoculturalist) or *pluriculturalista* (pluriculturalist) groups—that is to say, it divided indigenous communities into those that were considered to be "isolated" culturally or truly indigenous and those that had intermingled at some level with nonindigenous cultures. Indigenous people were excluded from decision-making at the national policy level, though there was some limited participation at the provincial level. In Formosa, for example, provincial authorities named three indigenous advisors to the local process and began appointing indigenous teaching assistants in the classroom to help build knowledge of the Spanish language, a process the federal government estimated could take up to three years.[56]

Officials in Neuquén planned to collect indigenous-language expressions in a Spanish-language handbook while in several other provinces school curriculums were developed to stress work skills and prepare students to participate in the government-sponsored crafts marketing project. The military saw the integration of indigenous peoples into a larger national project as related to other aspects of *proceso* social and political goals. Because many of Argentina's indigenous peoples lived in border areas, military authorities imagined their project as one of national security and tied the bureaucratic language of indigenous advancement to the fight against subversion. Authorities planned to eliminate poor housing and sanitation as a means of ending Chagas disease and other diseases transmitted by insect vectors (these were endemic in many northern provinces). At the same time they worried about indigenous peoples who encountered foreign merchants (who came across the border from Chile, Bolivia, and Paraguay to sell provisions and alcohol), non-Catholic evangelists, secretive sects, and *empresas colonizadoras* (colonizing companies). In an odd twist on the long-standing erasure of indigenous Argentines from national identity, promoting indigenous rights became a question of defending national territory and identity during the dictatorship.[57]

Despite its concerns about Catholic missionaries, the military government saw the promotion of Catholicism as an intrinsic part of indigenous community life in rural Argentina, just as it promoted the Catholic Church as a key arbiter of new Argentine moralities. The Special Committee on Education and Catechism of the Catholic Church was charged with developing a new pastoral strategy for aboriginal Argentines. The Sub-Secretariat of Social Action of Chaco province began working with the Church to build chapels to honor the Virgin Mary in indigenous communities; the goal of this project was to block the efforts of other faiths. The federal Sub-Secretariat of Faiths moved to gain a better knowledge of Protestant groups working among indigenous peoples with the intent of regulating those contacts and blocking what authorities described as the corruption of biblical instruction by poorly trained missionaries and the resulting syncretic or fanatical religions that were emerging among indigenous peoples. According to the sub-secretariat, this was aggravating fatalistic tendencies in indigenous communities.[58]

The military government used the promotion of indigenous rights as a pretext for identifying and eliminating small evangelical Christian churches working among indigenous Argentines. Working with federal authorities, the Administración General of the Instituto Provincial del Aborigen de Formosa (General Administration of the Provincial Aboriginal Institute of Formosa Province) recommended better supervision of all Protestant pastors and missionaries working with indigenous communities. Government officials in Formosa and Buenos Aires found that too many were leaving the communities they were attending in spiritual crisis. Formosa authorities also proposed that Protestant pastors should represent the state by promoting respect for national symbols, that non-Spanish-speaking foreign pastors should learn Spanish, and that religious leaders should stop promulgating the notion that poverty was divinely favored.[59]

The military government's supposed promotion of indigenous rights was similar to its ostensible support of human rights more generally in

Argentina. In both cases, the government used ostensibly progressive political and social agendas to fight subversives. In this case, the government became interested in the modernization of indigenous society as a way to identify what they called marginal sects (evangelical Christians) attracted by the exoticism of indigenous groups, by the allure of indigenous lands, or by the chance to engage in moving contraband and other criminal acts.[60]

Provincial authorities embraced the military's business plan for integrating indigenous groups into modern society. That plan dovetailed with the regime's economic vision for a prosperous Argentina that was free of government strictures, a vision that stressed independent initiative. The government's plan called for indigenous communities to generate incomes of their own and, in so doing, to strengthen indigenous families and promote the interests of indigenous women. There was strong support from provincial governments for the installation by the Fondo Nacional de Artes (National Arts Fund) of a new Mercado Nacional de Artesanias (National Crafts Market) in Buenos Aires. The Fondo estimated that the market would immediately provide work for 80,000 indigenous Argentines and assure a constant supply of newly produced indigenous arts and crafts from around the country. It would improve quality control and foster independent artistic expression, while at the same time promoting a market-driven model of indigenous life.[61]

Despite the fanfare that surrounded the government's proposed program for integrating indigenous people into Argentine society, the dictatorship never achieved its goals. This was partly because of economic decline in Argentina, partly because of the Malvinas War, partly because of the collapse of military rule, and partly because of the impossibly large scope of the project. Nevertheless, the dictatorship successfully used its purported defense of indigenous rights, women's rights, and refugee rights in the international community to reinforce the notion that Argentina was not the pariah state that Amnesty International and other rights groups claimed it was.

As it launched its new program for indigenous Argentines, the dictatorship announced another key expression of its support for human rights with great fanfare. In 1979, the Argentine government began to work with the UN Refugee Agency to welcome Vietnamese refugees, the so-called boat people who had fled their homeland under precarious circumstances. The military kept its promise to admit Vietnamese refugees for three years. But as in the case of indigenous Argentines, the military's vision of a pro–human rights agenda was tempered with a moral ordering of the lives of the refugees in a way that was designed to integrate them into Argentine society according to strict norms. They were settled in areas chosen by Argentine authorities rather than by the refugees themselves and in accordance with what military authorities decided were "normal occupations" for this group. The refugees were banned for three years from moving to poor neighborhoods in Buenos Aires or to within 100 kilometers of that city. They were also blocked from moving to several other cities in an effort to "avoid urban demographic congestion." The refugees could establish permanent residence in two years and become citizens in seven years, after they had shown themselves to be responsible potential Argentines.[62]

The "pro–human rights" successes of the Argentine government served as a form of diplomatic capital in the international community. The military government's claims did not convince skeptics in France or the United States, where the government's posturing on indigenous rights or boat people never carried much weight. But for nations with their own human rights problems (that is to say, many Asian, African, and Eastern European states), these Argentine success stories presented an opportunity to offer diplomatic support for the *proceso* with the unstated understanding that such support would be reciprocated.[63]

Shortly after the coup d'état, some in the international community had tried to isolate Argentina in important international venues because of its violations of human rights. In September 1976, Gabriel O. Martínez, the Argentine representative to the United Nations in Geneva, wrote to the foreign ministry that he could not have predicted the recent attacks on Argentina in the UN Sub-Commission on the Prevention of Discrimination and Protection of Minorities. The previous month, the sub-commission's Working Group on Communications had responded to new accusations of human rights violations in Argentina by voting 4 (Ghana, Nicaragua, Pakistan, and Soviet Union) to 1 (United States) against bringing the information to the attention of all sub-commission members.[64] But when other members became aware of human rights violations in Argentina, they reversed the Working Group's decision to bury the evidence. Drawing on submissions from Amnesty International and the International Commission of Jurists, the French representative on the sub-commission raised the issue of juridical insecurity in Argentina. Dutch and British members pointed to the 20,000 political prisoners in Argentina and the rampant political violence there. The Soviet Union came to Argentina's defense, saying that its critics had relied on unreliable media sources about the human rights situation in Argentina—the same kind of sources UN diplomats had used to build a case against the abuse of psychiatric hospitals in the Soviet Union. In response, a "western group" emerged on the sub-commission comprised of delegates from the United States, France, Great Britain, Italy, Austria, and the Netherlands. This group rejected the Argentine government's denials and, according to Martínez, harbored a "deliberately hostile attitude" toward the dictatorship.[65]

When the western group moved to isolate Argentina, Latin American delegates to the UN either supported Argentina (Nicaragua and Costa Rica) or abstained from taking a position (Mexico, Colombia, and Ecuador). Members of the Non-Aligned Movement (NAM) were largely steadfast in their support of Argentina. Argentine diplomats had used movement solidarity to appeal to the UN representatives from these nations. They won support from each of the NAM members on the Sub-Commission, which included Iraq, Nigeria, India, Egypt, Kenya, Pakistan, Ghana, and Iran. Among "socialist" nations within the NAM, Yugoslavia and Romania backed Argentina without reservation, while the Soviet Union expressed strong support. In diplomacy as in commercial relations, Argentina and the Soviet Union were generally able to overcome ideological differences despite the dictatorship's fixation on an international Marxist menace.[66]

In 1978, the attack on the Argentine human rights record was more forceful and more sustained in the international community than it had been before that time. On 11 July, Amnesty International sent a report to the Sub-Commission on the Prevention of Discrimination and Protection of Minorities that accused Argentina of rampant human rights violations. Confident in their UN allies, the Argentines declined to comment, instead circulating a very brief note from the Argentine embassy in Great Britain. The government also chose a low-key response to a report on 5 June by the International Federation for Human Rights, rejecting what it called the feeble methodology of the federation's investigation but offering to get to the bottom of individual cases of disappearance and torture the report cited. When the government was notified in June that the

Women's International Democratic Federation had accused it of human rights violations, it simply ignored the report.[67]

In mid-1978, the UN Economic and Social Council (ECOSOC) communicated its concerns about gross human rights violations in Argentina to the UN Secretary General through resolution 728F (XXVIII). The Argentine government responded by accusing enemies inside and outside the UN of attempting to discredit it and its "advances" in the area of human rights. It claimed, as always, that the military had come to power in 1976 to defeat a terrorist menace and the human rights situation had improved since the coup d'état. Moreover, the Argentine government insisted that what some cast as human rights violations were in fact a necessity of war that went far beyond the question of Argentine terrorists fighting the Argentine government. The dictatorship's self-assessment of its war on terrorism was contradictory. On the one hand, it routinely claimed success. At the same time, it maintained the illusion of an ongoing terrorist menace, arguing that eliminating the domestic terrorist threat was beyond the scope of "the rulers and of the Argentine people" because domestic terrorism was tied to international threats and to an ill-defined "similar precedent in the darkest periods of our civilization."[68]

The military frequently modified and updated its narrative of its defense of human rights. At the UN, Argentine officials were inclined to stress a larger history of international terrorism. For the military, Argentina had become an international battlefield "where hundreds of persons, men, women and children, civilians and military alike, [were falling] victims to violence and terror." Ill-defined international pressures led the military to apply articles 14–18 of the 1853 Constitution. The generals reasoned that these articles supported a state of siege, the coup d'état itself, and the denial of habeas corpus.[69] Other authoritarian governments that were members of ECOSOC accepted the positions of the Argentine military at face value, never questioning its interpretations of constitutional law or precedent. In a rare admission of potential human rights violations, Gabriel Martínez excused possible abuses by citing the "peculiar characteristics of this period of time" and by balancing guarantees of individual rights with "respect for and protection of the rights of others." As the government had done on many previous occasions, Martínez noted that the current state of siege had come into effect during a previous government on 6 November 1974.[70]

In 1982, bolstered by its "successes" with Vietnamese boat people and indigenous peoples, Argentina cast itself as a defender of human rights in the international community in its role as a member of the UN's Sub-Commission on the Prevention of Discrimination and Protection of Minorities. No country ever challenged Argentina's record in this forum. The work of the sub-commission had been slowed to a snail's pace by the 28,000 reports it received of human rights violations around the world each year and by the intense politicization of human rights at the United Nations. In 1982, the sub-commission considered whether to submit reports on human rights violations in several countries to the Commission on Human Rights for further study. Argentina charged one of its most experienced and sharpest diplomats, Juan Carlos Beltramino, with advancing Argentine interests in this forum. Beltramino had three objectives. First, he sought to avoid any criticism of the Argentine human rights record that would single out his nation or, worse still, transform Argentina into a pariah state for its violation of human rights. Second, he was to quash any criticism of Argentina through thoughtful diplomacy. Finally, he was to execute a diplomacy that combined maintaining a low profile for Argentina on human rights issues and suggesting that Argentina was a defender of human rights, using the examples of indigenous peoples and Vietnamese boat people.[71]

Beltramino believed that Argentina faced unique challenges. On the one hand, Argentine diplomats could count as a success that their nation had not been relegated to pariah status, like Paraguay or Chile. At the same time, he believed that Argentina faced an uphill struggle on human rights in part because African and Asian countries facing accusations from Amnesty International and other groups were able to avoid the spotlight by invoking ongoing liberation wars against colonialism and racism to justify their actions. In other UN forums, the Pinochet dictatorship served as a foil for Argentina; it could escape the designation of pariah state that was assigned to Chile thanks in part to its record on indigenous rights and refugees. The Argentines worked frequently with delegates from other NAM nations that were facing human rights charges, such as Morocco, Iran, and Indonesia. When the sub-commission considered a report on rampant human rights violations in Chile, Argentina quietly set itself apart from Chilean state terror by adding to a unanimous vote to pass the document on to the UN Commission on Human Rights for further action and possible sanctions.[72]

Despite the fact that motions before the sub-commission often marshaled different coalitions in support or opposition, Beltramino identified five nations as having a "more marked political and ideological attitude" (that is to say, a less malleable position on human rights or a position less amenable to Argentina's elaborate defense of its human rights position). Russia tended to defend its Cold War allies when accusations of human rights were made. Norway, Great Britain, Belgium, and France were more problematic because of their tendency to accept the reports of Amnesty International at face value and to vote accordingly. Beltramino found that he was able to work effectively with developing-world governments that were not as committed to a particular political or ideological stance.

The vagaries of human rights diplomacy were evident in a debate that came up in the context of accusations of human rights violations in Paraguay. The issue was how long countries would have to respond to charges related to human rights violations. Argentina supported longer response times. That proposal was voted down. Paraguay was generally regarded as a hopeless human rights violator, and for Argentina or other allies in the region, it was scarcely worth defending in light of their own human rights problems. The accused nation was given no time to defend itself before the Paraguay report was passed on to the Commission on Human Rights.[73] East Germany and Poland, in contrast, were given a year to respond to human rights violations charges.

In the day-to-day workings of the sub-commission, topics of discussion were so varied and so poorly defined that Argentina could avoid any serious attack on its human rights record. The most serious threat Beltramino faced came in the sub-commission's acceptance of critical communications from the Argentine human rights organization Centro de Estudios Legales y Sociales (CELS; Center for Legal and Social Studies) about the conditions of prisoners in Argentine jails; from the Comisión Ligas Agrarias Argentinas (Commission of Argentine Agrarian Leagues) about the disappearance of rural workers in the province of Santa Fe; and from Amnesty International about forced disappearances and political prisoners.[74] The Argentine government prepared official responses to these accusations. The Moroccan delegate gave Argentina its measured support by suggesting that the documents be passed on to the Commission on Human Rights without debate. Argentina received stronger support from the Soviet Union. With diplomatic room to maneuver that

Chile or Paraguay did not have, Beltramino correctly interpreted this support as a defense of East Germany and Vietnam; the Soviet Union wanted to help these nations avoid a consideration of their human rights records at the UN.[75]

The reports from the three Argentine organizations were passed on to the Commission on Human Rights, but this was only a modest defeat for Argentina. Although serious questions about human rights in Argentina remained open and the documents remained on the table in the UN, Beltramino had avoided a debate over human rights in Argentina within the sub-commission. In his efforts to block the transfer of documents to the Commission on Human Rights, Beltramino argued that the sub-commission might take into account favorable developments on the human rights front in Argentina since 1980 (including Argentina's efforts on behalf of boat people and indigenous rights), plans for free elections in 1983, and the recent legalization of political parties.

Argentina exercised quid pro quo diplomacy. Even though East Germany was a frequent critic of the Argentine dictatorship and a key destination for many Argentines seeking refuge from the military, Beltramino rejected criticism of that nation for violating human rights and voted to block the transfer of the East German case to the Commission on Human Rights. In doing so, he allied himself with majorities led by the Soviet Union and voted against western European delegates. On the question of rights violations in East Timor, Argentina backed another ally on the committee, Indonesia. Beltramino argued that a document before the committee that was critical of Indonesian actions in East Timor should be quashed on a technicality and that the criticism did not adequately distinguish between human rights violations and the supposedly distinct issue of East Timor's right to self-determination. Though Argentina abstained on a committee vote that condemned Indonesia, Beltramino offered a spirited defense of the Indonesian government by arguing that the committee was not competent to assess the right to self-determination in East Timor or anywhere else. Beltramino also condemned human rights abuses in Iraq in exchange for diplomatic support from Iran (based in part on strong Iranian-Argentine nuclear ties). He sided against French and Norwegian diplomats in voting against condemnations of Morocco, Great Britain (in Northern Ireland), and Pakistan. These decisions combined support for friendly Moroccan and Pakistani delegations and a rejection (in the British case) of Argentina's nemesis, Amnesty International, which had drafted each of the condemnations.[76]

Here and in other international forums, Argentina rarely deviated from its cautious human rights policy, one that emphasized its own supposed domestic successes, called in political favors from other nations, and backed those whose support the Argentines could count on at a later date. Occasionally, Argentina supported other countries accused of violating human rights when the particular accusation might later be relevant to charges against Argentina and when a defense of the other nation might set a useful precedent that might later serve Argentine interests. In 1982, Beltramino felt that a motion to condemn human rights violations in El Salvador would have a direct impact on his nation because it said that Salvador was not governed by a legitimate constitutional authority. He vigorously attacked this statement as erroneous. The issue alarmed the Argentine government as potentially dangerous to the dictatorship's elaborate defense of its own coup d'état and the state terror that followed. Argentina was one of only three countries to vote against the motion, which easily passed. More commonly, Argentina established its human rights credentials on easy votes, where it could build on its diplomatic and political capital by siding with the majority on human rights cases that had what seemed like no moral or legal application to the Argentine case. In 1982, when Israel invaded Lebanon, Argentina joined the majority on the sub-commission in condemning Israel. The only vote against the motion came from the United States, and the only abstentions were voiced by Belgium and Great Britain. As a representative of the Argentine dictatorship, Beltramino found many opportunities within the Sub-Commission on the Prevention of Discrimination and Protection of Minorities to argue that Argentina's record on human rights was admirable rather than deplorable.[77]

Although they were never able to convince domestic and foreign critics of Argentina's human rights credentials, government officials achieved their goal of maintaining close contact with a majority of their trading and diplomatic partners. In 1979, Argentina's reputation as a human rights violator did not prevent its election to the Human Rights Committee of ECOSOC and to the Executive Committee of the Office of the UN High Commissioner for Refugees. Argentine diplomats were also present at the Seventh Session of the United Nations Environment Programme Governing Council.[78] Ambassador Alberto Dumonty led the Argentine delegation to the Second Session of the UN Disarmament Commission in Czechoslovakia. The UN Secretary General named Argentine diplomat José María Otegui to a group of experts on regional disarmament. The Argentine government backed the incorporation of Spain into the UN Economic Council for Latin America as an observer, announcing on that occasion that it would receive 1,000 families of Vietnamese refugees. And—to the applause of diplomatic colleagues—Argentina doubled its contribution to the Office of the UN High Commissioner on Refugees for 1980 (from US$25,000 to US$50,000).[79]

Argentina triumphed at the United Nations by avoiding critical scrutiny of its human rights record and by continuing to work effectively with most other nations in a way that promoted a range of Argentine interests. That ongoing Argentine integration with the international community drew on the politics of normalizing state terror as a necessary prelude to the return of democracy. At home and abroad, the military mounted a political and legalistic campaign to defend its takeover of the government and the internal war that followed. While many in Argentina and the international community remained unconvinced by this argument, many more assented or raised no significant objections. The military government took pains to disseminate information about new initiatives that supposedly showed evidence of a strong pro–human rights agenda. These included promoting a free market–inspired plan to benefit indigenous populations and welcoming Vietnamese refugees. Neither of these projects altered a history of gross human rights violations, but each was integrated into Argentina's successful defense of its human rights record at the United Nations and in other international venues.

3

The Frank War, the Fabrication of an Ongoing Menace, and the Jews

Carlos Beltramino and a host of other Argentine diplomats and policymakers presented an image of Argentina as different from "violent" societies such as Paraguay or Uganda. However, the military's trumpeting of Argentine rectitude on human rights depended on ongoing contradictions. *Proceso* leaders felt they had to project a notion of continued crisis in the successful but difficult war against "subversives." At the same time, they had to convince Argentines and others that the government was on track in its project of building a new, progressive Argentina. It was in the regime's interest to suggest publicly that the military takeover had quickly achieved what it set out to accomplish—the destruction of the guerrilla menace in the north. But precisely because the guerrilla threat had never been as significant as the military had argued and because the kidnappings and executions the military perpetrated far exceeded the number of rebels fighting the government in Tucumán and elsewhere, there was an ongoing need to construct a fictitious "subversive" enemy. Despite overwhelming evidence of a decline in the guerrilla menace that the military itself accepted and even welcomed as a victory, the fiction of a subversive enemy helped justify long-term repression and the fantasy that the Argentine dictatorship was a supporter of human rights.

Throughout the dictatorship, the Argentine military framed its project for national regeneration in the context of an ongoing terrorist menace that was the "true" violator of human rights in Argentina. An April 1978 memorandum for the press from the Ministry of Foreign Relations revived the danger-of-subversion argument in an even more elaborate form than the arguments the military had put forward at the time of the coup. However, the language such statements used to describe the ongoing dangers Argentines faced evoked the domestic and international criticisms of the Argentine military. The military frequently referred to the false danger of a return to political breakdown and urged Argentines to remember the wave of kidnappings and assassinations that had terrorized the innocent. "Fear, insecurity, and chaos were the predominant ingredient of daily life."[1]

Military officers argued that their actions in 1976 was the opening salvo in a third world war against international communism. This invoking of an international communist threat became crucial to how the dictatorship presented the menace of disorder to Argentines as ongoing. This argument constructed the 1976 coup as both a victory and a defeat. The Argentine government called pre-1976 leftist guerrilla terrorism a "dirty war" and the military response a "frank war" that was waged openly with the backing of the "principals and traditions of the west." The frank war had been successful in dismantling the daily menace of terrorist assaults. By 1978, the argument went, the frank war had enabled the government to regain almost complete control of the polity. But this image of a battle almost won was accompanied by an unending image of defeat. Although the "terrorist apparatus" had been shaken and leftist terrorists (generally unnamed) had been reduced to engaging in isolated acts in Argentina that had only limited significance (and frequently the military manufactured such "acts"), the "frank war" had come at a price. "But just as we've begun to benefit from our victory over terrorism, enjoying a peaceful and calm environment, we must recognize that the war has come with costs," an internal intelligence document conceded. One of these was the attacks on Argentina's image overseas.[2]

The Argentine military conflated a domestic terrorist menace (left over from the almost-won war against terrorism), international Marxist influences, and foreign criticisms of Argentine authorities about human rights violations. The military told the public that its victory over terrorism and its destruction of terrorist networks and the popular support for such networks had forced leftists to flee abroad, where they had created new bases of operation and were succeeding in disguising their "nihilistic essence" behind a mask of democratic values. According to the military, much of the international campaign of falsehood against Argentina over human rights violations was, in fact, the work of exiled Argentine subversives.

Argentine authorities went further still. They asked Argentines why this had happened. Why had well-intentioned people in other countries who were concerned about human rights abuses succumbed to the false arguments of Argentine terrorists in exile on the issue of human rights in Argentina? For the military, the answer was that Europeans, North Americans, and others simply did not grasp the magnitude of the war the Argentine military had fought and continued to fight. Foreigners, in short, were dupes of Argentine terrorists who were now disguised as exiled victims of military repression.

The state intelligence agency, the Secretaría de Inteligencia de Estado (SIDE), repeatedly identified that menace as being located both inside and outside the country. Argentina kept watch on what it perceived as the ongoing activities by subversives in neighboring countries and beyond. In early 1981, for example, the SIDE identified twenty "subversive" actions by Chilean nationals in Chile and noted the appearance of rural guerrillas near Valdivia. In this and other instances, the Argentine military fed its paranoia by noting Chilean military intelligence reports on the capture of three guerrilla camps in Chile: while some of the rebels had escaped, others had made their way toward the Argentine border, the Chileans reported ominously.[3]

There were no follow-up reports on whether the so-called subversives had ever crossed into Argentina. That was scarcely the point. Despite the fact that most of what Argentine intelligence investigations turned up only hinted at possible enemy activity, SIDE operatives followed such leads as though they were based on evidence, fueling a sense among some in Buenos Aires that a threat of internal subversion also persisted. In one respect, nothing changed from 1976 to 1983 in how the military portrayed its enemies: It was unwilling or unable to distinguish between actual opponents of the regime and the more ambiguous notion of "subversives." In July 1981, for example, the Mexico City–based Trabajadores y Sindicatos Argentinos en el Exilio (Argentine Workers and Unions in Exile), an innocuous group of expatriate opponents of the regime, published an appeal for support in the left-leaning newspaper *Uno más uno* (based in Mexico City). The Argentine foreign ministry viewed the fact that a group of seventy Argentine exiles had met to protest peacefully in front of the Argentine embassy in Mexico City as a potential threat. Of further alarm to Argentine authorities was an advertisement in *Uno más uno* that called on Argentines in Mexico to remember the death of Eva Perón; signatories included Esteban Righi, the exiled minister of the interior from the Peronist administration of Héctor Cámpora.[4]

Often military intelligence officers could not see the difference between innocuous public protest (which the Argentine Constitution protected as a free speech right) and what might, in fact, be an effort by an Argentine guerrilla group (or what was left of it) to reorganize overseas. Between 25 July and 22 August 1981, Argentine diplomats and intelligence agents in Mexico City conflated a series of "threats." These included Argentine Political Prisoner Week at the Colegio de Economistas (College of Economists, which the SIDE referred to as the "College of Marxists"); a concert at the Teatro de Bellas Artes in Mexico City given by Argentine pianist and human rights activist Miguel Angel Estrella (whom the Argentine government had identified as a security threat through his music)[5]; a remembrance ceremony at the Colegio de Economistas on the fifth anniversary of the death of Mario Roberto Santucho (the leader of the People's Revolutionary Army who had been killed by the Argentine military); a ceremony organized by the Sindicato de Trabajo de la Universidad Nacional Autonoma de Mexico (which was communist inspired, according to SIDE) to pay tribute to Argentines struggling against dictatorship; a public request signed by Luis Rivera Terrazas, president of the University Council of the Universidad Autonoma de Puebla, asking for the release of Argentine political prisoners Jorge Taiana (who was never affiliated with a revolutionary movement) and Montonero leader Ernesto Villanueva[6]; and a brief note in the newspaper *Excelsior* (based in Mexico City) criticizing a possible Argentine military intervention in El Salvador. By conflating the potential (though weakly presented) threat of a subversive menace with acts as innocuous as peaceful public protest, the military regime kept its guerrilla enemy alive.

Hazy information from other countries helped the dictatorship promote the notion of an ongoing subversive threat. This included reports of the activities of the Red Brigades in Italy and unsolved killings and robberies in Chile. Sometimes the SIDE seemed well informed, as when one of its agents in Lima predicted correctly that the Maoist Sendero Luminoso would increase its violent efforts to destabilize the Peruvian government. But here and elsewhere, what any of this had to do with Argentina was never clear beyond the military's insistence that an international communist conspiracy meant that each of these and other threats would "naturally" be tied to equivalent groups in Argentina.[7]

Although Argentine authorities could never show a clear and immediate link between an overseas terrorist threat and an Argentine equivalent, they collaborated with right-wing regimes in Central America that were intent on waging wars against internal threats from leftist guerrillas. In 1980, Argentine military authorities identified Guatemala as a threat when their counterparts in that country informed them that a handful of revolutionary groups, including the Ejercito Guerrillero de los Pobres (EGP), the Fuerzas Armadas Rebeldes, and the Partido Guatemalteco del Trabajo, had joined forces in a single command structure to plan and carry out attacks.[8]

Argentine authorities found ways to back repressive regimes in Guatemala because the two countries were allies in an international struggle against communism. As a strategy to combat subversion, Argentine leaders decided to support Guatemalan candidates for leadership positions in international organizations. They invited Guatemalan entrepreneurs and political leaders to Buenos Aires (in one instance under the auspices of the Comisión Nacional de Investigaciones Espaciales, the Argentine National Commission on Space Investigation). They provided aid and technical support for Guatemalan mining and agriculture. Moreover, the Argentine government scheduled visits of Central American business and political leaders to Buenos Aires in an effort to promote the idea that Argentina was a defender of human rights.[9]

The fact that hemispheric allies saw the same sorts of dangers as Argentine government officials did help convince Argentine officers that

their analysis of an international communist menace was correct. Guatemalan leaders promoted strong relations with the Argentine military
because they feared subversion at home and wanted to improve security
and order in Guatemala. Like the Argentines, the Guatemalan military
viewed strong international relations with other right-wing dictatorships
as a way to create a counterweight to U.S. and European policies on human rights in the Americas. Honduran leaders also supported Argentina. In a private conversation, the Honduran foreign minister told the
Argentine ambassador to Honduras that his nation would maintain a
neutral position on all Argentina-related discussions in the Organization
of American States (OAS) and the Inter-American Commission on Human Rights (CIDH). Honduras would not judge Argentina; the common
enemy of both nations was the extreme Marxist left. But it was clear to the
Argentines that the Hondurans would expect quid pro quo on issues related to nuclear questions. Honduras had requested technical assistance
from the Comisión Nacional de Energía Atómica (CNEA, the Argentine
National Atomic Energy Commission) regarding uranium prospecting,
radioisotope manufacturing, atomic security, nuclear legislation, and
other issues. The Argentine foreign ministry urged fast action by CNEA
to assure Honduran support for Argentina on human rights.[10]

The Argentine military positioned itself as the victim of unjustified assaults on its human rights record. Leaders spoke privately of going on the
offensive to combat foreign "lies." On 30 March 1981, the Argentine president instructed government departments to "attack" foreign enemies on
human rights questions instead of remaining constantly on the defensive.
As was frequently the case, Argentina's overseas enemies remained unnamed, but according to Argentine government authorities, they were
responsible for fabrications that were generally accepted in other countries and at the UN and the OAS.[11]

For the dictatorship, the most serious of the supposed foreign fabrications centered on the dual accusation that Argentina was violating human rights and that a key target of military rule was Jewish Argentines. In
many cases, it was never clear whether Jewish Argentines were targeted
because they were Jews or because they were supposed subversives. The
military brought a major public image problem on itself by detaining Argentines, Jewish and otherwise, on flimsy or nonexistent evidence. This is
what happened when the military detained José Siderman, a hotel owner
and entrepreneur from Tucumán province. Siderman was falsely targeted

by military authorities as a threat and imprisoned; while he was detained, military officers looted his property. Far from retreating in the face of international protests, authorities in Tucumán laid multiple charges against Siderman that included business fraud. Siderman escaped to the United States, where he established residence in 1978. He was later detained by Interpol at the request of Argentine authorities while he was traveling in Italy. That detention prompted a call from the Argentine ambassador in Washington, Raúl Castro, for legal action against Siderman in the United States.[12]

Castro's advice was not heeded, nor was it clear that Siderman's unlawful detention had anything to do with his Jewish identity. (Two decades later, in a landmark case in international law, his family sued the government of Argentina in a U.S. federal court for torture and loss of property. Argentina settled with the Siderman family out of court and agreed to pay them millions of dollars, a fraction of the value of the property the military government had seized.) Like the Siderman case, the cases of Jacobo Timerman and other Jewish Argentines prompted predictably intense foreign scrutiny of the dictatorship. While not all military officers cared much one way or the other about Jews, enough did to make it clear that anti-Semitism guided the thinking of *proceso* leaders, many of whom included on their list of enemies of the government a supposed international Jewish conspiracy. Such anti-Semitism led to unusual attention in the international community to the disappearance of Jews such as Siderman. When Trotskyist student leader Mariano Levin disappeared in late 1976, his parents, biochemist Emilio Levin and oncologist Rosita Levin, quickly mobilized support in the international scientific community. While nobody can be certain what prompted Mariano's release days later, his mother speculated that perhaps his captors had cringed at the possibility of an outcry over the detention of another Jew.[13]

Military authorities were deeply aware of how foreigners, particularly in the United States, quickly conflated dictatorship, human rights abuses, and anti-Semitism. The response of the dictatorship was contradictory. On the one hand, some diplomats and policymakers adopted a pragmatic approach that emphasized a forceful denial of Argentine anti-Semitism and attempted to generate support in the United States and elsewhere for the view that the dictatorship upheld human rights for all. At the same time, though, many in the Argentine military interpreted high-level international scrutiny of the treatment of Jews in Argentina as "evidence" that Argentine Jews were working with Amnesty International, communists, and other enemies, to discredit the Argentine government. The folly of the belief of some in the military that Argentine Jews were linked to the persistence of a terrorist threat likely did more damage to the dictatorship overseas than any other aspect of the dictatorship's internal war.

Alicia Partnoy and Jacobo Timerman were the most famous of dozens of Jewish Argentines who told stories of guards at illicit detention centers hurling anti-Jewish insults at prisoners. Such accounts had no discernible impact on the constituencies Carlos Beltramino and other Argentine officials courted in the international community, but they did shape public opinion in Western Europe and North America. Timerman became the most famous Argentine victim of human rights abuses and helped circulate evidence that while Jews comprised only 2 percent of the population, they may have accounted for as much as 10 percent of disappeared people.[14]

Jailers told Blanca Brecher, a prisoner in Olmos jail, that she was tortured more regularly than other prisoners because she was Jewish. Inez Vázquez reported that although pregnant women were generally not tortured, an exception was made in the case of Esther Herzberg because she was Jewish.[15]

Timerman's published account of his imprisonment, *Preso sin nombre, celda sin numero*, had a dramatic impact internationally when it appeared in 1980 and again when an English translation was published a year later. A distinguished journalist with connections and friends among highly placed Argentine politicians and military officers, Timerman was surprised when he was detained, tortured, and imprisoned. His account in *Preso* emphasized the taunts and violence inspired by anti-Jewish sentiment that he faced while he was behind bars. According to Timerman, anti-Semitism seemed to be a constant in Argentina's detention centers and seemed to be at the core of why the Argentine military tortured and killed. One guard kicked Timerman every time he passed by; Timerman learned eventually that this was because he hated Jews.[16] Timerman's captors questioned him repeatedly and under torture about what he knew about an Israeli plan to invade Patagonia. The so-called Plan Andina was paranoid mythmaking that may have reached as high as the junta itself. Timerman's jailers believed it to be true. To his jail guards, Timerman's Jewishness made him a subversive.[17]

Timerman's exposé in *Preso* of how central anti-Semitism was to the military's internal war was not his only dramatic revelation. He wrote that he was "stunned—amazed, almost unable to encompass" what he began to understand as the passivity of Argentina's Jewish leaders in the face of the dictatorship's deadly attacks on Jews.[18] Timerman's vision of Argentina under the dictatorship evoked the Nazi past and Jewish collaboration with Nazis in the Warsaw ghetto and other European ghettos during World War II. For many Jews and non-Jews, Timerman's riveting commentary was their first in-depth look inside a violent South American dictatorship. Timerman was featured on the front page of the *New York Times Magazine* and in dozens of newspaper articles in North America and Europe. Despite the dictatorship's insistence that Timerman's release was the consequence of due process, pressure from U.S. Jews and many others is what forced the junta to liberate Timerman. His citizenship was revoked and he moved to Israel. So important was his ongoing criticism of the military regime that the Argentine government mounted an elaborate disinformation campaign in Argentina and the United States to try to discredit his claims.[19]

Alicia Partnoy's *The Little School* (1986) also provides evidence of the links between anti-Semitism, Argentine military ideology, and the violence of state terror. Though less convinced than Timerman that anti-Semitism was a cornerstone of military repression, Partnoy notes anti-Jewish feeling among prison guards and the complicity of many Argentine Jews in the military's actions. "So many rabbis thank God for the coup that has saved them from 'chaos,'" she wrote bitterly.[20] She described how a range of odd and chilling anti-Semitic tactics characterized the *proceso*. Cases were reported of efforts to carve Stars of David or crosses onto the bodies of Jewish prisoners. Swastikas and anti-Semitic slogans were routinely painted on the walls in detention centers. Jews in detention were regularly accused of disloyalty to Argentina for their supposed Zionism.[21]

The military government saw Timerman and Partnoy's descriptions of anti-Semitism within the dictatorship and the responses they generated in some countries as evidence of a Jewish conspiracy. The military imagined a Jewish enemy in varied forms. A disproportionate number of supposed overseas "subversives" were Jews. Some military officials fantasized that Israel (and Jews abroad more generally) was part of an amorphous and dangerous threat to Argentine sovereignty that included Amnesty

International, the Soviet Union, and French socialists, among others. Some officers highlighted the writings of three Jews—Albert Einstein, Karl Marx, and Sigmund Freud—as dangerous to the fabric of Argentine society. The military targeted psychologists and psychiatrists with particular ferocity, many of whom were identified as Jews and, as such, a threat.[22]

At times, the military regime identified an amorphous Jewish enemy as responsible for foreign criticism. As early as September 1976, the Anti-Defamation League's (ADL) Burton Levinson reported to a special U.S. House of Representatives session on human rights in Argentina that anti-Semitism was a factor in illicit detentions.[23] In response to this and other linkages in the United States between the dictatorship and anti-Semitism, Argentine leaders came to see American Jews as dangerous, unrelenting opponents. In the international campaign to undermine the dictatorship and expose its brutality, there was likely no one more tenacious, more active, or more prominent in the media and in U.S. political circles than Rabbi Morton M. Rosenthal, director of the Department of Latin American Affairs of the ADL—and Argentine leaders knew it.

Rosenthal came to his opinions cautiously. At first, he even sympathized in stark Cold War terms with the dictatorship's campaign against international communism. Rosenthal, though, led a growing contingent of Americans who came to identify human rights violations in Argentina with anti-Semitism, a linkage that set the tone for how many U.S. policymakers understood human rights violations in Argentina. Many Americans saw the military government as Nazi-like for the unusual ferocity of its attacks on Argentine Jews. The linkage shook the Argentine military, who believed that Jews wielded an undue influence in U.S. political circles. In fact, while there was no Jewish conspiracy against the Argentine regime, Rosenthal ably fostered a sense among key U.S. political leaders that the Argentine regime bore similarities to Nazi Germany and the Soviet Union's persecution of Jews. Some of those political leaders were Jewish, including Senators Jacob K. Javits and Abraham A. Ribicoff, both honorary chairs of the ADL's National Commission, but most were not.[24]

In 1978, Rosenthal wrote a letter to the Argentine ambassador in Washington, Jorge Aja Espil, that exemplified his strategy of highlighting anti-Semitism as a problem in Argentina and tying it to broader issues of human rights violations. The letter criticized what Rosenthal described as a vapid response by the Argentine government to the problem. Aja Espil, one of Argentina's most senior diplomats, interpreted Rosenthal's missive as evidence of the "power" of the Jewish lobby. Unlike their condemnations of other opponents of the regime, Argentine military officials never condemned Rosenthal as part of the "communist" conspiracy against them. This was perhaps impossible, even for a right-wing military regime that was capable of tying the Jimmy Carter administration, the French socialist government, and Amnesty International to that supposed cabal. Rosenthal was often cautious to wear his Cold War right-center politics on his sleeve, both in order to generate support among political leaders in the United States and to try to avoid alienating an Argentine government that he hoped, in the end, might be willing to liberate (or be coaxed or pressed into liberating) political prisoners.[25]

In the 1978 letter to Aja Espil, Rosenthal expressed his Cold War leanings by opening with condolences on the terrorist assassination of the Argentine sub-secretary for economic coordination, Miguel Tobias Padilla, thereby acknowledging at least in part the Argentine military's position that their internal war was the result of an ongoing leftist guerrilla assault on the nation. "Our hope," Rosenthal wrote, "[is that] this barbarous act will be condemned by all fair-minded people." The letter also thanked the ambassador for having received a delegation of "young ADL leaders" in Washington. But Rosenthal went on to excoriate Aja Espil for having suggested that Nazi literature and anti-Semitism in Argentina "have not been serious problems." Rosenthal told the ambassador that not only were his denials disconcerting but they missed the point of the problem of anti-Semitism entirely: "A crucial question is not whether it exists but government policy toward it. Much of the criticism directed against your country on the issue of anti-Semitism is due to the perception that the Argentine government has, at times, failed to take timely and effective action to halt or prevent anti-Semitism."[26]

The ADL excelled not only at exposing how the dictatorship targeted Jews but at linking those acts to larger questions of human rights violations. Moreover, Rosenthal wanted to make it clear that the ADL was effective. He made no secret of precisely how often he interacted with U.S. political leaders and Argentine officials. Rosenthal wanted it clear that the ADL had contributed to influencing the dictatorship on human rights and perhaps had been responsible for decisions the junta had made to release prisoners and about other issues. On 17 March 1982, for example, Rosenthal wrote to ADL regional offices to report that "Rafael

Rey and six other prisoners on whose behalf we have intervened are now free men. The seven are part of a group of sixty prisoners who have been under a form of parole called 'supervised liberty' (libertad vigilada). Now that their parole status has been eliminated and they are entirely free, Rafael Rey can be reunited in Israel with his wife and his six year old daughter, whom he has never seen." Rosenthal's memorandum also reported on the contacts he had made with the Argentine embassy in Washington, instructed regional ADL offices about what news to report in press releases, and provided an update on other developments, including the fact that Argentine authorities had given broadcasters permission to air the 1978 television series *Holocaust*.[27]

The Argentine military's approach to its perceived Jewish opponents was quite complicated. It had a paranoid, anarchic, and irrational quality that manifested itself in the experiences of Jacobo Timerman and other Jews and was evident in how the authorities attacked their perceived enemies more generally. But it also had a very methodical element. An anti-Semitic and exaggerated concern about foreign Jewish influences, particularly with regard to U.S. politics, informed an important aspect of the dictatorship's growing obsession with the fact that so much pressure about human rights violations came from foreign governments and international organizations. The belief among high-ranking Argentine military officers that Jews in the United States and elsewhere somehow controlled U.S. economic and other policies toward Argentina helped prompt the government's strategy of defending Argentina's human rights record by pointing to its actions regarding indigenous rights.[28]

The Argentine government linked and even blamed Jewish organizations for Jimmy Carter's position on human rights violations in Argentina. A defense ministry memorandum about a proposed visit to Buenos Aires in 1980 by Maxwell Greenberg, Abraham Foxman, and Morton Rosenthal of the ADL emphasized the intimate relationship between B'nai B'rith and the human rights bureaucracy of the Carter administration. One of the objectives of the visitors was to learn more about the state of the Argentine Jewish community, but Argentine officials felt that the ADL was unlikely to change its firm position or moderate its accusatory tone. Moreover, the government worried that the proposed visit would generate conflicts within the Argentine Jewish community because the ADL had repeatedly criticized Argentine Jewish leaders for downplaying anti-Semitism and had accused the country's Jewish community of collaborating with the dictatorship. Interior ministry officials felt that the visit should be approved but that the Argentine government should establish contact in advance with both the local Jewish community and the Israeli embassy to avoid a new round of negative publicity about anti-Semitism.[29]

If Carlos Beltramino's diplomacy and related successes in the international community can be read as the high point of Argentina's policy of human rights obfuscation, the site visit of the Inter-American Commission on Human Rights to Argentina in 1979 was a nadir for Argentine officials who sought to present the dictatorship as a defender of human rights. The decision of the CIDH to go to Argentina came in part because of multiple reports of anti-Semitism. The Argentine military approved the mission hesitantly, recognizing it as a necessary evil if accusations linking human rights to anti-Semitism were to be successfully challenged. Contradicting its lofty language on indigenous rights, the dictatorship set about to conceal evidence of human rights violations and crack down on groups that might leak the truth to commission members. The Argentines worried about the specifics of the commission's itinerary requests—including meetings with Timerman, who was still in jail, and ex-president Isabel Perón—as well as the potential ambiguities and surprises the visit might hold.[30]

Like the Office of the United Nations Commissioner on Human Rights, the CIDH had received hundreds of petitions from Argentines and others about the tortured and disappeared. Cases such as that of Graciela Mellibovsky were at the core of what the CIDH hoped to resolve in Argentina. Mellibovsky's father, Santiago, told both the CIDH and the UN's Commission on Human Rights a familiar story. At dawn on 25 September 1976, some twenty heavily armed people in civilian dress had descended on the family home in Buenos Aires. The group threatened the family and announced that they were looking for Graciela, "a subversive delinquent." But Graciela was not home that morning. The family learned later that she had been detained the day before on a street in downtown Buenos Aires. They also knew that after she was arrested, she survived at least a week in prison, but after that, they had no information. The military authorities rejected the information the family provided. The interior ministry's response to the family's request for a writ of habeas corpus was that an exhaustive search had determined that Graciela Mellibovsky was not in any government detention facility.[31]

The military's response to the impending visit of the CIDH was multifaceted. Drawing on reports to the CIDH and other human rights bodies that were in the public domain, it altered the physical spaces where torture and executions took place. At the ESMA, for example, officials removed an elevator in response to reports that blindfolded prisoners remembered hearing the sound of an elevator in a clandestine torture center. Authorities instructed diplomats to increase their efforts in international arenas regarding suggestions about Argentina's leadership on human rights. The government even proposed an inter-American convention to make torture an international crime and issued new instructions to police and military authorities about how to interpret international norms on human rights violations more effectively. In addition, personnel in each branch of the service were ordered in early 1979 to assess the cases of all of those who had been detained. Even as the junta was protesting foreign characterizations of the regime as one that systematically ignored the judicial system, this ad hoc review of cases—which was to conclude no later than May 1979—entrusted officers in charge of those in illegal detention with determining whether prisoners were "innocent," "guilty," or "doubtful." The interior ministry ordered that those who were found innocent be freed immediately. In each of these actions, the government was conceding secretly and internally that it was holding innocent prisoners like Graciela Mellibovsky. "Guilty" prisoners were to be hustled from illicit detention into the formal penal system.[32]

For the most part, members of the CIDH mission saw only what the government wished them to see. Visits to prisons proceeded only when commission members agreed to respect Argentine sovereignty. In practice, this meant that Argentine authorities would not permit the visitors to question what they offered as evidence of the state of human rights. The government allowed CIDH visitors to interview whoever they wanted to in federal or provincial police custody, a strategy meant to reinforce the Argentine military's position that extralegal detentions, executions, and torture did not exist. However, commission members were not allowed to visit military facilities or detention centers.[33]

Without naming groups or individuals, the government cast doubt on the accuracy of some of the accusations about the disappeared. It also rejected categorically the accusations—which were later confirmed—about the birth of "disappeared children" in detention centers and jails and about the capture of children along with their disappeared parents. The military's defense, as always, was to deny the existence of prisoners in any facilities but legally sanctioned jails and to invoke Argentina's laws and procedures about the treatment of children of detainees, whether taken or born in custody. "If a woman gives birth in detention," the government claimed, "while the child remains in his mother's care at first, his care is subsequently determined by applicable regulations in regard to the moral and physical protection of the minor." This was a deliberate obfuscation of the fact that the nation's child welfare system had been destroyed by military officers who arbitrarily, secretly, and without documentation assigned the children of the disappeared to couples who were sympathetic to the political objectives of the military regime.[34]

Despite the Argentine military's preparations for the visit from the CIDH representatives and the limitations on the CIDH's access to detention facilities and prisoners, the dictatorship was unable to contain the criticisms of the members of the commission who came to Argentina. CIDH representatives were able to meet with several human rights activists in Argentine cities, although they were carefully prevented from seeing the worst Argentine atrocities. In early 1980, they issued a scathing condemnation of the regime. Officials from a number of ministries denied what they could. Officials in the Ministry of Foreign Relations claimed that the conclusions of the CIDH were wrong and constituted a dangerous interference in Argentine affairs. They also claimed that the accusations jeopardized the functioning of the Organization of American States.

After the failure of Argentine efforts to undermine the CIDH investigation at every turn, the government marshaled a final challenge to the findings of the commission. The objectives of the military remained unchanged in the face of this new international condemnation. The government insisted that there were no government-sponsored human rights violations, that the government was in fact a staunch defender of human rights, and that where violations occurred, they were the work of unnamed opponents of the regime. The government insisted again that it "shared the discomfort of the Commission with regard to those who were supposedly disappeared." Without acknowledging whether there were or were not any disappeared in Argentina, the government indicated that its various agencies and organs had been mandated to locate all of those listed as disappeared. Moreover, Argentine authorities insisted that they were doing everything possible in every disappearance case to inform all interested individuals and institutions of their progress in locating the person in question.[35]

While the CIDH repeatedly pressured Argentine authorities about the Timerman case, it is hard to know what role the visit played in helping to bring about Timerman's release. The visit coincided with a Supreme Court decision on a petition for a writ of habeas corpus that paved the way for the junta's decision to implement a loss of citizenship order in Timerman's case, which allowed him to be deported to Israel. It is also clear that concern over pressures from Jews about the Timerman case overlapped with the government's more generalized worry about foreign influences. In January 1979, the SIDE determined that the Timerman case was the most pressing issue in Argentina's relations with the United States in the area of human rights. While the SIDE blamed the "Jewish community around the world" for the campaign to free Timerman, it found that international pressure went far beyond the Jewish community and had been organized simultaneously in the United States and Western Europe. As it did in other episodes related to criticism of Argentina's record on human rights, Argentines saw a conspiracy. They also worried about international perceptions of Argentina and the dangers posed by individual antagonists. In the Timerman case, the SIDE singled out the work of New York Times correspondent Juan de Onís as particularly damaging, noting that he had abandoned any pretense of objectivity toward Argentina in his reporting on Timerman.[36]

The anti-Semitism crisis waned after 1980 partly because of the election of Ronald Reagan as U.S. president. This change brought a favorable policy shift toward Argentina that the dictatorship had correctly anticipated. Reagan administration policymakers and Argentine authorities shared priorities about what both saw as a communist menace. Moreover, and to the delight of the Argentine regime, the Reagan administration had no interest in wielding human rights policy in the international community like a club. In addition, U.S. policymakers now saw human rights as less important than larger Cold War strategic issues. According to Reagan administration officials, Carter had misunderstood the Argentine government's record on human rights and criticizing the Argentine military on human rights would weaken the international authority of a Cold War ally.

In May 1981, when the Fundación Carlos Pellegrini, a pro–free enterprise right-wing Argentine foundation, co-sponsored the Inter-American

Symposium in Washington with its American homologue, the Council for Inter-American Security, organizers could count on the attendance of high-ranking U.S. government policymakers, something that would have been unthinkable under the Carter presidency. They included James Lucier, legislative aide to conservative senator Jesse Helms (R-North Carolina); General Gordon Summer, former head of the Inter-American Defense Board and a member of the board of the Council for Inter-American Security; American Enterprise Institute member Michael Novak (who had recently been appointed to represent the United States on the Inter-American Commission on Human Rights); and General Vernon Walters. The State Department had confided privately to the Argentine embassy in Washington that Summer would soon be named ambassador-at-large for Latin America. Argentine officials were jubilant about the shift in attitude the new administration heralded.[37]

They read a statement that Secretary of State Alexander Haig made privately about Guatemala to some Republican members of the House Foreign Relations Committee as a signal on Argentina. While the U.S. government faced "some difficulties" in sending military aid to the Guatemalan government because of the human rights situation in that country, it would not abandon its Central American ally in the fight against "subversion." American authorities did not abandon human rights as a policy objective in Argentina and elsewhere in Latin America. But Argentine authorities understood immediately that the concern would be much more perfunctory than it had been under Carter and much less important than renewed Cold War priorities in Washington.[38]

The international human rights community reacted negatively to the U.S. shift in emphasis. In August 1981, Nobel Prize Laureate Adolfo Pérez Esquivel told reporters at McGill University in Montreal that there been no halt to the torture and disappearances in Argentina to warrant the U.S. policy swing. He argued that Reagan had deemphasized human rights in foreign policy to "create military alliances in Latin America and to support and to help all regimes favorable to U.S. interests."[39] Meanwhile, the Reagan administration changed U.S. policy on several fronts. In July 1981, Assistant Secretary of State for Political Affairs Walter Stoessel appeared before the House Human Rights and International Organizations Sub-Committee to explain the changes in U.S. policy. He told liberal chair Don Bonker (D-Washington) that the Reagan administration hoped Congress would eliminate section 701 of the Foreign Assistance Act, which prohibited the United States from sending assistance through international financial organizations to governments that were deemed to be human rights violators. Stoessel told the sub-committee that although Reagan's opposition to human rights violations would be firm, the new administration would favor what he called "traditional diplomacy," avoiding what Stoessel described as the paternalism and arrogance of section 701. The State Department relied heavily on the Argentine government's own assessment of the human rights situation in Argentina and its narratives of chaos, the coup, and what had taken place after March 1976.[40]

The state department maintained that since de facto president Roberto Viola had visited the United States earlier in 1981, there had been a notable improvement in human rights in Argentina because of "changes" in Argentine policy (and not as a consequence of pressure from the United States or other nations). Moreover, since Viola's visit, there had been no reports of disappearances, and the Argentine embassy in Washington had confirmed the "resolution" of 59 cases before human rights organizations.[41]

In July, the Reagan administration announced an end to what Haig viewed as kneejerk American votes in international organizations to pressure Latin American military regimes accused of systematic human rights violations. The United States reversed the Carter administration's policy and voted at the World Bank and the International Development Bank in favor of $483.8 million in loans to the four notorious South American human rights violators—$310 million for Argentina, $126 million for Chile, $40 million for Uruguay, and $7.8 million for Paraguay. The state department also convinced Argentine authorities that newly appointed Assistant Secretary of State for Latin America Thomas Enders would soon tour Latin America to announce a "mini Marshall Plan."[42]

At his confirmation hearing before the Senate Foreign Relations Committee as ambassador-at-large to Latin America, General Vernon Walters described the Reagan administration's emphasis on quiet diplomacy as the most effective way to win respect for human rights internationally. Walters condemned the Carter presidency for its criticism of foreign governments because of human rights abuses, a strategy that he argued could never work effectively. In addition, Secretary of State Alexander Haig referred to the human rights situation in Argentina positively in a speech to the Foreign Policy Association. Haig rejected the reports of Amnesty International and claimed that the situation had improved in Argentina.

He argued that the efforts of the international community to ostracize and isolate so-called human rights violators had failed and that his own quiet diplomacy would achieve much more.[43]

In August 1981, Assistant Secretary of State Ernest Johnston appeared before the House Banking, Finance, and Urban Affairs Committee to defend the government's decision to support applications to international lending agencies from Argentina, Chile, Paraguay, and Uruguay. Here as elsewhere, the Reagan administration took the Argentine military at face value echoing dictatorship assertions that the human rights problem was being resolved. Johnston told committee members that while human rights continued to be a problem in Argentina, it was essential to recognize key improvements and the steps toward improving human rights that Argentina and other countries in the Southern Cone had made. Johnston presented data on Argentine progress in ending disappearances, the growing power of the Argentine judiciary, the normalization of union activity, and the growing freedom of the press that had been leaked to the Argentine embassy before he testified: It was precisely the material that Argentine authorities had provided to the Reagan administration.[44]

At the same time, the Reagan administration signaled the Argentine embassy in Washington that the newly appointed U.S. ambassador to the OAS, John W. Middendorf, was coordinating sympathetic members of the Senate to work toward the abrogation of the Humphrey-Kennedy amendment to the Foreign Assistance Act of 1976.[45] The amendment had ended arms sales to and military training programs with Argentina until the administration could demonstrate to Congress that the Argentine government had made notable progress on human rights. Not only had U.S. policy shifted significantly, but the Reagan administration was now secretly cooperating with the dictatorship to formulate a policy that would dovetail with Argentine military thinking on human rights. In an October 1981 communiqué to the Argentine government, Vernon Walters indicated eight issues that would shape the evolution of bilateral relations. The United States was hoping that Argentina would agree not to interfere in Bolivian political crises; would avoid conflict with Chile; would revisit its trade ties with socialist states; would ratify the Tlatelolco Treaty on nuclear disarmament; would provide assistance to the government of El Salvador; and would send peacekeepers to the Sinai desert.[46]

Two other issues touched on human rights. In each case, the way the issues were framed suggested that human rights was less important to the Reagan administration than it had been for President Carter. Walters asked Argentina to free individuals who had been imprisoned for "political ideas and to dismantle 'paramilitary' groups." He also asked Argentine authorities to show "their willingness to collaborate in the defense of democracy." Walters's language was vague. His reference to political prisoners gave legitimacy to Argentine claims that most of those whose release was sought by human rights groups were detained for subversive, violent actions. His comment on paramilitary groups affirmed the military government's false assertion that the abuses of the human rights of leftists in the 1970s had been committed by the Argentine Anticommunist Alliance and other nongovernmental groups.[47]

Argentine authorities moved quickly to support the opposition of the Reagan administration to the Nicaraguan Sandinistas and left-wing revolutionary groups in other Central American countries. In 1981, the Salvadoran government accused France and Mexico of supporting the leftist rebel groups Frente Democrático Revolucionario (FDR) and Frente Farabundo Martí de Liberación Nacional (FMLN). The Argentine embassy in San Salvador passed information to Salvadoran authorities that Mexico and France had promised the FDR and FMLN immediate diplomatic recognition if the two groups were to occupy and maintain a "liberated zone." This so-called intelligence was almost certainly false. It was as improbable that Argentine authorities had such news as was the accompanying information that Canada, East Germany, and "another European country" would also recognize a revolution in El Salvador. This is an example of the risky game Argentine authorities were playing in their geopolitical region. They were simultaneously providing a covert military assistance program to armed forces in Honduras and El Salvador and launching a disinformation campaign that was designed to discredit some of the governments that had been most critical of Argentina's human rights record. At the same time, their actions worked to support the counterinsurgency warfare of the Reagan administration. A communication from the Salvadoran government thanked Argentine authorities for the intelligence and mentioned cryptically the "peaceful assistance" (likely meaning diplomatic support) the Argentine foreign minister had offered El Salvador in Washington.[48]

The timing of the disinformation Argentina spread in Central America about the French government suggests that early 1981 was a key moment in Argentina's international reputation on human rights. France's newly elected president, François Mitterrand, was a staunch and vocal opponent of military rule in Argentina, and the Argentine military predicted trouble from the French about its human rights record. But Argentine authorities also thought that the new French regime might act pragmatically and put human rights issues on the back burner. Although Mitterrand quickly canceled arms contracts with Chile and Argentina and banned any new exports of arms, in May 1981, unnamed sources in the new French government reported to Buenos Aires that Mitterrand was unlikely to curtail further trade with Southern Cone nations (with the possible exception of Chile). In addition, the president of the French Union of Industrial Exporters confided to the Argentine embassy in France that even though Mitterrand had saved his strongest attacks on human rights issues for South Africa, his government had quietly renewed contracts to purchase South African coal. Commerce might well trump human rights as a foreign policy priority for Mitterrand. However, the Argentines worried that the results of upcoming parliamentary elections might mean that Mitterrand would be pressured by a stronger body of socialist and communist *députés*. They also worried about some of those in high positions in the new administration, particularly Régis Debray.[49]

In the minds of paranoid Argentine strategists, France had assumed a place similar to that of Amnesty International or Cuba—it was a socialist nation with a socialist president. The new French government was a threat to Argentina on issues of human rights for several reasons. First, three members of Mitterand's cabinet had openly subscribed to the statements of the Argentine Commission on Human Rights, which, of course, were highly critical of the dictatorship. Second, although Mitterrand immediately adopted an anti-Soviet, independent foreign policy that could not reasonably have been lumped with that of Cuba or other enemies of the Argentine generals, he fit the rigid profile of an "enemy."[50] In response, the Argentine government aligned itself more firmly with Washington by voicing a strong anti-French position. When Mitterrand announced his opposition to U.S. policy in Central America, citing in particular a rejection of the Reagan administration's characterization of the Salvadoran revolutionary left as "communist subversion," the Argentines seized a strategic opportunity and issued a statement: "French socialism proposes a rejection of the danger [the] pro-Soviet regimes installed in Central America represent to continental security and that slice the hemisphere in two." For Argentina, this meant that France posed a strategic risk to the region, especially to oil reserves in Venezuela and Mexico and to the Panama Canal.[51] For the dictatorship, the new French government was the enemy for many reasons, including its opposition to the United States, its antipathy toward Argentina because of the latter's human rights violations, and its sympathy for Argentina's antagonists in the Americas, such as Cuba and Grenada and leftist insurgencies in Central America.

While dictatorship officials celebrated the installation of Reagan; Haig; Jeane Kirkpatrick, the new U.S. ambassador to the UN; and others they regarded as friends, they braced themselves for more problems related to human rights violations. As Reagan was moving U.S. foreign policy on Argentina away from criticisms based on human rights abuses, the American media was very focused on reports of Argentine rights abuses. In September 1981, *Life* magazine published "The Disappeared in Argentina," an article by Steve Robinson that reported dramatically on the hundreds of dead across Argentina, the majority of whom had been "innocent victims of a reign of terror."

In addition, Timerman was reaching the height of his fame. As vociferous as he was in his criticism of anti-Semitism in Argentina and of the complicity of the dictatorship in the mistreatment of Jews, he was almost as harsh in his denunciations of newly installed Reagan administration officials. This plus his opposition to the Israeli government gave Argentine authorities an opening to some in the Reagan administration and in right-wing political circles. In May 1981, relations between Argentina and the United States improved markedly. The State Department issued a white paper refuting the widely circulating belief that the Argentine government was behind a campaign of anti-Semitism and rejecting the claim that the "anti-terrorist campaign" in Argentina had targeted Jews.[52]

Seizing an opportunity, the dictatorship immediately circulated information to potentially sympathetic members of the U.S. Congress and others on the putative links between Timerman and David Graiver, who was suspected of having financed the Montoneros. The generals told their American contacts that Graiver had bought a 45 percent stake when Timerman co-founded the Buenos Aires newspaper *La Opinión* in 1971. Until Timerman's detention in April 1977, the two men had worked together on several publishing ventures. When the government detained Timerman, one of the accusations it made against him was that his ties to Graiver made him a subversive. In 1981, William F. Buckley and *Wall Street Journal* columnists Irving Kristol and Seth Lipsky repeated the dictatorship's line on Graiver in their portrayals of Timerman.[53]

Turning the tables on the critique of Argentine human rights abuses as anti-Semitic, Kristol called Timerman a "Solzhenitsyn of the left" and attacked his liberal supporters in the United States for criticizing friendly authoritarian governments in Argentina and elsewhere instead of criticizing the Soviet Union. Kristol took up the Argentine government's refrain in asserting that Timerman had not been detained as a Jew or a Zionist but rather because of his links to Graiver. Kristol accused Graiver of having bilked two American banks out of $40 million in his efforts to finance the Montoneros in Argentina. Buckley also explained Timerman's detention in Argentina as a function of his ties to Graiver. When Buckley tried to turn the dictatorship-Nazism linkage on its ear by denouncing Timerman for having tried to impede the work of Nazi-hunter Simon Wiesenthal, Wiesenthal asserted that Buckley's claim was not true. At the same time, Mario Gorenstein, president of the Delegation of Jewish Associations of Argentina (DAIA), said that Timerman's version of anti-Semitism in Argentina was an exaggeration. Timerman responded by comparing Gorenstein's declarations to those of Jewish leaders in 1930s Nazi Germany who downplayed government state terror. In *Prisoner without a Name*, Timerman wrote that he felt humiliated not because he was tortured but because the leaders of the Argentine Jewish community had been silently complicit in the government's torture of Jews.[54]

For Argentina, the stakes were high. Through the early summer of 1981, Argentine authorities followed the emerging frenzy around Timerman closely with the hope of ending criticisms about Argentina's human rights record once and for all. But unwelcome controversy and publicity continued to grow. On 23 May, the *Baltimore Sun* published an editorial about Argentina's "virulent anti-Semitism" that supported an initiative by municipal council member David Shapiro to withdraw permission for the Argentine frigate *Libertad* to dock in the port of Baltimore. Fearing a chain reaction of similar acts in the United States and elsewhere, Argentine authorities reacted with alarm. They contacted the State Department, which warned municipal authorities in Baltimore of the Reagan administration's special interest in having the *Libertad* dock in Baltimore.[55]

That same month, Timerman appeared, uninvited, at Senate Foreign Relations Committee confirmation hearings for Reagan's nominee for assistant secretary of state for human rights and humanitarian affairs, Ernest W. Lefever, a right-wing ideologue. Though Timerman was not asked to testify, he was introduced by committee chair Charles Percy to loud applause. Representative Richard Ottinger (D-New York) wrote Timerman that if the committee rejected the candidate, it would be "clearly attributable to your efforts."[56] (Lefever was in fact rejected.)

At the same time, after Mario Gorenstein appeared before the House Committee on Foreign Affairs and downplayed anti-Semitism in Argentina, committee chair Clement J. Zablocki (D-Wisconsin) met privately with Argentine embassy officials in Washington. During the Carter administration, Zablocki had adopted a moderate line on human rights; he was supportive of the president's initiatives to punish human rights violators but was not among those in the House who advocated the harshest responses to state terror in Latin America. Now, Zablocki complained to Argentine diplomats that Gorenstein's testimony had been "lukewarm" and was not forceful enough to convince some members of Congress that there was no massive mistreatment of Jews in Argentina. Zablocki suggested to the Argentine government that it press Gorenstein for a follow-up letter to the committee restating his positions on Timerman's accusations. Zablocki's suggestion prompted the Argentine chargé d'affaires to ask Gorenstein for the letter, and Gorenstein agreed to write one if the DAIA board approved. Argentine-U.S. diplomatic and policy collaboration had never been more complete. Argentine authorities breathed a sigh of relief as they began to feel that the controversy Timerman had created with his accusations of anti-Semitic human rights abuses had begun to shift in their favor.[57]

The crisis wasn't over, however. Timerman's arrival in the United States put him at the center of an internal political debate that had influenced some members of the Republican Party, who were now potentially inclined to view Argentina more negatively. The Argentine government believed that this internal debate culminated in June 1981, when the Reagan administration withdrew its nomination of Lefever for assistant secretary of state for human rights.[58] The Argentines felt that Reagan's hand had been forced in part by a Public Broadcasting System (PBS) program titled *The Timerman Debate and Human Rights*, a panel discussion moderated by journalist Bill Moyers. This had aired on 250 PBS stations across the

United States. Argentine foreign minister Oscar Camilión complained to the U.S. government of "false allegations" made in the program. Argentine authorities categorized the panel discussion participants as either friends or enemies: "The program presented four public voices against our country ([Patricia] Derian, [Morton] Rosenthal, [Richard J.] Barnet, and [Robert] Cox) and four supporters of the Reagan administration's policy of human rights silent diplomacy ([Mark] Falcoff, [Fred] Siegel, [David] Sidorsky, and [Ernest] Lefever)."[59]

The PBS program was part of a media frenzy about the Timerman case. The impact of Timerman's book was far-reaching. Despite the sympathetic report in May 1981 from the state department, the Argentine government remained in damage control mode. In a July 1981 interview with the state department's sub-director for the Southern Cone region, Frank Alberti, the Argentine ambassador to Washington, perceived a possible shift in U.S. policy on anti-Semitism in Argentina. While he did not condemn the dictatorship, Alberti expressed his government's concern about reports of anti-Semitism that included the circulation of racist pamphlets and reported attacks on Jewish community institutions. He made clear that the expression of concern was one the U.S. government "knew" the Argentine government shared.[60] That same month, uneasy Argentine authorities circulated to key Washington figures an official list of individuals who had been liberated from government detention between March and July 1981. Moreover, the embassy responded to accusations of anti-Semitism in a letter to the Argentine president that had been signed by 67 members of the U.S. House of Representatives, with documentation that portrayed Argentine Jewish contributions to society in a positive light and emphasized the "real participation of Jews in the political and cultural life" of Argentina. These actions were necessary because thanks to Timerman, Argentine officials said, the "forces tending to represent Argentina as a decidedly racist society, with a government that tolerated anti-Semitic activities" had multiplied.[61]

Argentine officials faced a daily onslaught sparked by Timerman and his supporters. Late in July 1981, Americas Watch sponsored a press conference in Washington at which Timerman's son Héctor denounced the existence of "concentration camps" in Argentina. Argentine authorities reacted to this and other examples of the upsurge in international criticism of human rights abuses in Argentina in three ways. First, they continued to deny publicly the existence of the illicit detention centers and to maintain the fiction that all incarcerations in Argentina were made through the judicial system. Second, and privately, they not only continued to view the secret detention centers as a necessary component of their internal war on communism but rejected out of hand what Héctor Timerman's term "concentration camp" implied; the Argentine military refused the international characterization of their government as in any way related to Nazism. Theirs was a battle conceived of and executed in a Cold War context. Finally, the Argentine military continued to deny outright that massive disappearances and torture had characterized their regime.[62]

The international scope of the Timerman crisis was troubling to Argentina's leaders. In August 1981, the Argentine foreign ministry called on the Israeli counselor in Buenos Aires, Eliezer Palmor, to express the government's dissatisfaction with reports in the Israeli media of Argentine anti-Semitism. He said that Timerman was the source of ludicrous reports of the expatriation of some 350,000 Argentine Jews to Brazil. Palmor expressed his sympathy for the Argentine government's position, noted the potential negative effect of such reports on Argentine Jews, and promised to bring an Argentine proposal that both governments disavow the reports to the attention of his government.[63]

In the United States, Timerman's influence continued to appear larger than life to uneasy Argentine officials. Robert Teinstein, an owner of the powerful publisher Random House; Orville Schell, a former president of the New York City Bar Association; and Patricia Derian, who had been assistant secretary of state for human rights in the Carter administration, co-founded the American Friends of the Madres de Plaza de Mayo in April 1981. The Argentine government blamed Timerman for this development because Random House had published his book. The International Federation of Human Rights and the International Commission of Jurists announced that the Timerman case signaled that an independent judiciary no longer existed in Argentina after March 1976. The Argentine government countered with its usual line that people outside Argentina could not know the intensity of the attacks of "subversive organizations" on the nation: "Aggression of extraordinary intensity demanded an appropriate level of response drawing on provisions in the National Constitution." The Argentine response to subversion, then, was always in proportion to attacks against the nation. The government argued that its response to the threat Timerman posed had been both measured and "defensive."[64]

The military also invoked article 483 of the 1951 Military Code of Justice to justify the fact that Timerman had been tried by a special war council: "This is not a question of [arbitrary] courts set up to judge members of subversive organizations; that would be an unacceptably subjective connotation." The military repeatedly cited earlier legislation and decrees to justify its turn to military tribunals in the Timerman case and on other occasions. Law 18.232 (1969) authorized the president to create war tribunals (though that law was abrogated by the elected government that came to power in May 1973). The 1969 law cited as an antecedent Law 15.293 (1960), which had also authorized the creation of war tribunals to try individuals and groups accused of crimes "against the public order and tranquility." The dictatorship also cited a 1962 Supreme Court decision that authorized the trial of civilians by military tribunals.[65]

Despite all the publicity the Timerman case generated internationally, there were no significant commercial, strategic, or diplomatic consequences for Argentina as a result of Timerman's spring and summer of fame in the United States in 1981. Thus, the Argentine response can be reasonably analyzed as a strategic victory for their approach to human rights. Argentine diplomacy and policy was nimble, aware, and responsive to overseas perceptions. The Reagan administration based its decision to improve ties with Argentina on the assessment of the CIDH. Despite its concerns, the CIDH confirmed that it had found no evidence of an official policy of anti-Semitism in Argentina during its 1979 visit. In a chilling confirmation of the extent to which Reagan administration positions on human rights in Argentina confirmed those of the dictatorship, the Reagan administration conceded that a disproportionately high number of Jews had disappeared during the dictatorship, but it reasoned that this was because a disproportionate number of Jews were members of terrorist groups. In addition, Reagan took President Roberto Viola's comments at face value in 1981 when Viola testified before a joint meeting of the Senate Committee on Foreign Relations and the House Committee on Foreign Affairs that he was aware of anti-Semitism in Argentina and was taking action against it.

Even though the Timerman case began to fade in the international imagination after 1981, the Argentine government continued to track

Timerman's activities. In mid-1982, the SIDE noted that the volume of pro-Timerman material in the international media was decreasing. It also pointed out that in Israel, he was being attacked for his connections to the so-called "Graiver terrorist group" and for his "false pro-Zionism." "Timerman," the SIDE reasoned, "has the support of only one Jewish group in the United States, which uses him to attack the Reagan government from the perspective of his old terrorist ties." When Timerman was promoting his book *Prisoner without a Name, Cell without a Number*, the SIDE noted that he regularly tried to show that Jews were being persecuted in Argentina. "In this latter area," the SIDE observed, "he has not achieved the desired result. In general, each of the Jewish organizations in the countries that he has visited have rejected his accusations. Because of this, Timerman and his campaign will continue to wane quickly."[66]

The Argentine military was right. Living in exile in Israel, Timerman emerged as one of the most vociferous and harshest critics of that country's 1982 invasion of Lebanon. That highly publicized stand complicated his relationship with pro–human rights groups outside Argentina, including Human Rights Watch, which had trouble reconciling the image of Timerman as a victim of human rights violations with his journalistic polemics.[67] After he returned to Argentina in the 1980s, he had difficulty finding a national role that would give him the cultural and journalistic importance he had achieved after his imprisonment.[68] Nevertheless, Timerman, more than anyone else, publicized the notion of a link between Argentina, dictatorship, and human rights violations that would persist into the period of democratic rule after 1983.[69]

The Reagan administration's position on human rights in Argentina veered sharply to the right during this period. In October 1981, during a debate on the Foreign Assistance Act (1982), the Senate took up the 1977 Humphrey-Kennedy amendment.[70] A voice vote approved an amendment to suspend Humphrey-Kennedy. The amendment to the Foreign Assistance Act that Senators Nancy Kassebaum (R-Kansas), Charles H. Percy (R-Illinois), and Richard Lugar (R-Indiana) proposed suspended the requirement of the Humphrey-Kennedy amendment that the president had to prove to Congress that Argentina had made notable progress on human rights before arms sales to Argentina could resume. Influenced by Walters, Middendorf, and other Reagan administration members, the new amendment affirmed the Senate's satisfaction with actions taken by the Argentine government in defense of human rights and its hope that the (fictional) progress the government had made in finding the disappeared would continue. Despite the vociferous opposition of several senators who cited ongoing human rights abuses, including Daniel Patrick Moynihan (D-New York) and Edward Kennedy (D-Mass.), the Humphrey-Kennedy amendment was suspended.[71] Reagan administration intelligence "confirmed" what the Argentine military had been saying for over two years, that the political crisis had passed in Argentina and that the military was returning the nation to democracy.

While military leaders kept the fanciful notion that Argentina was under threat from a subversive menace alive through the 1980s, they were unable to contain the conflation of the concepts of the Argentine dictatorship, anti-Semitism, and Nazism in international media. Even so, and partially as a result of the election of Ronald Reagan, the Argentine military managed to avoid long-term damage to its international commerce, its standing in international organizations, and its relations with most countries.

4

Democracy and the (Re)Shaping
of Human Rights Politics

After Argentina lost the Malvinas War, the military trumpeted what it described from mid-1982 through presidential elections in December 1983 as the nation's transition to democracy, one more piece of evidence that it supported human rights. In April 1983, a year after the war, the generals reported to the Inter-American Commission on Human Rights that "the evolution of the political process in Argentina has led to an ample debate, involving key interest groups on the problem of human rights generally, and of the disappeared more specifically."[1] But after the war, the military government lacked the aggressive confidence it had once shown. The generals back-pedaled. They knew that democratic rule was just around the corner, so to shore up their own credentials as democratic leaders they acknowledged the recent discovery of mass graves in Buenos

Aires and the vicinity and provided information about the discoveries to international human rights organizations.[2]

But this was too little too late. The military's record on human rights and the many lies military leaders had told spoke for themselves. When the dictatorship fell at the end of 1983, Argentines embarked on a three-decade search for answers and justice. The new government of President Raúl Alfonsín, which was elected in December 1983, did not wipe the slate clean regarding human rights. Alfonsín, who had been elected in part on his reputation as a *proceso*-era human rights lawyer, faced immediate intransigence from military officers who were determined to maintain the illusion that the dictatorship had defended human rights. It was not until the 1990s, after Alfonsín had come and gone, that Argentines were able to begin to resolve the problem of a lingering military culture that was dedicated to promoting the false memory that the dictatorship had supported human rights. That process could begin only after the majority of senior and mid-level officers of the *proceso* era had retired and a younger officer corps who were trained after the end of military rule rose to power.[3]

Early in 1984, though, Argentines were hopeful that the ousted military leaders would receive swift justice. The Alfonsín administration quickly set out to make Argentina an international leader on human rights, establishing mandates and deadlines for results that were impossibly optimistic. Almost all of the priorities of the new government's foreign policies were directly tied to human rights.

Alfonsín saw domestic and foreign policies on human rights as intertwined, and his government focused on the issue of human rights internationally and domestically. However, his government was just as inclined to cite historical precedents for Argentine international leadership on human rights as the military regime had been. Like the dictatorship, for example, the Alfonsín government often held up the 1853 Constitution and its provisions for protecting individual rights and liberties, including those of immigrants.[4] In part, the Alfonsín government's commitment to human rights was a response to unrest in some military circles that created an ongoing threat of a return to military rule—a threat that lasted until the fall of his presidency in 1989. As late as mid-1988, high-ranking military officers were arguing that there was a persistence of "subversion" in Argentina that could be linked to the return of democracy and moral decay since the end of military rule.[5]

After 1983, Alfonsín, a member of the traditionally centrist Radical Party, led a government dominated by a Radical Party majority in Congress. In power, Radicals claimed that they were approaching human rights neither as realists nor as pragmatists. They referred to an "ethical-juridical" dimension of human rights in foreign policy as a key Argentine contribution to intergovernmental organizations.[6] Argentines voted for Alfonsín in part because they viewed Peronist leaders as dinosaurs who were unable to chart a new democratic direction after the *proceso*. In fact, Radical Party language on human rights signaled that the Radicals had adopted much of what had defined the Peronist movement for decades in terms of social and economic policy. This included a commitment to expanding the social welfare state and recognizing the Confederación General del Trabajo (the General Confederation of Labor, a Peronist anarchist trade union) as the legitimate representative and political voice of working people.[7]

By the time Alfonsín came to power in late 1983, Peronists and Radicals had been the dominant forces in Argentine national politics for almost forty years. Originating in the late nineteenth century, the Radical Party had come to represent the interests of immigrants, working people, and a burgeoning middle class before World War I. Soon after the war, the Radicals abandoned their pro-labor roots and shifted to a more explicitly pro–middle class position. But the military governments of the 1930s marginalized the Radical Party politically.[8] As military rule ended after World War II, a new movement, Peronism, took on the cause of working people, particularly those who had migrated over the preceding decade from the country's interior to Buenos Aires and other cities. As Perón's governments moved to enact revolutionary social policies favoring working people, the Radical Party—which opposed Perón at the national level through the late 1950s—crafted a role for itself as the critic of authoritarian tendencies in both Peronism and military rule (and Radicals came increasingly to conflate the two as one menace) and as the defender of liberal democratic traditions. Alfonsín was known in the 1970s as a liberal democrat in that context, particularly among urban middle-class supporters of the Radicals, who saw that party as the one most able to promote civil and human rights. Worn down by decades of Peronism and military dictatorship (which many viewed as two sides of the same authoritarian coin), middle-class Argentines saw Alfonsín as their best hope for lasting democracy.[9]

After 1983, the official and public position of the Argentine government was that Argentines would lead aggressively but fairly in international organizations to defend and promote human rights. This position was congruent with the Radical Party's defense of liberal democracy. At the UN Commission on Human Rights, Argentine authorities highlighted their leadership in the creation of the UN Convention Against Torture (1984), particularly the diplomacy involved in removing dictatorship-era roadblocks to the treaty, including language that weakened international supervision of the accord. Argentina became a vociferous opponent of apartheid in South Africa and, in an important rethinking of human rights in the late Cold War period, began to press other UN delegations to consider the nuclear arms race as a human rights problem. In 1986, Argentina and India drafted a UN resolution designating the nuclear arms race a global menace to human rights. Argentina also pressed for international conventions that sought to prevent the violations of human rights that had taken place under the dictatorship, including an article in a proposed convention on the rights of children to protect the young from illegal identity changes.

In the first three years of the Alfonsín administration, the Argentine Congress ratified five important international human rights agreements. These were the American Convention on Human Rights (or San José Pact; in Argentina, Law 23.054); the International Convention on the Suppression and Punishment of Apartheid (Law 23.221); the International Covenant on Civil and Political Rights; the International Covenant on Economic, Social and Cultural Rights (Law 23.313); the Convention on the Elimination of All Forms of Discrimination against Women (Law 23.179); and the Convention Against Torture (Law 23.338).[10]

As part of a larger political project to acknowledge Argentines who had been forced into exile by the dictatorship and entice them to return home, the Radical government moved quickly to make Argentina a haven for refugees. Linking the problem of refugees to human rights, under Alfonsín, the Immigration Department of the Ministry of the Interior shared responsibility for refugees in Argentina with the newly created Sub-Secretariat for Human Rights within the Ministry of Foreign Relations. More important, bureaucrats would no longer make decisions about refugee claims behind closed doors. Executive Order 464/85 (1985) created the Comité de Elegibilidad para Refugiados (CEPARE), an independent committee responsible to the president that had the authority to consider and make decisions about each potential refugee's application to enter the country. Formally, CEPARE would apply standards established by the 1951 UN Convention on the Status of Refugees, which as a result of new national legislation in 1984 (Law 23.160) would no longer apply solely to refugees from Europe. Informally, the question of which refugees the government would admit was politicized by Radical Party politics that placed the issue of human rights policy front and center and that invested the party with responsibility for maintaining the human rights of the nation in the context of the ongoing threat of a return to military dictatorship.[11]

One clear indicator of how the Radicals redefined human rights after the fall of the dictatorship was how the SIDE approached the problem. In early 1987, for example, the spy agency that had once tracked and kept files on human rights activists in Europe was reporting on the deterioration of human rights in Ecuador as an issue that had policy implications for the Argentine government. The SIDE reported on 40 cases of assassination, 170 arbitrary arrests, and 60 cases of torture in Ecuador at the hands of a right-wing government.[12] As they reprogrammed dictatorship-era bureaucracies for democracy, the Radicals drew on the enemies of the former dictatorship—key national and international human rights organizations—to establish policy standards. The government depended on a longtime opponent of the Chilean dictatorship, for example, the Vicaria de la Solidaridad, to assess the validity of the claims of individuals who had applied for refugee status from Augusto Pinochet's Chile and to gather data for hearings.[13] When María Teresa M. de Morini, director of the foreign ministry's Human Rights Office, reported on the cases of five Chileans who had applied for refugee status in Argentina in March 1987, she relied on information provided by the Vicaria. She supported the case of Paulo Valenzuela Muñoz because of the Vicaria's view that he "had had serious problems of personal security" in Chile. While the Vicaria had no information on another applicant, Rosa Toro Valladares, it offered to find out more. Morini's advice about a third applicant, Rodrigo Heraldo Lagos Cerda, was only that "the Vicaria has no information on this case."[14]

In February 1984, Foreign Minister Dante Caputo laid out the contours of the new administration's policy in a speech before the UN Commission on Human Rights in Geneva. In his opening lines, Caputo underlined both transition and the break from military rule:

Nuestro pais ha salido de una larga noche en la que los derechos esenciales para la dignidad de la persona humana fueron brutalmente desconocidos, menoscabados o violados—hechos de esa magnitud no tuvieron precedente en la Argentina, pais precursor de los derechos humanos, que ya en 1813 habia abolido la esclavitud y la tortura.

Our country has emerged from a long night during which basic rights to human dignity were brutally ignored, impaired or violated—acts of such magnitude had no precedent in Argentina, a pioneering nation in human rights that had, by 1813, abolished slavery and torture.[15]

In addition, Caputo made clear that while state terror was the cause of human rights violations before 1984, both Peronism and the military were ultimately to blame. In his account of the history of abuses that predated 1976, he also pointed to authoritarian rule as a precursor to social disorder. Caputo's use of the language "authoritarian rule" was meant to tie Peronism to military governance as a progenitor of governance by force and the denial of political liberties—and to highlight *radicalismo* as the only legitimate democratic counterweight to the country's violent past. Authoritarian rule had created a violent climate, Caputo argued, in which frustrated youth had found an outlet in the "apostles of violence, terrorist groups of varied ideologies" that adopted as their political method the destruction of the right to life and liberty. "That was how the terrorists, "moved by the delirium of their supposed liberation and prompted from overseas, won over many young people to cruel and irrational killings and kidnappings," Caputo continued, referring to the Peronist-era revolutionary left.[16]

The new discourse of the Radical government on human rights overlapped with that of the military in two ways. First, like the dictatorship, the Radicals claimed that Argentina had a long history of defending human rights and tied themselves to that tradition. Second, the Alfonsín administration blamed Peronist thugs and terrorist groups for human rights violations. At the same time, Alfonsín wanted to present his government as the antithesis of military rule and to demonstrate that it was the only viable democratic option in Argentina.[17]

Caputo made clear to the international community that the Alfonsín government's actions on human rights would be swift and far-reaching. A new National Commission on the Disappeared (CONADEP) would gather information about thousands of crimes, and Caputo singled out the issue of disappeared children. His government would also prosecute military perpetrators of rights abuses. Congress had already begun work to dismantle military law and incarcerate convicted perpetrators of rights violations. Capital punishment would end and those convicted by military courts between 1976 and 1983 would be freed. Military courts would be limited in the future to cases specifically relevant to military crimes. Torture would be punished with sentences equivalent to sentences for homicide. Those found to have been in a position to prevent cases of torture would be charged with crimes of omission. Torture resulting in death would yield a sentence of life in prison.[18]

The Alfonsín administration presented its role in restoring and advancing human rights in Argentina as the nucleus of an ethical rebuilding of national identity. For Alfonsín that meant an aggressive pro–human rights stance at home and abroad.[19] In close conjunction with its efforts to address the crimes of the Argentine military, the Alfonsín government took strong pro–human rights positions on key international problems. Shortly after Alfonsín came to power, Argentina began to reduce diplomatic ties with South Africa. The foreign ministry did not appoint an ambassador to Pretoria. The Argentine Congress and the Alfonsín administration repeatedly spoke in support of the liberation struggles of Africans in South Africa and Namibia. On 22 May 1986, Argentina broke diplomatic ties with what it termed the racist government in Pretoria.[20]

During this period, Argentina's foremost international concern was its growing international debt—what Deputy Foreign Minister Jorge Sábato called "a Marshall Plan in reverse."[21] The new Argentine government viewed the nation's massive foreign debt as a political problem that had been created mostly by the outgoing military government and as a threat to democracy and human rights in Latin America. Economic issues figured prominently in Argentina's promotion of human rights in the Americas. Advocacy of free trade and the free movement of capital had long been hallmarks of regimes that had engaged in massive human rights violations. The Alfonsín administration took the position that although military governments had touted the ideal of an efficient economy for half a century, they had repeatedly left the country in economic shambles. On a related front, the new Argentine government sought the political and economic integration of South America as the only reasonable path to a more equitable treatment of poor nations by the economically powerful, which in turn would foster democratic and human rights.[22]

A first priority for Alfonsín was dismantling the apparatus of repression. This was done on moral grounds, but it was also done for political reasons. It reinforced the linkage between democracy and human rights and strengthened the Radicals' bid to position Argentina as a human rights leader internationally. In late 1983, the president asked CONADEP to investigate and report within six months on disappearances and other atrocities committed by the military dictatorship.[23] The commission brought together prominent and respected Argentines, including journalist Magdalena Ruiz Guinazú, novelist Ernesto Sábato, Rabbi Marshall Meyer, and cardiologist René Favoloro. The commission published its findings, which were drawn from the testimony of thousands of witnesses, in the form of a book titled *Nunca Más*.[24]

Despite the importance of CONADEP's work to document military atrocities and although it provided the evidence needed to try senior-ranking military officers, many of the commission's findings merely confirmed what human rights groups inside and outside Argentina had long known. CONADEP did little to uncover new evidence that related to the thousands of unresolved cases of disappearances. Nevertheless, the Alfonsín government successfully used CONADEP's findings to enhance its image overseas as a defender of human rights. One key finding of CONADEP was that there had been a methodology of repression in Argentina. Perpetrators had deliberately hidden their identities to avoid future prosecutions. This differed from the interpretation of journalist Jacobo Timerman and others who argued that unlike Augusto Pinochet's Chile, where the machinery of repression was strictly hierarchical, repression and human rights abuses in Argentina had been much more anarchic. Whether or not a detainee was tortured and abused had depended on the whims and interests of the military or police authorities who presided over a particular region or neighborhood.[25]

The CONADEP report provided a statistical and deeply emotional account of state terror. There had been 340 detention centers. The living conditions of prisoners had been subhuman, and they had been treated sadistically. CONADEP also made clear that there would be much for the Alfonsín administration to resolve. "People were executed with their identities obscured. In many cases their bodies were destroyed to avoid subsequent identification," it reported.[26] CONADEP also concluded that military authorities had destroyed extensive documentation on the disappeared. Argentines and others read these results as a starting point from which to approach the new democratic government for information on lost loved ones. However, the Alfonsín administration insisted that democratic authorities could not be held responsible for identifying the disappeared. They would do their best, but the military had done much damage with its obfuscations and lies, and it had destroyed many official records. Despite this caveat, Argentines and others put enormous pressure on the government to prosecute human rights violators and provide answers to the thousands of questions about the disappeared.[27]

Alfonsín struggled to distance his government from problems that were attributable to the dictatorship. With some success, Alfonsín's government convinced the international community that there had been a sea change in human rights in Argentina—that the new government had consigned human rights violations to the past. In 1987, in keeping with that scenario, the UN Commission on Human Rights' Special Rapporteur on Torture, Peter H. Kooijmans, visited Uruguay and Argentina to learn more about how a society could transform its human rights record from atrocious to exceptional. Kooijmans wanted context that would help him understand current problems in Mexico, Peru, and Colombia.[28]

While the government had commissioned CONADEP to create a collective memory from the recent past, Alfonsín's claims that all problems related to past and present human rights abuses were being quickly and effectively resolved were false. In 1984, when the Ministry of the Interior reported on crime and punishment in response to a UN questionnaire, it suggested that Alfonsín had ended abusive prison conditions from the period of military rule in less than a year.[29] In its responses to the UN survey, the new government sought to distinguish itself from its predecessor in a number of ways, particularly focusing on quality-of-life issues for prisoners such as provision for religious services, libraries, personal hygiene, and medical care. For more than 150 issues relating to the treatment of prisoners, Argentina claimed that it subscribed to minimum UN standards. But did this mean that all problems with prison conditions had been solved? It is true that the clandestine detention centers where the worst sorts of abuses had taken place no longer existed. The government claimed that overcrowding also was no longer an issue because the police, the judiciary, and the prison system now supposedly worked well together and communicated effectively with one other. In addition, the government quietly cited reforms made during the period of military rule, including the construction of a handful of new penitentiaries beginning in 1979.

In its reports to international bodies on the number of disappearances during the dictatorship, the Alfonsín administration repeatedly chose the relatively low estimate of 8,960—a number heatedly challenged by domestic and international human rights groups. Moreover, the new government, which was now responsible for locating corpses and accounting for prisoners, claimed that data from the dictatorship years was accurate. These were figures that human rights groups had criticized for years. Despite protests from domestic and foreign human rights organizations, the new administration could find only 197 people in federal prisons who had been charged with subversion and like "crimes" as defined in dictatorship-era decrees.

In 1984, the new government passed three laws to address the most egregious of abuses of prisoners under military rule. Law 23.700, known as the sentence commutation law, paved the way for the liberation of many of the 197 military-era detainees the new government had acknowledged. The new government conceded that these prisoners had been held under unusually cruel conditions. Law 23.042 invalidated much of military law that had been applied to civilians through the end of 1983. Those who had been convicted by military tribunals now had recourse to habeas corpus, and this procedure resulted in the freeing of 90 prisoners. Law 20.070 substantially reduced the sentences of many who had been convicted after March 1976.[30] Because of this speedy judicial initiative, by July 1984 only 70 of the original 197 remained behind bars.

Justice was not swift for all, though. The Alfonsín administration continued to hold Hilda Navas de Cuestas, José Cuestas, Juan A. Tejerina, Fernando Gaura, and eight others as leftist terrorists through 1987, for example, thus accepting the *proceso* "justice" that had identified these prisoners as dangerous subversives. The military, then, was not the only group in Argentina that recognized a terrorist menace on the left.[31]

Responding to ongoing international scrutiny, Alfonsín made the elimination of cruel and unusual punishment a priority. Here, though, as in other juridical attacks on the human rights legacy of the dictatorship, the government was most effective on paper; perpetrators of human rights abuses went largely unpunished while much of the new legislation had little (if any) immediate impact. Law 23.409 (1984) established the norm that civil justice had precedence over military justice and mandated an aggressive role for the civilian court system in investigating dictatorship-era crimes and prosecuting the perpetrators. Law 23.097 (1984) incorporated specific torture-related prison terms into the Argentine criminal code for the first time. Officials who were found guilty of inflicting torture would be subject to 8–25 years of imprisonment, while those who had known of torture but had not acted promptly to stop it would face 3–10 years. None of these laws, though, had any immediate relevance to cases before the courts or to the legacy of torture and killing.[32]

Executive Decree 3090 (1984) created a new Sub-Secretariat of Human Rights (SDH) within the Ministry of the Interior. The SDH came into operation when CONADEP's mandate ended. Its function was to continue working on disappearances, human rights violations, and other problems as defined by CONADEP. In 1984, it negotiated a contract with the Editorial Universitaria de Buenos Aires (EUDEBA) to publish, promote, and distribute CONADEP's final report. The contract ensured that the price of the report would make it widely accessible and that there would be subsequent agreements with foreign publishers to distribute the report around the world. Published under the title *Nunca Más: Informe de la Comisión Nacional sobre la Desaparición de Personas*, the two-volume report contained the original text of CONADEP's report to Alfonsín as well as a list of those who had disappeared and a list of clandestine detention centers. It was a crucial early victory for the Alfonsín administration in its efforts to establish the government's strong links to an international culture of human rights by assaulting the military's legacy. As often as middle-class Argentines bought *Nunca Más* to pore over, they acquired it to sit on a table in their living room in memory of those who had been killed.[33]

Almost 1,000 people were present at the 28 November 1984 book launch for *Nunca Más* at the San Martín Cultural Center in downtown Buenos Aires, including the municipal secretary of culture, Mario "Pacho" O'Donnell; members of CONADEP; and representatives from embassies in Argentina (some from countries with unresolved petitions for information on the disappearance of their citizens). By the end of the year, the first run of 40,000 books had been followed by three more editions. There were eight editions by 1987, totaling 225,624 copies—a massive best seller by Argentine standards. In addition, contracts were quickly signed with prestigious foreign commercial publishers, including Seix Barral (Barcelona), Faber & Faber (London), and Farrar Straus Giroux (New York).[34]

Through *Nunca Más* and other SDH initiatives, the Alfonsín administration constructed a recorded memory of human rights violations under the dictatorship. This record became its own core political credential, one that became essential to the president as his economic record came increasingly into question. The record also helped maintain the support of the urban middle class throughout the decade. In addition to the CONADEP report, the SDH also created an archive of human rights violations, starting with records that CONADEP had considered in drafting its report. In June 1985, the SDH entered into an agreement with the Centro de Estudios Legales y Sociales (CELS) to open a photographic archive of disappeared persons. While this work sought to preserve memory and safeguard for and disseminate information to those seeking to right past wrongs, the government also had another objective. By controlling access to its archive, the SDH began to regulate human rights organizations and thus define what did and did not constitute a human right.[35]

In January 1985, the SDH created a protocol for consulting the materials it had archived. It allowed only nine human rights organizations to have access to the archive.[36] These organizations had been formally recognized by the SDH's secretariat. While the materials housed were also now available to "interested individuals," the implication of the distinction was twofold. First, the Alfonsín administration had become an arbiter of the legitimacy of human rights organizations and of what would constitute a human right. Second, human rights were a function of specific dictatorship-era problems and thus a function of the political fortunes of the Radical Party. The SDH asked the nine organizations it recognized to name official representatives as a condition for their access to warehoused documentation. All did so, with the exception of the Madres de Plaza de Mayo.

Shortly after, the SDH moved to increase its control of human rights data. Using the ostensible and improbable goal of "preserving the information contained in the CONADEP archive," the SDH won passage of Ministry of the Interior's Resolution 851 (1985), which assigned a "reserved" designation to all archived material on human rights. Thus, no one could use the official record of military-era human rights abuses without the explicit permission of the SDH.

Other ministries wanted a hand in orchestrating the Alfonsín administration's human rights agenda. The foreign ministry had played a key role in defining human rights before 1984, and its leaders wanted to preserve that role in democratic Argentina. Its officials forged ahead quickly to place Argentina "on the side" of human rights, picking up where their colleagues a year or two before had left off.[37] Within the foreign ministry, a second Human Rights Sub-Secretariat (MRE-SDH) was created and given administrative responsibility for a range of concerns. The MRE-SDH created two new directorates: the Directorate on Women and the Human Rights Directorate. The Department of Legal Studies, which was charged with reconciling domestic legislation in Argentina with the UN Convention on the Elimination of all Forms of Discrimination against Women (1981), was part of the Directorate of Women. The Department of Multilateral Organizations was responsible for UN and OAS activities relating to the rights of women.[38]

The Human Rights Directorate was composed of the Department of Humanitarian Affairs, a second Department of Multilateral Organizations, and a Department of Bilateral and Legal Affairs. Each department had sweeping responsibilities that illustrated the Alfonsín administration's broad approach to human rights. The Department of Humanitarian Affairs dealt with the Red Cross, the UN High Commission on Refugees, and ad hoc problems of a humanitarian nature (for example, aid to Mexico during that country's 1986 earthquake). The Department of Multilateral Organizations addressed a range of issues within the UN and the OAS, including apartheid in South Africa and the work of the Inter-American Court of Human Rights. The Department of Bilateral and Legal Affairs worked with nongovernmental organizations and with foreign governments that sought information on those who had disappeared during the military era.

Many of the problems this second human rights bureaucracy was charged with addressing had ostensibly already been human rights priorities for the dictatorship. For example, Alfonsín was not the first president to present Argentina as a leading defender of women's human rights. In many cases, Argentina's human rights foreign policy changed little through the transition to democracy.

Alfonsín's human rights credentials were his greatest political asset during the 1983 campaign. Through the mid-1980s, Alfonsín understood that as other problems proved increasingly difficult to resolve, such as rampant inflation, escalating foreign debt, the implications of the Semana Santa uprising of the military in 1987,[39] and his government's failure to bring the vast majority of military torturers and killers to justice, his pro–human rights positions were crucial to buttressing domestic and international support for his government. At the same time, Alfonsín was on the defensive on issues of human rights even before he took office. He was deluged with foreign and domestic requests for information on the disappeared, but throughout his term, he often had no information to offer.

On 30 May 1984, Ambassador Horacio Ravenna, the director of the newly created MRE-SDH, wrote to CONADEP president Ernesto Sábato to ask for help. Ravenna wanted all data on clandestine detention centers, disappeared children, and CONADEP procedures for processing evidence to be made available for distribution to embassies abroad.[40] In addition, concerned about the possibility of a new military *putsch* against democratic rule, the new government immediately tried to limit the power of the military in civil society with Decree 23.040, which repealed the military government's Law of National Pacification (1982), which had sanctioned "the use of terrorist methods to combat terrorism" after the fact.[41] This was the first executive order issued under democratic rule, and it provides another layer of context for Alfonsín's strong attention to human rights. Throughout his presidency Alfonsín faced the prospect of a coup d'état, and government officials believed that the faster they moved to buttress a new human rights regime, the more unlikely it would be that the military could come back into power.[42]

In his most forceful pro–human rights decision, Alfonsín asked the Supreme Council of the Armed Forces to bring Lieutenant General Jorge R. Videla, Lieutenant General Roberto E. Viola, Lieutenant General Leopoldo F. Galtieri, Admiral Emilio E. Massera, Admiral Armando R. Lambruschini, Admiral Jorge I. Anaya, Brigadier General Orlando R. Agosti, Brigadier General Omar D. R. Graffigna, and Brigadier General

Basilio Lami Dozo to trial for their leadership of the *proceso*. The charges stemmed from violations of military law and constitutional norms. Videla and Massera both received life sentences, and Agosti, Viola, and Lambruschini received lesser terms. These were the first convictions of military dictators in the Americas and were a remarkable triumph for Alfonsín.[43]

At the same time, under Alfonsín and the new democratically elected Congress, there was a rapid and extensive bureaucratization of human rights as a problem. The new bureaucracy was designed to erase the legacies of military rule and create a culture of human rights that celebrated the victory over dictatorship-era abuses. Yet the SDH was located in the branch of government that had presided over and planned the mechanics of repression, disappearance, and state terror. Its mandate was not unlike one important objective of the dictatorship-era Ministry of the Interior—organizing educational and community activities that reaffirmed the importance of human rights (though, to be sure, how the government understood human rights had changed radically).[44]

The government launched a massive propaganda and educational campaign to promote human rights and to tie such rights to a broad range of cultural, social, and political cornerstones of *radicalismo*. As part of its human rights campaign, the Argentine government returned to the policy of open and free admission to public universities. It legalized the activities of student organizations, which had been proscribed by the military, in both secondary schools and universities. While the government argued that the goal was promoting human rights, such policies were also part of a larger project to tie the politics of human rights to Radical Party politics. At both the university and high school levels, the Radical Party immediately dominated student government and began to wield considerable power over curriculums and the choice of university administrators.[45]

The Consejo Nacional de Investigaciones Científicas y Técnicas (CONICET), which had been decimated by the military, was rebuilt. Ousted scientists were reinstated. The Radicals created a system of fellowships for those who had been persecuted by the military. By 1987, some 80 exiled scientists had returned to Argentina in response to offers of positions at CONICET and funding for research. The new government also worked to tie CONICET and other pro–human rights reforms to a consolidation of Radical Party political authority. During the 1980s, most new CONICET positions went to Radical Party backers and anti-Peronists, so that while ostensibly the organization's restructuring was directed against the legacy of military rule, another objective was to con-solidate Radical Party authority.[46]

Argentine authorities tied domestic human rights projects to larger international objectives in a way that suggested that the Alfonsín admin-istration was at the forefront of the struggle for human rights. Often, the government trumpeted the results of such policies as triumphs. In reality, they frequently fell far short of stated objectives and instead reaf-firmed the long-standing role of the Radicals as a party of the middle class with little to offer working Argentines. For example, the Alfonsín administration set out to reform institutions as a means of increasing access to political participation, increasing equality of opportunity, and increasing universal access to basic goods and services. The Ministry of Health launched dozens of new programs such as school lunches, orga-nized sports for poor neighborhoods, and a new fund to provide medi-cine for the poor. These projects were presented as examples of distribu-tive justice. But none of them stopped the decline in living conditions for the majority of Argentines during the 1980s and the growing poverty in Argentina. To be fair, the Alfonsín government cannot be blamed for increasing poverty that was a symptom of both long- and short-term problems. These include disastrous dictatorship-era economic policies that led to massive deindustrialization and a devastating and exponential increase in foreign debt.[47]

The Alfonsín government counted among its accomplishments the Primer Festival Latinoamericano de Teatro (the First Latin American Theatre Festival), the Foro Nacional de Bibliotecas (the National Library Forum), and the Segundo Festival de Orquestas Sinfónicas Nacionales (the Second National Symphony Festival). The government promoted such expressions of popular culture as a triumph of democracy, human rights, and *radicalismo*. A new Secretariat for Social Promotion was cre-ated at the federal level to emphasize the government's commitment to human rights as a way to end poverty. Regrettably, like other Alfonsín-era human rights initiatives, secretariat rhetoric trumped substantive results. The secretariat set out to find ways to increase the income levels of the poorest Argentines and to work with urban and rural communities to create new mechanisms of political participation and organization at the grassroots level. The activities of the Secretariat combined a sensitivity to the linkages between human rights and democracy with high ideals. But the government had no links to traditional *peronista* organizing practices in neighborhoods or other communities, so it failed to transform the lives of ordinary Argentines in any meaningful way.[48]

The results of the secretariat's efforts to improve the lives of Argentina's indigenous people were mixed and, for the most part, as ineffectual as military-era programs. When the Alfonsín administration came to office, the best estimate of the country's indigenous population was 150,000—a number that had been haphazardly put forward in 1968. The Alfonsín administration revisited this number and found that there were 200,000 indigenous people in the republic, including members of thirteen ethnic groups distributed in twelve provinces. While indigenous people represented only 0.11 percent of the population in Buenos Aires Province, the figure in Jujuy Province was 16.85 percent. Congress passed Law 23.302 (1985), which made the government responsible for preserving the cultural and linguistic identity of indigenous groups and for promoting the "historical repair of [indigenous] communities, dispossessed unjustly from their lands."[49]

The legislation provided for a new system of indigenous justice based on traditional norms and practices. Indigenous communities would have greater control of their traditional lands, a policy that would include ending the sale of land to nonnative peoples. There would be bilingual education in rural schools and a stricter application of laws protecting workers in indigenous communities. Despite these advances on paper, there was no improvement in education or working conditions among indigenous Argentines.

Provincial legislatures passed equivalent laws, which included land distribution projects in Formosa, Chaco, and Neuquén. Depending on the indigenous group in question and on local traditions, land was sometimes distributed to communities and sometimes distributed to families.[50] However, the Radicals failed repeatedly to provide immediate aid to Toba, Mataco, and other northern indigenous communities that were repeatedly battered by flooding in the 1980s. Larger projects of the sort the military had attempted in order to bring indigenous Argentines out of poverty were unsuccessful. In some areas, the approach of democratic Argentine authorities was disturbingly similar to the approach their military predecessors had used. Although the Alfonsín administration presented Argentina as a leader in protecting the human rights of indigenous peoples, nothing substantive changed for indigenous peoples during the 1980s. Much of what the Argentine government said was ambiguous rhetoric. Law 23.302 (30 November 1985) addressed indigenous politics and aboriginal communities. According to the Alfonsín administration, the passage of this legislation would preserve indigenous cultures and languages and provide "historic reparations" to indigenous communities that had been unjustly dispossessed of their lands. But the law did none of these things.[51]

There were some measured successes. As during the period of military rule, provincial authorities followed the federal lead. Law 6373 (1986) in Salta created an Aboriginal Institute to be directed by an indigenous person. Law 5758 (1986) in Tucumán brought provincial legislation into compliance with Law 23.302. Through 1986, the federal government sponsored multiple programs to benefit indigenous groups in Chaco, Chubut, Formosa, Jujuy, Misiones, Neuquen, Rio Negro, Salta, Santa Cruz, and Santa Fe provinces.

By 1987, though, even the government conceded privately that Law 23.302 had been largely ineffectual. A frustrated Alfonsín went to Congress to pass a handful of changes to the law that would allow for rapid and effective advances in efforts to alter the lives of indigenous Argentines. The government now insisted on tougher requirements for compliance with labor laws in indigenous communities. One change revised the definition of an indigenous community, favoring cultural and anthropological markers over geographical/historical guidelines. This meant opening government programs to more indigenous groups and setting aside a long-standing government position that indigenous groups were only those that had been present at the time of the Spanish conquest in what was now Argentina. The Chiriguano people, for example, who had only been in Argentina for four decades, could now count themselves as "indigenous."[52]

Redefining the concept of who belonged to an indigenous community was a key shift. Until 1987, indigenous communities had been legally defined in civil and commercial terms. After 1987, the definition of an indigenous community was expanded to include members who were simply living in the group. Many communities had "disappeared" for want of commercial activity or formalities related to civil status (census numbers, for example), but now a community would continue to exist as long as it had a statute that indicated how its legal representatives were chosen. The government acknowledged the relationship of indigenous peoples to land in ways that emphasized cultural identities and sought to end loss of land by reforming laws so that individuals who had not been born in a given community could not buy land within the community. By the mid-1980s, the Radicals recognized that their educational reforms were of limited value to indigenous peoples because they often used uniform standards and materials at the expense of attention to traditional indigenous knowledge. A new version of Law 23.302 stressed bilingual and multicultural programs that would make it possible for curriculums to incorporate indigenous cultural values and spirituality.[53]

The Council for the Consolidation of Democracy (which was responsible directly to the president) was one of several bureaucracies established to promote the linkages between *radicalismo*, governance, democracy, and human rights. It proposed constitutional reforms that would include creating the office of prime minister and expanding popular consultation through plebiscites and referendums. For the most part, Argentines were unimpressed with these changes because of ongoing economic problems and an unresolved human rights legacy.

Finally, in 1988, the Alfonsín government began to recognize its failures. Most important, despite the initial success of obtaining convictions for a handful of top military officers, Alfonsín was not able to win further cooperation from military tribunals in the investigation of crimes committed during the military regime. More ominously, an internal Ministry of Foreign Relations report noted that there were "still institutions in all areas of public life that have remained impenetrable to democratization."[54] The dictatorship culture persisted in police forces, judiciaries, and other bureaucracies where corruption, a reluctance to prosecute dictatorship-era crimes, and the ignoring of police violence were commonplace.

As the economy faltered, the Alfonsín government became less certain about what the correct human rights policy should be. In June 1986, for example, the Argentine Congress tried to abrogate Law 22.546, which had been approved under military rule in 1981. The law provided for a bilateral Treaty on the Protection of Minors that had subsequently been ratified by Uruguay and Argentina. Though many cited this as an important instrument for providing restitution to the victims of the dictatorship, during the Alfonsín administration, Argentine legislators interpreted the document as an instrument designed to protect kidnappers and prevent the return of stolen children to their families. María Teresa M. de Morini, director of the foreign ministry's Human Rights Office, like many Argentine legislators, felt that the document was a troubling legacy of the dictatorship that ought to be repealed. But Foreign Minister Susana Ruiz Cerutti disagreed, citing the pro–human rights component of the treaty and arguing that legislators would contravene the Argentine Constitution if they tried to repeal the accord. She pointed out that the power to make treaties (and the power to repeal a treaty) rested in a co-operative agreement between the president and the legislature.[55]

More troubling for the Alfonsín administration was the fact that as early as January 1984 it faced immediate, overwhelming, and persistent pressure to make the disappeared reappear. Like its military predecessor, it could not begin to keep up with the continued onslaught of requests for information. While the Alfonsín administration was sympathetic to such queries, it was often unable to offer useful information or restitution. Although those who wanted information supported democratic rule, the requests came as a demand for action from the Argentine government. Frequently, requests were made for information that the petitioner knew the Argentine government had in its possession. By mid-1984, dozens of groups and individuals were pressuring the Alfonsín administration to release information. In most cases, the administration was less than co-operative for fear that answers would lead to new questions about pros-ecution and criminal responsibility.[56]

Within months of coming to power, the Alfonsín administration was ignoring, deflecting, and refuting the mounting queries from overseas, much as its military predecessor had done. There was immediate and mounting pressure from the Swiss government and Swiss citizens, for example, over the case of Mariana Zaffaroni Islas, who had been impris-oned at the age of 18 months with her mother on 27 September 1976. She was adopted and given the name Daniela Romina Furci. In 1983, she was identified and found in the home of Miguel Angel Furci, a retired army officer. Within months, she had disappeared again. Not only did the democratic government face mounting criticism from Switzerland and elsewhere because a new disappearance had taken place on the Radicals' watch, but there was a growing chorus of criticism of the government because it had not included the kidnapping of children in its list of crimes that would lead to the conviction of Argentine generals.[57]

In 1985, a federal court in Rome asked Argentine authorities for information about the disappearance and detention of children, underlining the failure of Argentine courts to produce the disappeared and the seeming incompetence of the Alfonsín government. The Italians sought information on José Abdala Sabino (born 27 July 1974 in Mercedes, Buenos Aires; kidnapped with his parents on 16 March 1977); Gabriel Matías Cevasco (born 14 October 1976 in Buenos Aires; disappeared with his mother on 11 January 1977); and Eva Paula Logares (born in June 1974; disappeared with her parents on 18 May 1978; found by the Abuelas de Plaza de Mayo as "Paula Luisa Lavallén," the daughter of police officer Rubén Lavallén). The Abuelas human rights groups, who were dissatisfied with the progress of the democratic government on these and dozens of other cases, had provided information on these and other cases to the court in Rome.[58]

Often the Alfonsín administration had no answers. In the case of three Swiss citizens (Carlos Eduardo Wagner, disappeared 14 September 1977; Victor Hugo Hoper, disappeared 29 April 1976; and Norberto A. Habegger, disappeared August 1978), the Argentine government attempted to locate the disappeared with no results. In January 1987, ten federal court jurisdictions began investigating Habegger's case. In 1986, the Federal Court of San Nicolás began a new consideration of Hoper's disappearance. In late 1985, the Federal Court in Rosario began working on the Wagner case. None of these investigations yielded new information.[59]

The case of Israeli citizen Jacobo Isaac Grossman highlighted the Alfonsín government's failure to eradicate the sins of the dictatorship completely. Grossman, who had been picked up by military authorities in July 1976, was charged with extortion, kidnapping, and possession of explosives and weapons. He was sentenced to 10 years, 22 years, and 7 years, respectively, for these crimes. According to both the Alfonsín administration and the dictatorship, the Israeli government had recognized privately in 1976 that while Grossman had acted as an agent for the Montonero guerillas, he had also worked for the Israeli secret service under the chargé d'affaires of the Israeli embassy in Buenos Aires. In 1987, the ADL's Morton Rosenthal pressed for Grossman's release. While the Alfonsín administration rejected Argentine military intelligence as unacceptable in many cases, in this case it confirmed the validity of Grossman's sentences. He remained imprisoned even though his detention in

1976 had been illegal; it had been a street-level kidnapping by the Operations and Intelligence Group of the Third Infantry Division, a notoriously violent military unit and the same group that planned and executed an attempted coup d'état in 1989.[60]

The case against Grossman was complicated for Alfonsín. He believed that Grossman had been justifiably prosecuted by the military for crimes related to his membership in the terrorist Montoneros. Thus, Grossman remained behind bars despite legislation that had promised his release as a prisoner of the military.[61] Rosenthal likely understood that Grossman was guilty of the charges for which he had been convicted, but the Alfonsín administration was aware that the case could jeopardize its relationship with the ADL and others in the international Jewish community who were strong supporters of the democratic Argentine government. Rosenthal claimed that Grossman could not have committed one of the principal crimes for which he had been convicted because he was being held in federal prison in Buenos Aires at the time. He cited a document in his possession that purportedly showed that Grossman was being detained by Argentine authorities on 6 July 1976; one of the crimes for which he had been convicted was committed two days later. Rosenthal also tried to provide Alfonsín with a way of by-passing the question of guilt or innocence. He argued that Grossman might be released on humanitarian grounds, thus enabling him to provide spiritual and financial support to his elderly and ailing mother, who had moved to Israel.[62]

The government denied Rosenthal's request that Grossman be released, insisting privately that Grossman's convictions by military courts had been arrived at justly.[63] Although military authorities saw a Jewish conspiracy abroad, no one in the Alfonsín administration accused Rosenthal of cooperating with Israeli authorities. However, Rosenthal was not the only one who was interested in Grossman's case. Israeli National Radio (Kol Israel) had been pressing for information about Grossman, specifically whether Israeli or Argentine officials could confirm that he had been working as an Israeli agent under the direction of the Israeli ambassador in Argentina at the time of his detention in Buenos Aires. In addition, the Israeli embassy in Buenos Aires had been asking for information from the Argentine government about the Grossman case for some time; Shimon Peres planned to take up the case with Argentine officials during a 1986 visit that, in the end, never took place. But the Alfonsín administration was convinced that Grossman had been advising the Montoneros about managing large sums of money and infiltrating industrial security, although it never released statements about these activities to the public. The administration also believed that Grossman had been working for Israeli intelligence, receiving instructions from the Israeli ambassador in Buenos Aires.[64]

The Alfonsín administration had multiple foreign policy objectives with regard to human rights. Frequently, the principal objective was the same as it had been before 1984. The tactics the government used to achieve its foreign policy goals also often did not change. This became apparent in how the government interacted with individuals and groups seeking information related to human rights. Throughout the 1980s, the UN Commission on Human Rights Working Group on Enforced or Involuntary Disappearances pressed the Argentine government for information it could not provide. The content of the requests from the Working Group for information during the Alfonsín presidency was strikingly similar to the content of its requests during the dictatorship. But the Alfonsín administration cooperated much more fully than the military had done. At the same time, Argentine officials saw some of the same dangers and risks that the military had perceived in confronting foreign pressures to provide information about disappeared individuals. In early 1984, the Working Group began considering a site visit to Buenos Aires to collect information, to meet with relatives of the disappeared and human rights organizations from the region, and to hold a regularly scheduled Working Group meeting. Horacio Ravenna of MRE-SDH recommended that the Foreign Relations Minister approve the visit, emphasizing that the visit would help improve Argentina's international image. According to Ravenna, "It would be politically convenient for the improvement of the country's foreign image to invite the Working Group" to Buenos Aires because it would give the government an opportunity to "show the visitors the progress that had been made" on human rights.[65]

When Working Group members visited Buenos Aires in June 1985, they were received by the Argentine foreign minister, the interior minister, and the chair of the Senate Foreign Relations Committee. The government used the occasion to turn over information on forty cases that included twenty-two missing Paraguayans and five Chileans who had been thought incorrectly to have been taken to Chile.[66]

The Argentines took the Working Group's choice of Buenos Aires as a meeting place as a signal of the UN's confidence that the Argentine government had respect for human rights. The decision by Argentine authorities to treat the event like a state visit was an effort to promote the notion that Argentina was a strong defender of human rights.[67] But this was hardly the case. Most requests for information that came to the Alfonsín administration came with a summary of what the Working Group or other organizations already knew about particular cases, information that these groups believed was already in the hands of Argentine authorities. The exercise, then, was less a sharing of information about a disappeared person than a confrontational effort to pressure the Argentine government to take decisive action to find individuals and initiate criminal consequences for the perpetrators of human rights abuses. In August 1985, only two months after it had visited Argentina, the Working Group asked for information about twenty-one cases, including the cases of five women who had been kidnapped while pregnant and two children who had been seized with their parents. Thousands of such requests were submitted through the Working Group and through other channels, and the material that accompanied such requests overwhelmed the Alfonsín administration with data on human rights violations. The government was unable to keep up with the many demands for news about thousands of cases.

In the case of Oscar Donato Godoy, for example, the Working Group had testimony from the missing person's mother-in-law that it passed on to the Argentine government in the hope that Godoy's disappearance would be resolved. The Argentines read the data as a sharp reminder from the UN that the Argentine government had a responsibility to solve what seemed to be a straightforward case. The Working Group made clear that "neither the *habeas corpus* petitions, nor [the family's] complaints to government authorities" had produced results. When it passed on information about Godoy's case, the Working Group was duplicating data that the Argentine government would already have received repeatedly from the impatient family.

In the Working Group's request for information, it included the information that Godoy had been kidnapped by unnamed Argentine authorities on 28 February 1978 with his wife, Olga Mabel Ferreyra de Godoy, who was nine months pregnant at the time. "About five days later," according to Ferreyra de Godoy's mother, "relatives of the disappeared learned that his wife had given birth at the Tigre Hospital. The disappeared's brother-in-law tried to visit [Ferreyra de Godoy] at the hospital, but staff refused him entry and told him that she was under arrest and could not receive visitors." The Working Group reported further that a police cruiser had been stationed outside the hospital at the time. Whether or not Godoy's captors could be identified and whether or not there was documentation of the birth, the UN was suggesting diplomatically but forcefully that there had to be at least a dozen people in Tigre who knew of the clandestine birth at Tigre Hospital in early March 1978. As in many cases, the Alfonsín government gave no response other than to acknowledge the request for information.[68]

Groups and individuals overseas saw Argentine authorities as either incompetent or obstructionist in their responses to this and hundreds of similar cases. Alfonsín had to balance his effort to cast Argentina as a human rights leader with the increasingly difficult task of defending his reputation against accusations that Argentina had been unresponsive to human rights problems from as far back as the early 1970s. In September 1987, the Argentine permanent representative to the United Nations in Geneva, Leopoldo H. Tettamanti, told the foreign ministry that he had received word from Luis Varela Quiros, a Costa Rican diplomat, that a campaign against the Argentine government was in the making from within the Working Group. There would be new denunciations, he wrote, "all in reference to old cases." Tettamanti fought back. He asked Varela Quiros to tell the Working Group that he anticipated "politically responsible" behavior from his Argentine colleagues. Tettamanti warned that were the Argentine government "attacked gratuitously, without evidence, or irresponsibly, it would be obliged to defend itself, with the risk of damaging the good relations maintained by the Working Group."[69]

That fall, Argentine authorities felt themselves under siege. The international community had begun to echo domestic criticism of Alfonsín for caving in to military authorities during the Semana Santa (Easter Week) uprising and its aftermath. Argentine diplomats fought the growing perception of the Working Group—fueled in part by the complaints of human rights NGOs—that the stalled process of releasing information about the disappeared was tied to new limitations on prosecuting military officers for crimes committed during the dictatorship.[70] Despite the Alfonsín administration's failure to resolve cases of individuals who had disappeared, middle-class Argentines remained deeply committed to the idea that good human rights practices were intimately tied to the democratic processes outlined by the Radicals. Many ordinary Argentines took it upon themselves to defend human rights in Argentina and internationally in a way that continued to construct human rights as a set of problems relating to dictatorship-era abuses but not, for example, to ongoing police brutality.

In October 1987, on behalf of himself and university colleagues, Victor A. Ramos, professor of geology at the Universidad de Buenos Aires, wrote a stern letter to the Colegio de Geólogos de Chile demanding an explanation for the assassination of twelve Chilean citizens by the government of Augusto Pinochet. Ramos noted that his indignation stemmed in part from the fact that one of the victims, José Valenzuela Levi, was the son of a colleague at the University of Stockholm, Beatriz Levi. Argentines had begun to pressure foreign dictatorships in the same way that foreigners had once pressured Argentine authorities in defense of human rights, in this case using the tactic of shaming Chilean academics under the watchful eye of a Swedish academic.[71]

Despite frustration from many quarters over the government's inability to produce information about the disappeared, members of the Alfonsín administration and the president personally were lauded for their defense of human rights both before and after the fall of the dictatorship. For example, after Alfonsín received the president of B'nai B'rith International, Seymour D. Reich, on 21 October 1987, Reich celebrated Alfonsín's role as a defender of human rights and praised the Argentine leader for his support of B'nai B'rith's position on the plight of Soviet Jewry in a thank-you note.[72] These celebratory moments could not erase the growing number of attacks on Alfonsín for his inability to provide justice in the aftermath of military-directed state terror.[73]

In November 1986, the Carter Center—at the specific request of former U.S. president Jimmy Carter—forwarded a strongly critical communiqué from Amnesty International (USA) to President Alfonsín. Amnesty International executive director John G. Healey wrote that very few of the dictatorship-era "missing children" had been returned to their families. Some children had been located in the homes of personnel connected with the military regime, but very few of these cases had been resolved, even when judicial proceedings had begun for the return of these children to their families.[74]

In addition, in dozens of cases, the Alfonsín administration had adopted the position of the former military rulers that sometimes a subversive was, in fact, a subversive. The case of Héctor Géronimo López Aurelli illustrates this point. By the time of the Easter Week rising in 1987, he had been a prisoner in the U.2 federal detention center in Buenos Aires for over a decade. The Alfonsín administration never questioned the judicial procedures that put him behind bars. He had been convicted and sentenced to life in prison in November 1979 by the First Circuit Court in Córdoba for possession of arms and munitions of war, the emblems of subversive organizations, materials destined for the creation of explosives, kidnapping, and murder. In October 1980, the Córdoba Federal Court confirmed the sentence on appeal, and a year later the Supreme Court rejected a new appeal.[75]

By the terms of Alfonsín administration Law 23.807, a system of reduced sentences was implemented for those who had served jail time between 24 March 1975 and 10 December 1983. For López Aurelli, this meant that on 14 February 1988, he would be in a position to petition for his freedom. In his case, though, the government argued that Law 23.807 was irrelevant. The Alfonsín administration judiciary repeatedly confirmed the conviction of López Aurelli as reasonable by all measures. In November 1984, he petitioned the justice ministry for his unconditional release and a reopening of the case. This was turned down, as was a second petition for a review of his case before the Federal Court of Córdoba.

On 18 October 1985, former air force captain Osvaldo Antonio López petitioned the Inter-American Commission on Human Rights, alleging that the Alfonsín administration had violated his human rights as protected by the American Convention on Human Rights.[76] There was widespread international press coverage of the case and on 30 June 1987, the commission declared López a political prisoner. The Alfonsín government went before the court to defend López's conviction at the hands of military authorities, beginning with its support of a 1976 ruling by the Appeals Court of La Plata.[77] On 29 April 1976, officers had found photographs and diagrams showing the locations of air force fighter jets hidden in the gas tanks of six Mirage III E aircraft at an air base in Morón. Authorities immediately suspected a "subversive" operation. The ranking officer took statements from all personnel on the base at the time. None admitted guilt or saw anything suspicious. López was one of those on the base at the time the cache of documents was found. He declared his innocence in a statement and later proved that he had never been alone during his shift that day. During López's trial, evidence showed that one of the gates to the base had been left open the night before the discovery and that there had been nobody at the duty officer's post. Results at this point were inconclusive, and the court refused to hear the case.[78]

In July 1977, masked assailants kidnapped López while he was leaving work. He was held blindfolded for eight days, at which point he managed to escape his captors. López immediately presented a denunciation to the Federal Court in Córdoba and went into hiding. Unnamed security forces searched for him in the homes of his family members on charges of desertion. When his family was threatened by the military, López turned himself in to the air force and was imprisoned at the Unidad VIII Air Force Base in Morón. Under torture, López confessed to a range of new charges that included having planted explosives in the Mirage aircraft, having met with members of the Ejército Revolucionario del Pueblo (ERP), and having provided ERP members with classified information on Unidad VIII. All of this, he now admitted under duress, was inspired by his love for Gladis Aoad, who had introduced him to Oscar Rosson, Aoad's former boyfriend and an ERP member. When the military detained Aoad, she denied having had political conversations with López (thereby absolving herself of intellectual authorship of the crimes) but confirmed that she had been López's girlfriend and had introduced him to Rosson (who disappeared at about that time and would later be named as a victim in *Nunca Más*).[79]

After these events, the military charged López before a military tribunal. Pretrial depositions from friends and family of Gladis Aoad all maintained that she had never had an interest in politics (which suggested that Aoad's testimony had been extracted by torture). Soldiers who had known and lived with López, his neighborhood bowling companions, and others all told the court that they had no idea that he was involved in politics. López's spontaneous admission of guilt could not be corroborated. It flew in the face of many details of the case and conflicted with much of what the air force investigation had revealed. When those who had been on the base at the time of the discovery of the documents were called back to testify a year after their original statements in 1976, they reconfirmed their testimony. In the meantime, while López was in prison, air force officers exacted a new statement from him. He now explained that during his shift that day on the base, he had placed explosives in the plane in broad daylight. Not only had explosives never been found, but the notion that someone might have placed them in an aircraft in broad daylight was absurd. López was convicted of an array of crimes and was notified on 18 May 1979 that he had been sentenced to twenty-four years in prison on charges that included illicit association, revealing national defense secrets, and an attack on an aircraft. He was turned over to the commander in chief of the air force to serve his sentence.[80]

The first component of López's appeal under the Alfonsín administration focused on the fact that the dictatorship had set aside military law. By ignoring his requests for earlier appeals, it had refused to respect his right to designate a public defender, and it had mishandled the case on several technicalities.[81] More important, when he appealed to the Inter-American Commission on Human Rights in 1985, he drew on a new interpretation of equality before the law (an interpretation that the Supreme Council of the Armed Forces and the Federal Court of La Plata had both rejected in 1984). Although he was an air force captain at the time of the supposed infractions, López reasoned that the circumstances of his detention, incarceration, and prosecution were equivalent to those faced by civilians under the dictatorship and therefore constituted violations of his civil rights by the military.

The Argentine Supreme Court had rejected a second line of appeal that López brought to the Inter-American Commission. He sought to nullify his convictions and incarceration because he had been repeatedly denied habeas corpus rights. Law 23.042 guaranteed that provision, he argued. It was meant to enable Argentine civilian courts to quickly and easily review convictions that had been made by military courts during the dictatorship.

On 26 March 1985, the Alfonsín government responded by defending both its own judiciary and that of the dictatorship. It argued that López's case could not be heard by the commission because he had already had complete freedom to exercise Argentine human rights protections, particularly Laws 23.040, 23.042, 23.070, and 23.077. Privately, the government recognized that this argument was weak because although the Supreme Council of the Armed Forces had determined that López's previous convictions and sentences were irrevocable, the court had reduced López's jail term from 24 to 22 years. The court had offered no explanation for this change. The Argentine foreign ministry observed internally that that decision would suggest to foreign observers that Argentine judicial institutions were weak. Worse still, it seemed to the foreign ministry that the Alfonsín administration was defending the ongoing detention of a prisoner who had suffered an indefensible incarceration during more than three years of democratic rule and that the case would strain international public opinion. The Inter-American Commission on Human Rights not only heard the López case but urged parties to reach a quick and amicable settlement that would lead to López's release. His on-going detention had indicated a failure of the credibility of the Alfonsín government's claim that it was defending the principle of equality before the law.[82]

Four years into his term, Alfonsín could boast about a long list of accomplishments on human rights. The interior ministry's Subsecretariat of Human Rights had launched dozens of investigations and made hundreds of recommendations about strengthening and protecting human rights in Argentina. Government-sponsored university and high school courses disseminated knowledge about the history, evolution, and protection of human rights in the international community. The government trumpeted new pedagogical styles that had made learning possible for hundreds of thousands of young people who had previously been shut out of the educational system. It also promoted the democratization of education by funding high school and university student centers (albeit often under the direction of powerful Radical Party affiliates) to encourage students to exercise their rights and freedoms. Law 23.114 (1984) created the Argentine Pedagogical Congress, a Radical Party–dominated forum to promote debate among educators, students, and others on democratization and human rights. Law 23.068 (1984) brought in a new university electoral system and new governing structures for students, graduates, and faculty members.[83]

Whether or not these were true human rights victories and whether they shaped the national consciousness on human rights are unclear. Frequently, as in the case of the link between structural reform, human rights, and university politics, they were tied to an assertion of Radical Party authority and ongoing efforts to link human rights to *radicalismo*.

In twists on 1940s classical Peronism and 1970s liberation theology, Alfonsín tied the promotion of human rights to social action (though again placing *radicalismo* front and center). He reformed federal government institutions to provide equal access to goods and services across class and regional lines. This included the creation of a national school lunch program, the Sports for All program, the Neighborhood Games program, and national health programs. The Radicals promoted a cooperative movement that linked nonprofit organizations to human rights issues. For example, during the first four years of the Alfonsín government, the Secretariat of Cooperative Action registered more than 2,000 new cooperatives and provided a range of new incentives for these groups. In addition, the president's Council for the Consolidation of Democracy proposed a set of modifications to the Constitution that included the creation of a new office of prime minister, a new parliamentary system, and new mechanisms for referendums and plebiscites.[84]

In October 1987, however, Argentine Nobel Laureate Adolfo Perez Esquivel claimed that killings and torture had continued with impunity in Argentina, despite the ostensibly democratic government that ruled. While the violence could not compare to the death toll under military rule, Perez Esquivel cited the deaths of some 300 people after 1983 at the hands of the provincial police in the province of Buenos Aires.[85] The response of the Argentine government to that accusation was an eerie reminder of the language of the dictatorship. Authorities simply noted that the 300 deaths Perez Esquivel cited could not be confirmed. Yet the *bonaerense*, the Buenos Aires provincial police, was a notoriously brutal force whose torture and killing of prisoners had been widely documented in the Argentine press since the coming of democracy. Eduardo Janus, Argentina's press attaché in Ottawa, offered in Kafkaesque deadpan that the accusations surprised him, "now that the human rights situation in Argentina had returned to normalcy."[86] The Alfonsín administration was now denying the accusations of some of the same groups and individuals that had decried human rights violations under military rule.

In early 1987, the Alfonsín administration counted the convictions of top generals one year earlier among its key human rights achievements. A federal court had sentenced Jorge Rafael Videla to life imprisonment for 66 counts of homicide, four counts of torture leading to death, 93 counts of torture, 306 counts of kidnapping, and 26 counts of robbery. Emilio Eduardo Massera had also received a life sentence, and Orlando Ramón Agosti had been sentenced to 4.5 years, Eduardo Viola to 17 years, and Armando Lambruschini to 8 years. In light of prominent cases of persistent injustice—like the continuing injustice to Osvaldo Antonio López—and the 1987 Semana Santa uprising, these accomplishments seemed meaningless to many Argentines. Even the work of CONADEP came under scrutiny by the public and the Alfonsín administration itself. When María Teresa M. de Morini asked her interior ministry counterpart, Subsecretary for Human Rights Eduardo A. Rabossi, to provide information about convictions that had come about as a result of CONADEP's report, Rabossi could report no data on trials and convictions. All the government could report to the public was the number of cases CONADEP had cataloged.[87]

The shift in public opinion from optimism about CONADEP to the decreasing capacity of that body to find what most Argentines might have considered justice reflected the relationship of the new democratic government to human rights. There were important successes, ranging from initiatives that helped transform the popular understanding of human rights to the unprecedented conviction of the dictatorship generals. At the same time, Argentines remained unsatisfied. New human rights complaints continued against the Buenos Aires Provincial Police and other federal and local authorities. The government left a sour taste in peoples' mouths by trying and failing to instill the notion of a link between democracy, human rights, and Radical Party politics.

On the world stage, while the Argentine government made human rights a priority, the new administration quickly found itself answering for dictatorship-era disappearances and defending military judicial processes. By the early 1990s, each of Argentina's neighbors had also undergone similar transitions from brutal dictatorship to democracy. State terror in the late 1970s and early 1980s had been coordinated in a secret multinational enterprise that was jointly conducted by intelligence agencies in Argentina, Paraguay, Brazil, Bolivia, Chile, and Uruguay. Programs of restitution, justice, peace, and reconciliation in the region, however, remained national and, as in Argentina, were often tied explicitly to a particular political movement and did not produce satisfactory results.

5

Finding a Cynical Center

Over the Easter weekend of 18–19 April 1987, Argentines watched anxiously as a group of rogue officers who adhered to dictatorship-era policies and ideals tried to overthrow the government. This event became known as the Semana Santa uprising. Alfonsín ended the crisis by announcing famously that "democracy cannot be negotiated" and "the house is in order." But when the government rushed the Law of Due Obedience into effect two months later (4 June 1987), many suspected that the president had given away the independence of the presidency in a democracy. An earlier Final Point law (24 December 1986) had established a sixty-day deadline for prosecutors to initiate cases against those accused of human rights violations during the dictatorship. If prosecutors could not prepare cases in that time frame, the officers in question would be left alone. Due Obedience pardoned all but the most senior military officers, reprising the failed Nuremberg defense that middle-ranking or junior officers were simply obeying orders when a prisoner was tortured or executed.[1]

While the government likely did not negotiate with the organizers of the attempted coup, it seemed clear to many that centrist military officers sympathetic to what they regarded as the imperatives their military colleagues had faced in the late 1970s had used the coup attempt as a political wedge to demand an end to the prospect of prosecutions related to human rights. Did Alfonsín agree to Due Obedience as a way of calming tensions in the Argentine military and avoiding the prospect of further coup attempts?

If Alfonsín believed that Due Obedience and Final Point marked a necessary end point in the defense of Argentine democracy, he paid a significant price for them in the realm of public relations. In November 1987, Amnesty International labeled Due Obedience a threat to the gains won with the convictions of the Argentine generals because it granted "impunity to all but the most senior officers for crimes committed during the repression." Amnesty chapters from many countries and Argentine human rights groups denounced Due Obedience because it contradicted a February 1984 Argentine law that specifically rejected the "due obedience" defense in cases involving "atrocious or aberrant" acts. Amnesty challenged the Alfonsín government's international position as an ostensible leader in the advocacy of human rights, arguing that the new law undermined the United Nations Convention Against Torture, which stipulated that "an order from a superior officer or a public authority may not be invoked as a justification for torture."[2]

The Easter Week military uprising and the ensuing Due Obedience and Final Point laws marked a watershed in human rights politics in Argentina. Because the nation's rampant inflation and other economic problems continued to increase through the mid-1980s, Alfonsín had already lost much of his post-dictatorship luster. After Due Obedience and Final Point, the national and international human rights constituencies took aim at what they felt were the president's growing weaknesses on human rights issues. When protesters demonstrated against the new laws outside the Argentine embassy in Copenhagen, Denmark, María Teresa M. de Morini, subsecretary of human rights, advised Argentine diplomats to avoid use of the terms "due obedience" and "final point," referring instead to the less inflammatory and less recognizable language "Law 23.492." Morini also stated that the groups that were helping to organize the growing protests in Denmark and elsewhere included the Madres de Plaza de Mayo, the Abuelas de Plaza de Mayo, Amnesty International, and five Danish human rights groups. Like the military government had, the Alfonsín administration now found itself watching the activities of human rights groups as a potential threat.[3]

· On 10 December 1987, actress Liv Ullman marched with the Madres de Plaza de Mayo in front of the presidential palace to protest impunity for human rights abusers within the Argentine military. The signs the protesters carried had a picture of the Argentine president standing at attention beside a military officer, both men saluting. Some 10,000 people joined the protest, and during her visit, Ullman issued public statements condemning the Alfonsín government's human rights record. She then visited the Villa Devoto prison in Buenos Aires, where ten political detainees were still in custody from the dictatorship era. On 11 December, the artist Sting visited the offices of the Madres de Plaza de Mayo. Hours later, some 10 million viewers in Argentina and Uruguay watched the Madres join Sting on stage at El Monumental, Buenos Aires' largest stadium. Argentines saw this joint appearance as a show of support for the group's opposition to the Alfonsín administration's wavering on human rights. It was the first time in two years that the Madres had appeared on state-controlled television in Argentina.[4]

As early as May 1987, the government was preparing for an onslaught of criticisms of Due Obedience and Final Point from overseas. In private, high-level meetings, government officials laid out the sorts of arguments they expected and the legal flaws in the new legislation. Legal precedents in Argentina and the nation's international positions had routinely cited the Nuremberg and Tokyo Charters, which emphasized international agreements that excluded due obedience as a reasonable defense against accusations of torture or as a legal provision that could be applied after the fact. Moreover, in refugee and asylum law, Argentine courts and legislators had explicitly rejected amnesty for acts considered crimes against humanity (including torture and kidnapping); those in Argentina who were seeking asylum but were found to have committed such acts were extradited immediately by Argentine law. Furthermore, Argentine officials were concerned that several high-level prosecutions would have to be abandoned as a result of Due Obedience and that the international public relations fallout would be a problem.[5]

Anticipating criticism, the Argentine government laid out its position on the issue of why there was no inherent contradiction between Due Obedience and existing law and precedent. It sought refuge in legalistic and questionably relevant explanations. The Nuremberg and Tokyo Charters, government officials argued, were irrelevant to Due Obedience. The former drew on very different circumstances that included a major international war. As a result, the crimes in question were war crimes, crimes against peace, and crimes against humanity—none of which were relevant in Argentina. Due Obedience was not an amnesty, the Alfonsín administration claimed, because amnesty implied forgetting past wrongs, while the Due Obedience law did not.

The government anticipated that the Astiz case would be more difficult. Captain Alfredo Astiz was one of the most infamous human rights violators of the Argentine dictatorship. He was accused in the torture and deaths of hundreds of prisoners at the infamous Naval Mechanics School detention center (ESMA) and was also accused of having kidnapped one of the founders of the Mothers of the Plaza de Mayo, Azucena Villaflor. Villaflor's remains were identified in 2005. Astiz was even more well known for his role in the kidnapping (and likely killing) of Dagmar Hagelin (who held both Argentine and Swedish citizenship), as well as for the assassination of Alice Domon and Léonie Duquet, two French nuns. When pressure came, it focused on Astiz and other high-profile cases like his. Foreign governments, human rights groups, and individuals pressed hard for Astiz's extradition to France (for the killing of the nuns)—a development Argentina resisted. Despite the fact that by the terms of Due Obedience, Astiz was not prosecuted for two of his most famous crimes (Hagelin and the nuns), the Argentine government made it known to international critics that it intended to prosecute him for his role in ESMA killings and torture. Those latter crimes went beyond the parameters of Due Obedience. Privately, and despite its public statements to the contrary, though, the government recognized that it had limited evidence in cases where Astiz had been accused of torture and other crimes; it was not likely that he would be convicted.[6]

Though Argentina was a signatory to the Inter-American Convention to Prevent Torture, Argentine officials breathed a sigh of relief when the treaty was not ratified internationally. Some of the provisions of that convention were at odds with Due Obedience. The United Nations Convention Against Torture, which Argentina had signed and ratified, also prohibited Due Obedience. For the time being, anyway, Argentina had also dodged that bullet: the Convention Against Torture did not enter into effect because only nineteen nations ratified it, one fewer than the required twenty.[7]

The Argentine government quickly became a victim of its own success in having cast itself a human rights leader. Denunciations came from around the world. The onslaught Alfonsín had anticipated came quickly from the European Parliament, the Inter-Church Committee on Human Rights in Latin America (Canada), Action des Chrétiens pour l'Abolition de la Torture (France), and some two hundred other groups and individuals. The criticisms, according to Morini, tended to be of "identical tenor."[8] Human Rights Watch accused Congress and the administration of having passed the two laws under imminent threat from a strongly armed elite whose intent was to put an end to democracy. It criticized Alfonsín for eroding judicial authority and independence by passing laws that made it possible for its decisions and sentences to be disobeyed.[9] The Medical Action Group of the rights organization Philippine Action Concerning Torture wrote a letter to Alfonsín to express its concern that the Argentine legislation might set a precedent for Philippine judicial decisions in the prosecution of Ferdinand Marcos–era human rights abusers in the Philippines.[10]

Morini coordinated the response to such protests through late 1987, mostly through formulaic, noncommittal, and obfuscating language that disappointed those who had raised concerns. She continued to make no mention of Due Obedience by name. Her language stressed that the law did not erase the truth and did not refute what was known publicly in Argentina. It placed responsibility for crimes related to human rights on those who materially executed an order, not on those who gave the order, she claimed. According to Morini, there was no amnesty in Argentina but rather a clarification of criminal responsibility.[11] When Alfonsín responded directly to his critics, the language was even more flowery and ambiguous. Writing to Jacqueline Westercamp, president of Action des Chrétiens pour l'Abolition de la Torture, the Argentine president noted that those primarily responsible for human rights violations had been punished—a first for any country. For that reason, he went on, the new legislation would have no impact on his moral and political convictions (as laid out during the 1983 presidential campaign) and would not have an impact on the future of his government's pro-democracy programs. In a risky move that drew on his political capital domestically and beyond,

Alfonsín referred to his moral authority on human rights, citing the "permanent recognition" he had received from European Community member nations for his "modest contribution" to the cause of human rights. This meant, in the end, he intoned, that there was a "spiritual and moral linkage" between his government and pro–human rights advocates.[12]

The Due Obedience law is evidence of Alfonsín's failure to transform Argentina in the way he had once promised to do. One of the clear illustrations of this was the case of Uruguayan Eduardo O'Neill Velazquez. Early in 1977, he was detained at a Buenos Aires police station. On 8 February, he was transferred to the custody of the First Corps of the Army, which was under the command of Colonel Carlos Guillermo Suárez Mason, one of the most notorious human rights abusers of the dictatorship. O'Neill Velazquez was never seen again. Now, even though prosecutors had abundant evidence that Suárez Mason was directly responsible for O'Neill Velazquez's disappearance and likely murder, Due Obedience meant that a conviction in the case would be impossible. In this and dozens of other cases, a range of human rights groups (including Americas Watch, the Abuela de Plaza de Mayo, the International Pro-Human Rights Federation, the Madres de Plaza de Mayo, and the Relatives of Those Detained for Political Reasons) joined the families of disappeared Uruguayans and the Uruguayan government to demand information from the Argentine government and to call for the criminal prosecution of the perpetrators. They had begun to request information in 1984, but after Due Obedience became the law in June 1987, there was alarm in many quarters. Under Due Obedience, all proceedings would come to a halt, except for charges relating to child-stealing and the illegal transfer of property. Rights groups feared that in this and in hundreds of other cases the trickle of information the Argentine government had released would slow even further. The Alfonsín government offered no information on O'Neill Velazquez and had no intention of prosecuting Suárez Mason.[13]

By September 1987, the Alfonsín government had brought 2,249 cases to a variety of courts and tribunals for investigation. CONADEP had concluded that the military had conducted an organized campaign of kidnapping and assassinations during the dictatorship. For each crime, those in charge—the commanders of the military units responsible for specific jurisdictions—had personally issued detention orders, had received detailed information on those held captive, and had decided about who would be released. That level of micromanagement by high-level officers suggested to the families of the disappeared and to human rights groups that reams of evidence existed on thousands of cases. Before Due Obedience became law, court orders could have forced the military to release such documentation. But after Due Obedience and Final Point, there were no new prosecutions, no new court orders, and no forced releases of documents. The Argentine government denied that the laws interfered with the pursuit of justice. Due Obedience, according to Argentine authorities, had been preceded by four years of investigations and the resolution of scores of cases of military repression, and that process would continue. The new law would not impede the flow of information or the possibility of new proceedings for cases relating to the kidnapping of children or the illicit transfer of property.[14] But few were convinced there would be much progress on old cases after the new laws were passed.

Moreover, the government began to face new accusations of human rights abuses, some specifically related to older cases. Graciela Beatriz Daleo, who had been kidnapped on 18 October 1977, had watched the case against her captors proceed to trial. But on 6 September 1988, she was detained and imprisoned at Prison U.3 in Ezeiza. Like her prosecutors and the military dictatorship, the Alfonsín administration believed that there was evidence that she had committed violent acts as a Montonero and that she had participated in the kidnapping of Jorge Born in 1975. Her lawyer told the government and the United Nations Working Group on Enforced or Involuntary Disappearances that her current detention was groundless and politically motivated. Moreover, the lawyer claimed, the basis for accusations of terrorism against Daleo came from testimony that prosecutors had presented from disappeared prisoners of the military regime, that is to say testimony that may have been obtained under duress. This case and others like it made it clear to many observers that 1987 marked a watershed for human rights in Argentina and that Alfonsín was in retreat.[15]

In May 1987, police threatened human rights workers and told them to stop their efforts on behalf of the families of three young men who had recently been killed in the community of Ingeniero Budge, outside Buenos Aires.[16] Noemí Diaz de Rivas issued a statement on 28 May 1987 that said that she had received a telephone call from someone ordering her to end her work with the Budge victims. That same day, a blue Ford Falcon[17] tried to run her over outside her home. Someone inside the car shouted at her "*que me deje de joder con los negritos de Budge*" [to quit fucking around with the Budge niggers].[18] She immediately reported these events to Interior Minister Antonio Troccoli, who never responded. The next day, Diaz de Rivas was kidnapped by four armed men. She was held for 90 minutes while she was insulted about the Budge killings.

International human rights groups watched these and other developments with alarm. On 30 July and 6 August 1987, the UN Economic and Social Council issued statements from its offices in Paris and Buenos Aires denouncing the intensifying crisis in Argentina's human rights situation. They tied that escalation to the new Final Point and Due Obedience laws. A new wave of repression was spearheaded by groups and individuals whose identities were largely hidden. Various members of the Madres de Plaza de Mayo were beaten, and Madres president Hebe de Bonafini was threatened. New assassinations, arbitrary detentions, kidnappings, and torture took place. The UN Economic and Social Council cited the cases of Osvaldo Villanueva, Juan Carlos Ridella, and Antonio Villas (each of whom was presumably assassinated); Noemí Rivas and Rubén Rodriguez (who were presumed to have been kidnapped); and German Schiller, Gloria Lopestri, Osvaldo Barros, Ana María Testa, Rodolfo Carballo, León Zimmerman, and Humberto Tumini (who were victims of threats). The Council asked for the intercession of the UN Commission on Human Rights to convince an unresponsive Argentine government to respect human rights and fundamental liberties.[19]

Dictatorship-era cases lingered in the courts, mired down in part by an overwhelmed judicial system. The response from the diplomatic community was severe. The unresolved disappearance of Swedish citizen Dagmar Hagelin generated hundreds of letters from overseas. A short letter from Swedish citizen Lars Jönsson about the Hagelin case prompted U.S. Senator Barbara A. Mikulski to write to the Argentine government asking for information "on the fate of this young woman." As in hundreds of similar cases, the Argentines were able to do no more than indicate that the case was before a federal court.[20]

Behind the scenes, Alfonsín built on the international commercial, strategic, and political successes of the dictatorship in his efforts to convince other governments to set aside human rights as a key problem in bilateral relations with Argentina. The case of the Alfonsín government's relationship with Canada is one example. Canadian members of parliament, church leaders, Amnesty International chapters, and dozens of other groups and individuals had been vociferous in their criticisms of human rights violations by the Argentine military after March 1976, although those criticisms had little impact on Argentina's international standing or on bilateral ties. Argentina's most important relationship with Canada was in the nuclear sector. In 1973, the two countries signed a nuclear accord that included a contract for Atomic Energy of Canada Ltd. to build Argentina's second commercial nuclear reactor. Despite public protests and political opposition in Canada to the dictatorship, the reactor was finished in April 1983, before the fall of the military and despite rumors in Canada that the military might use nuclear energy to fuel electric prods that were used as a torture device. Several delays in the supply of Canadian nuclear technology to Argentina had little to do with protests over Argentina's human rights record; they were primarily the result of changes in Canada's nuclear transfer regulations in the aftermath of India's detonation of its first nuclear device in 1974.[21]

Ten years later, the stresses in Canada's relationship with the Alfonsín government were due mostly to tensions over the Malvinas War. The war put the Canadian government in a difficult position vis-à-vis Argentina; the Canadians had no choice but to back the British recapture of the islands. At the time of the war, Canadian officials privately informed the military government that its position was complex. Publicly, the Canadian government supported the British government. Responding to a Canadian public that was sensitized to questions of individual liberties and abhorred military aggression, Canadian officials had felt it necessary to criticize (albeit vaguely) the Argentine invasion of the Malvinas Islands and to reduce diplomatic contacts with Buenos Aires to a minimum. But behind the scenes, its response was pragmatic; Canada made clear to Argentine authorities that it meant to keep lines of communication open so as not to jeopardize strong bilateral ties in the nuclear sector and in other areas.

Argentina envisioned a "post-Malvinas" period in bilateral relations in which full dialogue would be restored with Canada and other nations. Like the military government, the Alfonsín administration was convinced that human rights would be marginal to the practicalities of bilateral commercial and diplomatic ties.[22] In June 1984, the Canadian Department of Foreign Affairs told the Argentine ambassador in Ottawa privately there had been strong pressures from various domestic sectors for the Canadian government to decry ludicrous statements that the military government had made about a continued fight against subversion at the end of its tenure. Despite this pressure, Canada would not commit itself to comment. Alfonsín took the Canadian approach as a positive sign that Canada was interested in fast-tracking the improvement of bilateral relations. Both the military government and the democratic government in Argentina were well aware that even though the Canadian government had criticized the military government's record on human rights, Canada had improved its commercial ties with Argentina during the dictatorship. Both Argentina and Canada saw the new democratic government as an opportunity to establish better trade relations. Commerce had grown steadily in both directions through the *proceso* until the Malvinas War; the value of such transactions had reached 200 million dollars in 1979. Argentine exports to Canada, which were valued at 5 million dollars in 1967, had reached 66 million dollars in 1981.[23]

The dictatorship had established other points of contact with Canada that Alfonsín hoped to build on. For example, in October 1980, in conjunction with a meeting of the Canadian Association of Latin American and Caribbean Studies, the Argentine embassy in Ottawa had helped organize a seminar on Argentina that was attended by Argentine and Canadian government representatives and by members of the Canadian business community. That led to both governments signing an Economic, Commercial, and Industrial Cooperation Agreement that Alfonsín wished to expand. In another example, in 1981, the provinces of Alberta and Ontario had each sponsored trade missions to Argentina. It was the Malvinas War, not the problem of human rights, that had disrupted bilateral ties. But even Canadian protests against the Argentine invasion were "relatively mild given [Canada's] ties to the United Kingdom." That was how the Canadian government characterized the protests to the Argentine government, and that was how the Argentines chose to see them.[24]

When Canada joined the United States and some European nations in supporting economic sanctions against Argentina during the war, no one in Argentina responded to the issue with blustering excuses. Canada made it clear to Argentine diplomats that its links to Washington made supporting sanctions the only viable option. The military took the explanation at face value, as did the new Alfonsín administration almost two years later. The problem for Argentina in early 1984 was that the break in trade had left its mark. Even though prohibitions on exports had lasted only from 26 May to 22 June 1982, the disruption had caused a decrease of 40 percent in trade with Canada compared to 1981 levels, the lowest point since the beginning of the dictatorship. By early 1984, Argentina's economic difficulties were exacerbated by mounting problems attributable to its delays in repaying foreign debt. The Export Development Corporation, for example, cut all financing for sales to Argentina by Canadian exporters. Alfonsín adopted the military's wait-and-see approach with the Canadians, hoping for a propitious moment to press for a renewal of good relations. In mid-1984 there were positive signs. Both governments seemed interested in a new wide-ranging trade agreement, and both governments opened negotiations for an agreement to transfer nuclear technology.[25]

Ironically perhaps, one of the first of the Alfonsín administration's initiatives toward Canada did not distance it from the dictatorship but instead underlined continuities between the two regimes. When the Canadian government invited Brigadier General Sebastián Marotta (a dictatorship-era official who was representing the new democracy) to tour satellite research and production facilities in Canada, Marotta made a favorable impression on his hosts. The brigadier general, who was also the director of the National Space Investigation Commission, laid the groundwork for new cooperative agreements in several areas. After Brazil and Canada signed an agreement to transfer satellite technology in 1984, the Alfonsín administration hoped that Marotta's good relations with his Canadian counterparts would lead to a technology transfer agreement that would pave the way for a new generation of Argentine satellites.[26]

Through the 1980s, Alfonsín's most important challenge in bilateral ties with Canada remained precisely what it had been since 1974. Canada had signed nuclear nonproliferation agreements that made it a proponent of levels of security when transferring nuclear technology that Argentines felt impinged on their sovereignty rights to develop a peaceful nuclear program. In addition, despite the fact that Argentina had insisted for decades that it had no nuclear weapons plans, in return for the export of nuclear technology, Canada demanded international inspections of every Argentine facility where some use could be made of the exported materials or know-how. In addition, it demanded such inspections of nuclear facilities that had no relevance to Canadian exports. This final point was galling to Argentine authorities, both military and civilian.[27]

Canada's nuclear program mattered to Argentines both before and after December 1983 for precisely the same reasons. First, Canada was the leader in non-enriched uranium technologies; Argentina had no facilities for uranium enrichment. Second, Argentine officials had long viewed Canada as a counterweight to its dependence on ties with Germany, the only other notable player in the non-enriched uranium technology sector. Alfonsín continued the same policy the dictatorship had adopted on nuclear technology; Argentina would continue to press Canada diplomatically for what Argentine officials called a "flexibilization" of Canadian nuclear policy, meaning a relaxing of restrictions on the technology flow from North to South.[28]

Not much changed substantively after 1983 in how human rights issues affected bilateral ties between Canada and Argentina. Like the dictatorship, Alfonsín understood that Canada had long played an active role in promoting human rights in Argentina. The goal of the Canadian government had been to "satisfy or neutralize a domestic [Canadian], activist public opinion" on human rights.[29] As the military dictatorship had done, Alfonsín regarded Canadian positions on human rights as both ineffectual and marginal.

Many of Argentina's positions on human rights after 1983 were neither ineffectual nor marginal. They were public relations exercises. Although the Alfonsín administration reported progress in efforts to locate the disappeared, the results were a patchwork of a few successes outweighed by many failures. In 1984, authorities found Ramón Angel Pintos, a child who had disappeared with his parents during the dictatorship. A judge returned him to his biological family in 1986. Though Mariana Zaffaroni Islas, another missing child, was found, her captor, Miguel Angel Furci, a former SIDE operative, managed to escape with his wife, Mariana, and police were not able to locate them after they escaped. Rosa Luján Tarato de Altamiranda had last been seen in July 1977 in the Campo de Mayo detention center outside Buenos Aires, where it was reported she had given birth to a daughter named Rosita. Despite intense pressure by her family on Argentine authorities through CONADEP and other avenues, the Eighth Circuit Court of La Plata was unable to locate either Tarato de Altamiranda or her daughter.[30]

Sometimes the Alfonsín administration dragged its feet in response to requests for information about those who had been imprisoned by the dictatorship. At other times, the government seemed overwhelmed and unable to coordinate action from bureaucracy to bureaucracy. In June 1986, Colonel Timoteo Gordillo wrote to Morini on behalf of Military Court No. 71 to request information on the case against dictatorship leader General Luciano Benjamín Menendez and others. Gordillo wanted the names of 129 Argentines listed as disappeared in the CONADEP report but who had appeared alive suddenly in 1985 in Mexico City at the time of the earthquake there. He repeated the request on 21 July. On 22 September, Morini finally replied. There was no list, he said. Because the Argentines' efforts to aid earthquake victims had been humanitarian and the information about the location of disappeared people in Mexico City had been transmitted to the Ministry of Foreign Relations exclusively in that vein, the list of the 129 had been discarded. Gordillo asked whether the list had ever been sent to the media or to other government bureaucracies. Morini never responded to that question, raising the possibility that she was not interested in providing a military court with evidence that, in this case at least, the "disappeared" were simply somewhere else, as the military had always claimed.[31]

When the Radical government became overwhelmed by foreign and domestic pressures, it used a device the military government had also used to discuss the state of human rights in the republic: it noted the juridical and constitutional record (often citing the same acts and clauses the military had cited), as though the record in and of itself meant that there were no violations.[32] As Argentina continued to grapple with long-standing racism toward people of color and with new forms of racism associated with a growing immigrant presence from neighboring countries and from Asia, the Alfonsín administration claimed that the problem simply did not exist. In 1988, for example, the UN Economic and Social Council asked Argentina, as it did other nations, for information on what the national and provincial governments were doing to counter racism and discrimination. The Argentine government insisted that there was no racism—precisely the same type of denial the dictatorship had offered in response to accusations of disappearances and torture. Authorities made an absurd case that there was no possibility of discrimination in Argentina because of provisions in the 1853 Constitution.[33] Article 16 defended the principle of equality among all citizens while the International Convention for the Prevention and Sanction of the Crime of Genocide

(1956) had been incorporated into Argentine law. The Alfonsín administration cited these as well as a number of other legal and constitutional precedents that had been ratified and sanctioned before 1984.[34]

The Alfonsín administration did move away from the strategies of its predecessor in the mechanisms it put in place for denouncing and countering racism. The government cited the creation of the Sub-Secretariat of Human Rights in the Ministry of the Interior (SDH) as the most important of these changes; its mandate included receiving denunciations of human rights violations that included racist actions. But this gesture was somewhat hollow, as the government denied that racism existed. It proclaimed that "our nation is based on the integration of immigrant groups of diverse origin, race, and religion who have built this country by leaving us generations of Argentines. This explains the harmonious coexistence of distinct ethnic groups in our territory and the resulting incompatibility of the privileging of one group over another."[35] This statement included no mention of Argentina's indigenous peoples or of Argentines of color, who were the majority population.[36]

Stranger still, the Alfonsín government bolstered its human rights credentials by drawing on advances it claimed had been made during military rule. It cited a 26 June 1980 Supreme Court decision that gave Jehovah's Witnesses freedom to practice their religion. That decision was the first in more than twenty years to address the rights of religious minorities and the first to guarantee religious freedom in Argentina. The decision of the Court struck down Resolution 8795/76 (1976) of the Dirección Nacional de Migraciones, which had been affirmed by Resolution 655/79 of the Ministry of the Interior; that resolution denied permanent residence to a Jehovah's Witness living in Argentina, said that his presence in Argentina was illegal, and ordered him to be expelled from the country. The two resolutions had drawn on Decree 1867/76 (1976) of the Dirección Nacional de Migraciones, which declared the religious activities of Jehovah's Witnesses illegal in Argentina. In the 1980 decision, the Court found that constitutionally guaranteed civil rights and the right of the man to live in Argentina were directly contravened by Decree 1867/76. It threw out Decree 1867/76, which falsely assumed that the religious activities of Jehovah's Witnesses represented a "danger or risk to national security." The Court found that assumption inherently and unconstitutionally discriminatory.[37]

The Court rejected the government's claim that the expulsion order should be upheld because Jehovah's Witnesses would not show appropriate respect for the symbols of nation. The Court instructed that if it could be shown that a Jehovah's Witness was disrespectful of an Argentine national symbol in a manner that contravened the law, legal action could be taken on an ad hoc basis. More important, the Court found that Jehovah's Witnesses were free to exercise their religion as a function of the derogation of 1867/76 and because of Law 21.745 (1979), which established the National Registry of Religions.[38]

Unlike the case of the Jehovah's Witnesses, there was no mistaking Alfonsín's break with the dictatorship on policy toward South Africa. This issue emerged as a key focus of Alfonsín's drive to transform Argentina into a human rights leader. After Argentina scaled back diplomatic ties with Pretoria in early 1984, it cast itself as a leader in isolating South Africa. In March 1985, it established diplomatic relations with Zimbabwe, and it opened an embassy in Harare two years later. It did break ties with South Africa, although it did not do so until 22 May 1986. That year, Congress approved the International Convention on the Suppression and Punishment of the Crime of Apartheid (Law 23.221). Under that convention, the racially discriminatory practices of the South African regime were considered a violation of human rights. Argentina also established formal relations with the Southern African Development Coordination Conference (the forerunner of the Southern African Development Community), established informal contacts with high-ranking members of the African National Congress, exerted pressure on South African authorities to liberate Nelson Mandela and other political detainees, and even gave money to help rebuild the Mandela family home after it was firebombed.[39]

Argentina practiced a strict boycott of sports events held in South Africa and pointed out frequently that Aerolinas Argentinas had stopped flying to South Africa in 1981. While the state could not prevent citizens from traveling or trading with South Africa, the Constitution permitted Alfonsín to block sales of materials that were considered to be strategically significant, such as oil or arms. The Argentine government rigorously adhered to UN resolutions, including its insistence that Namibia become independent immediately and that the new nation's territory include Walbis Ba (which at the time was occupied by South Africa and was specifically named in UN Security Council Resolution 435). Argentina recognized the Southwest African People's Organization as the only legitimate representative of the Namibian people. That group's secretary-general, Herman Andimba Toivo ya Toivo, met with officials of the Argentine Ministry of Foreign Relations on 21 August 1985.[40]

The delegates at the 1986 International Conference of the Red Cross in Geneva were polarized over the issue of South Africa. After complex negotiations, they approved a motion that expelled South Africa from the conference. African nations drove the opposition to South Africa, which was backed by most Latin American countries but was opposed by several Western European countries and some Asian nations. At first, Argentina's lead diplomat, Morini, argued to her superiors that Argentina should remain on the margins of the debate and not vote so that Argentina could preserve good relations with countries on both sides. She followed the long-standing argument of Great Britain and some other governments that suspending South Africa from the Red Cross would harm black South Africans whose interests would be better served if South Africa was a part of the Red Cross.[41]

Once the severity of the division became apparent, the foreign ministry realized that it would have to take sides. As a conference delegate, Morini had voted in favor of expelling South Africa, but she noted to her superiors that South Africa expelled the Red Cross from its territory immediately after the vote. What she failed to grasp was that for her superiors, the Argentine government's positions on international human rights issues had become an exercise in international power politics; they were not concerned about the day-to-day workings of the Red Cross in South Africa. At the 1986 conference, Argentina was rewarded for its position when conference organizers included it in a small group of nations (that also included the United States, the Soviet Union, Denmark, Zimbabwe, Libya, and Indonesia) that was mandated to come up with resolution language that all parties could accept.[42]

At times, Morini found herself without support inside the Argentine government on the politics of human rights. In 1986, for example, drawing on international refugee law and Argentina's international commitments in this area, Morini supported the claim of Dara Rauf Esad Al-Haidari for refugee status in Argentina. Born in Baghdad, Al Haidari was living in a refugee camp outside of Tehran, a victim of Saddam Hussein's authoritarian terror and the Iran-Iraq War. Morini encountered a cynical response from officials in the foreign ministry and other bureaucracies that were not willing to discard power politics to accommodate a morally strong human rights case. Vicente Espeche Gil, the director of the foreign ministry's Africa and Middle East Department, argued against Argentina taking any refugee from Iraq because of the potential "risk" to good relations with Saddam Hussein.[43] In the first nine months of 1986, Argentina received 613 requests for refugee status. The government reviewed 537 and declared 186 eligible. Of these 186, it refused 100 and approved 58, most of whom were refugees from Pinochet's Chile.[44]

Also in 1986, Argentina co-sponsored a UN Commission on Human Rights resolution on democratization, the return to constitutional rule, and the installation of a popularly elected civil government in Guatemala after long periods of authoritarian rule. In response to accusations from Amnesty International that human rights abuses in Guatemala were ongoing, the resolution noted that the council would continue to keep an eye on the rights situation there. Argentina took a moderate position. Germany and France pressed for stronger language on human rights violations in Guatemala before the resolution went to nations for ratification. Argentina's stance was an indication of Alfonsín's troubles at home related to how his government was handling the dictatorship-era legacy of human rights abuses and the ongoing threat of military intervention. Argentina appended a text to the resolution that distanced itself from the position of France and Germany and indirectly asserted the success of Alfonsín's pro–human rights politics. The Argentine text expressed satisfaction with President Marco Vinicio Cerezo and his efforts to promote human rights and confidence that his promise to establish a national human rights commission that would end "all efforts against the lives and the dignity" of Guatemalans would be fulfilled.[45]

Arab and Jewish communities were key ethnic constituencies in Argentina; in fact, four provincial governors were Arab Argentines. In May 1985, the Argentine government proclaimed that it was a high priority that "these communities live together in harmony and we want to keep things that way."[46] During this time, Israel faced increasing condemnation because of its human rights violations. Pressed on all sides, the Argentine government radically altered its policy on Israel in 1987. In May, at the forty-third session of the United Nations Commission on Human Rights, the Argentine delegation expressed its opposition to equating Zionism with racism and to referring to the Israeli occupation of Arab territory as a human rights violation. María Teresa M. de Morini had argued to her superiors that because Argentina was "practically the only Latin

American nation" to shift toward a more pro-Israel policy, its position would yield concrete benefits in terms of its economic and political ties with Israel.[47] Though her principal mandate was supposed to be concern for human rights, on this occasion, Morini backed the important policy shift for pragmatic political reasons.[48]

It is true that the Argentine government's policies related to human rights in the 1980s were conditioned by a genuine concern for human rights and a strong conviction that promoting human rights overseas would strengthen Argentine democracy, the position of the Radical Party in Argentine politics, and the strength of *alfonsinismo* within the Radical Party. However, while Argentina's public position always emphasized a strong concern for human rights, behind the scenes, Argentine officials often looked for diplomatic solutions that favored a range of Argentine interests nationally and internationally, at times sacrificing human rights principles for gains in other areas. In 1986, when the European nations proposed extending the European Convention on Human Rights to the Malvinas, Argentine authorities balked; the Argentine government refused to approve international resolutions or actions on the Malvinas that did not explicitly recognize Argentine sovereignty over the islands.[49]

Unlike the application of the European Convention on Human Rights to the Malvinas, which had nothing to do with human rights, Argentina's decision in 1987 to align itself more closely with the U.S. human rights policy vis-à-vis Cuba was driven by genuine concern for rights abuses. At the same time, the policy shift also drew on Alfonsín's desire to distance himself from governments further to the left within the Non-Aligned Movement and an interest in improving ties with Washington. On 6 May 1987, Raul Alconada Sempé, sub-secretary of Latin American affairs (MRE), met with Alan Keyes, director of international organizations within the U.S. Department of State. Also present was Robert Gelbard, deputy assistant secretary of state for South America. The two sides reached agreement on how to pressure the Cubans at the United Nations on their human rights violations, and they agreed about how difficult it had become for moderates within the Non-Aligned Movement to confront regimes that were more "radical." Keyes told the Argentines that the United States would find a way for its moderate friends within the Non-Aligned Movement, like Argentina, to cooperate more closely with future U.S. diplomatic and strategic initiatives. The rapprochement between the United States and Argentina was all the more striking because

Argentina owed a political debt to Cuba. Five years earlier, Cuba had been one of the first nations to back Argentina during the Malvinas War. Now Argentina was describing its former ally as a "radical" nation within the Non-Aligned Movement.[50]

In late 1986, at the forty-first session of the UN General Assembly, the United States redoubled its efforts to isolate Cuba by proposing a strong condemnation of human rights abuses on the island. Cuba countered with a resolution on the rights and liberties of African Americans and indigenous peoples in the United States and a related proposal on Puerto Rico. After heated debate, an Indian resolution passed that took both the Cuban and U.S. resolutions off the table. Shortly after, the tension between the United States and Cuba overflowed into the work of the UN Commission on Human Rights. When India put forward a motion to block any action against Cuba, Argentina was one of two Latin American countries that opposed the motion.[51]

Even though the Argentine government took an ostensibly apolitical position on human rights in international venues, it took clear positions on other issues. Argentina knew that the debate on Cuba at the UN would proceed to the UN Sub-Commission on the Prevention of Discrimination and Protection of Minorities. Five of the twenty-six appointed experts on the sub-commission were Latin American, and the Mexican, Antonio Martínez Baez, was the most senior of the group. When the Cuban expert sought the position of chair of the sub-commission, Argentina anticipated pressure from the United States to oppose that bid. Argentina did not want to face the consequences of what might be perceived as support if the Cuban was appointed. The solution was for Argentina to seek the presidency itself; it lobbied privately for the support of other Latin American delegates and tried to convince the Cuban not to run:

> In a word, what Cuba must understand is that if a Cuban were to direct the Sub-Commission, the United States would feel morally and politically obliged to condemn Cuba. If Cuba wants to go from victim to aggressor, it should weigh the consequences with care, particularly in regard to countries like ours that have paid a high price for our convictions, but that don't have to pay a penny to any country trying to turn all this into a business.[52]

Argentina hoped to convince Cuba that agreeing to an Argentine candidate for the chair of the sub-commission or accepting another candidate might represent a first step toward frank and open inter-American dialogue on human rights. What Argentine officials were not yet prepared to tell the Cubans is that they also hoped to encourage them to recognize the authority of the sub-commission to observe Cuba—that is to say, for Cubans to recognize their status as potential human rights violators. Argentina hoped to pressure Cuba in this direction with a secret promise that in return and in the future, the United States would keep human rights off the agenda of the UN Sub-Commission on the Prevention of Discrimination and Protection of Minorities. There is no evidence that this offer came, in fact, from the United States; the only evidence suggests that Argentina was speaking on behalf of the United States to Cuba. The Argentine government was keen for an opportunity to work more closely with the United States on human rights problems, and it wanted the sub-commission to move ahead quickly in its investigation of claims of human rights violations in Cuba. Such an investigation would allow nongovernmental organizations to step in and investigate.

The Argentine position on Cuba was duplicitous. On the one hand, Argentine officials presented themselves as a neutral third party, backed by the authority of Alfonsín's pro–human rights positions, that was anxious to help defuse Cuba's human rights conflict with the United States. On the other hand, the Argentine government had begun lobbying Cuban officials on behalf of Cubans who identified themselves as victims of rights abuses. One of Argentina's motives for pressuring Cuba was the goal of making clear to the U.S. State Department that Argentina "was not indifferent to the situation in Cuba."[53]

The Argentine government saw human rights and Cuba as an avenue by which, through U.S. backing, it might strengthen its leadership role in the Non-Aligned Movement and in Latin America by simultaneously reducing the influence of Cuba and other socialist members within the movement. The Alfonsín government projected its leadership in the movement at the same time that it worked to shift it to the right politically, toward greater proximity to U.S. Cold War strategic positions, without at the same time openly allying itself with Washington. At the May 1987 meeting between Alconada Sempé and Alan Keyes, Gelbard asked Argentina, as a representative of "moderate" (non-socialist) nations within the Non-Aligned Movement to consider pressuring Cuba.

To the Americans, Argentina presented its own prospective role in criticizing Cuba before the sub-commission as that of a "third party" and "in a manner that did not reflect the East-West conflict." The United States accepted the offer and the Argentines used Leandro Despouy, their expert on the sub-commission, to implement the plan. Alfonsín had transformed human rights diplomacy into high-stakes international power politics and a quiet alignment of Argentina's interests with those of the United States.[54]

Some Alfonsín-era policy shifts on the issue of human rights were not particularly bold. They brought benefits to the government at an insignificant cost. The decision to break ties with apartheid-era South Africa was an easy one. The government's reason for the break cited the institutionalization of a system of racial discrimination that was a severe and ongoing human rights violation.[55] Argentina's position on South Africa was its clearest departure from the foreign policies of the dictatorship, and it carried political capital because it shored up Argentina's international human rights credentials.

The consistency Alfonsín showed on South Africa, though, was unusual. What human rights meant changed as Argentine policy priorities changed. By 1987, the Argentine foreign policy on nuclear arms reductions had become a matter of human rights. In that year, Argentina sponsored a motion during the forty-second session of the UN Commission on Human Rights that linked the consequences of the nuclear arms race to the protection of human rights, peace, and the development of poor nations. Argentine officials tried without success to include language in the motion that favored nonnuclear zones that would have indirectly established its supremacy over the Malvinas and established a nuclear threat from the United Kingdom in the South Atlantic.[56] Where possible, Argentina also protected a relatively loose definition of human rights that would not confine Argentine policy domestically or internationally. During negotiations on a new protocol to the Inter-American Convention on Human Rights, the Argentine government recognized economic, social, and cultural rights as important protections. It also noted the interest of some governments in emphasizing the equivalence and interconnectedness of each of these areas of rights with civil and political rights. In addition, Argentina recognized that poverty in some countries—the absence of economic rights—meant that other rights would be difficult to achieve. At the same time, the Argentine government opposed the efforts of poorer Latin American governments to include language in a new protocol that might tighten up the definition of human rights. Alfonsín wanted no part of an international agreement that might lay out specifics on how rights of any sort should be protected.[57]

By the end of his term in office, Alfonsín was still facing ongoing human rights trouble. Although many of his initiatives were intended to take charge of and resolve outstanding human rights problems, hundreds of cases remained open and unresolved as far as international critics were concerned. Moreover, the ongoing search for information and demands for action from overseas underlined Argentina's inability to resolve its legacy of human rights violations. The Alfonsín government never lived down its attempt to present the Due Obedience and Final Point laws as the language of a government purportedly dedicated to human rights above all else. In July 1987, presidential advisors Claudia Maskin and Alejandra Fortuny wrote that the purpose of Due Obedience was to rigorously assign blame where appropriate, not to let anyone off the hook for human rights violations. But Maskin and Fortuny convinced no one.[58]

In 1988, the UN Working Group on Enforced or Voluntary Disappearances—which was still seeking information on hundreds of unresolved cases dating from the early 1970s—placed before Argentine officials requests for information on twenty-five cases from the period 1974–1978. The fact that some of these cases had been reported earlier by the Abuelas de Plaza de Mayo to no avail had increased tensions between Argentine human rights organizations and the government. The Working Group reported 3,452 cases to the Argentine government between late 1983 and the end of 1988, and the government had responded in 2,932 cases. But Argentine authorities had explained only 40 cases to the satisfaction of the Working Group. And among these 40 cases, the Working Group was able to identify only seven people who had been released from detention, four children who had been found, and fourteen bodies that had been located and identified.[59]

The 1987 Semana Santa uprising shook Argentines and suggested that military rule might again become reality. Alfonsín responded by moving to consolidate his government by strengthening more moderate factions within the armed forces. This he did by ending what many officers viewed as the "assault" on the records of their actions during the dictatorship. Although Due Obedience and Final Point may well have contributed to the marginalization of dictatorship-era figures within the armed forces, these laws severely damaged Alfonsín's reputation regarding human rights. Even as the government redoubled its efforts to control the damage that had been done, its human rights policy remained largely unchanged. In the face of dramatic economic challenges, human rights remained a low priority, despite Alfonsín's claims to the contrary. While new government bureaucracies responded to complaints and chased down information and perpetrators, only small numbers of disappeared were found and few perpetrators faced justice of any sort. In the international community, the Alfonsín administration became more cynical through the late 1980s. It was focused on human rights but was willing to compromise human rights objectives for the sake of improved commercial or strategic ties.

Epilogue

Saving Jorge Omar Merengo

Even though the Alfonsín administration could not right all its human rights wrongs, democracy brought remarkable, life-altering change for many. For one thing, it saved the life of Jorge Omar Merengo. In early 1977, Merengo was living with his common-law partner, Felisa Villalva, and an adopted son in a run-down section of Dock Sud, a violent working-class neighborhood in greater Buenos Aires. At one time, Dock Sud had been a port of note. Sailors from all over the world had come through with money to spend. Little of that economic hustle and bustle was left at the time of the March 1976 coup. When one of the many taverns where sex workers still plied their trade came on the market the following year, Merengo bought it for a song. The 22 was a bar with a reputation for drugs and fights. Merengo planned to clean it up, to make it a decent venue.[1]

Merengo and Villalva worked hard on improvements and renovations. They opened as a restaurant a few weeks after they bought the property. Just down the street, though, one of the traditional neighborhood bars, El Gato Negro, continued to function. Sex-trade workers outside the bar talked up clients, and inside they tried to sell dances and more. Clients began to find their way to the new 22 after a few hours at El Gato for drinks and a bite to eat. Despite Merengo's efforts to change the image of his refurbished restaurant, some of the old patrons continued to return to their haunt. He later told authorities that these returning customers harassed and insulted him.

Merengo worked long into the night trying to make a go of it at 22, sometimes leaving at 5 a.m. to head for his day job as a sailor in the Argentine navy; he was stationed at the headquarters of the naval police. He was thirty-six years old the night Carlos Ramón Lezcano stumbled into 22, drunk and in the company of a sex-trade worker known as Judith (later identified as Argentina Chacón). They had just come from El Gato. Details of the fight that ensued between Merengo and Lezcano remain unclear. Merengo later complained to arresting officers that Lezcano had brought "his dirty life" over from El Gato. A few days later, Merengo set a plan to kill Lezcano in motion. Just before dawn on 31 May 1977, Merengo, along with fellow naval personnel Víctor Francisco Rodríguez, Carlos Ramón Maidana, and Juan Martínez, stole a Chevrolet 400 and kidnapped both Lezcano and Chacón at the door of El Gato Negro. They drove their prisoners to an abandoned lot. The sailors raped Chacón and then killed both Chacón and Lezcano under a bridge over the Santo Domingo Canal.

In 1979, after a two-year trial, federal judge Antonio Borrás condemned Merengo to death for the killings. It was the first sentence of capital punishment in Argentina since 1916; the death penalty had been abolished in the 1960s for all but war-related crimes. In 1976, however, Law 21.388 of the dictatorship era had reintroduced the death penalty, and it was on that basis that Borrás issued his sentence. The sentence was delayed on appeal, and Merengo was not executed. The death penalty under the new democratic government was commuted to seven years in jail (capital punishment was again abolished in 1989). Merengo went free into Alfonsín's new Argentina.

The crime, the arrest, and the sentencing unfolded in a context that was removed from the immediacy of the state terror of the dictatorship.

The violence of the military was far less apparent in the Dock Sud sub-urb than it was in the center of the capital. The contours of Merengo's story, though, and the murders themselves place the case in late-1970s Argentina. The theft and use of a Chevrolet 400 by naval personnel was typical of hundreds of similar operations during military rule. Merengo's sense of outrage over what he viewed as moral turpitude and decay in Dock Sud echoed the pronouncements of the military government about moral decay, family, sexuality, and gender.[2] At the same time, this was not a typical crime committed with impunity under the dictatorship. In this case, the state reacted with the sharpest possible rebuke. Through the judiciary, it distinguished clearly between a task force in a Ford Fal-con (which generals regarded as a legitimate wartime mission) and the actions of a rogue gang of sailors who were in no way carrying out the work of the state. Is the distinction significant? Whether or not the Me-rengo case has specific relevance to the 30,000 cases of Argentines killed by the state between 1976 and 1983, it illustrates that despite the military government's ludicrous propaganda and lies about human rights and the law, at times there was an internal order to how the dictatorship ap-proached rights, crime, morality, and the law. Moreover, the sentence for the crime—which was reviled by the international rights community—reflected the government's harsh rejection of some violent crime.

Merengo's story does not contradict the central narrative of massive human rights abuses under the dictatorship, nor does it undermine the vital distinctions between military rule and the democracy that followed. But like the Alfonsín administration's inability to live up to its promise of a full accounting of human rights violations under the dictatorship and the Radical government's mixed record on important domestic and hu-man rights concerns, the shift from dictatorship to democracy combines both sharp breaks and disturbing transitions, the latter of which have been frequently ignored by middle-class Argentines. While Merengo's life was saved and capital punishment was abolished, the Alfonsín ad-ministration was unable to right past wrongs regarding human rights to the satisfaction of most Argentines. Nor was it able to eliminate the dictatorship's legacy of abuses and the consequences of those abuses. Alfonsín and other political leaders watched the early euphoria of the post-military period slip away as Argentines lost confidence in their new democracy. In the dual context of the nation's inability to move past the dictatorship with some sort of finality and the country's economic woes through the late 1980s, many wondered if there would ever be a full accounting of human rights violations under the military.

When Ernesto Sábato was named to chair CONADEP at the outset of the Alfonsín administration, he was a respected public figure. Sábato, who had been an atomic physicist present at the creation of the Argentine nuclear program in the 1940s, was also the country's most famous novelist. The appointment marked a reassertion of democracy and modernity through culture and the arts.[3] Although the authority Sábato lent to the truth commission process and the *Nunca Más* document asserted a forceful endpoint to the violence of the dictatorship, the artistic productions of younger, less-well-known cultural figures such as novelists Luisa Valenzuela and Ricardo Piglia and artist Marcelo Brodsky reflected ongoing unease and dismay in Argentine society over issues the truth commission could not resolve. These culture producers accepted the premise that what ailed Argentine society under the dictatorship had to be understood in the context of what had come earlier in the nation's political system, cultural life, and social life.[4]

These artists challenged Ernesto Sábato's conviction that the past could be left behind. This disagreement played out in other ways. *Nunca Más* proved unsatisfactory as a mechanism for bringing conciliation, memory, and justice to a society shaken by years of violence. Like Alfonsín's record, the document was incomplete. Despite its catalogue of data about many who had been tortured and executed, *Nunca Más* left too much unanswered. Most important, it gave no compelling explanation for how or why the country could have descended so quickly into such extreme violence. It offered no clarification of the motivations for or the decisions of the military leadership or of the mechanisms by which society accepted the supplanting of legal and constitutional norms.

After 1983, dozens of incidents reminded Argentines that murderers and torturers walked among them. Journalist Jacobo Timerman and writer Alicia Partnoy, both of whom were held and tortured during the dictatorship, were among many Argentines who ran into their former torturers on the streets of Buenos Aires. These meetings illustrated the facility with which human rights violators lived and worked in post-1983 Argentina. One of Timerman's torturers asked him at a chance meeting in the street how he was faring, how his health was. In a still stranger case, in July 2000 a group of human rights activists came face to face with torturer Julio "El Turco Julian" Simón in a downtown Buenos Aires café. Soon a small crowd surrounded him. El Turco was recognizable because the former soldier had made a career of appearing on television talk shows to defend his actions during the dictatorship and dismiss the concerns of those who sought to prosecute human rights violators as inconsequential. The police arrived in time to save Simón from a violent beating. For some, the fact that the crowd had confronted El Turco marked an important step forward for Argentine society, an incident that suggested that Argentina was confronting its past. For others, the episode was a reminder that the country could not put its past to rest. Later that year, El Turco Julian was arrested and charged for dictatorship-era crimes. But why then? Though they were heartened by the arrest, many Argentines understood the prosecution as a function of the café incident. Like the period of military rule itself, Argentine justice has been and continues to be capricious and anarchic—charging and convicting some, unable or unwilling to confront others.[5]

Judicial inefficacy and unpredictability is tied to corrupt politics and the fact that the military continued to play a strong political role in Argentina through the end of the twentieth century. Through the early 1990s, direct pressure from the military on the governments of Presidents Raúl Alfonsín and Carlos Menem meant that these executives were unwilling to tackle the problem of unprosecuted human rights violators. Instead, the respective governments of these two presidents retreated from plans to punish torturers and executioners. In 1990, shortly after coming to power, President Menem decreed a pardon for military officers who had been prosecuted and imprisoned in 1985. Each was released, and the problem (for the military) of the possibility that the government would seek a judicial accounting for human rights violations seemed to have come to an end. There the matter lay until a decade later, when federal judges in Argentina began to open new prosecution files against *proceso* leaders, who by that point were in their 70s and 80s. Although during Menem's decade in office the military lost power, the country moved no closer to the accounting that many sought for wrongs committed before 1984. One of Menem's most important political legacies was the fact that he reduced the power of the armed forces. However, this was part of an effort to enhance Menem's own power and the strength of the presidency. Among other moves, Menem's government seized control of the country's major airports and a number of industrial companies and other enterprises from the armed forces. It also froze military salaries, and by

154 · Consent of the Damned

the mid-1990s, many middle-class officers were struggling to maintain lower-middle-class status. Additionally, Menem made it more difficult for the armed forces to acquire weapons independent of civilian (Ministry of Defense) authority. These changes likely did far more to isolate the military from political power than the Alfonsín-era prosecutions of the generals.[6]

Many military hard-liners who had backed and continued to back the dictatorship into the 1990s began to retire. Many active duty officers who had come of age professionally after 1983 were not interested in defending the human rights violations of their predecessors. Few anticipated the sea change that was ushered in with the appointment of General Martín Balza as head of the armed forces in 1995. Balza, Argentina's most decorated officer during the Malvinas War, made it clear that while he did not favor a broad-based judicial attack on human rights violators, his position was dramatically different from that of his predecessors. One of the electrifying statements Balza made was that he believed strongly in the constitutional rule of law. By this he meant not that the constitution had justified military rule but that there was not and never had been a good reason for the military takeover of the government. He also decried the human rights violations of the *proceso*, indicating that there was never an excuse for torturing pregnant women and kidnapping children. In 1999, after he had retired, the Association of Retired Officers expelled him from their ranks. He responded that as long as he had his membership in the YMCA he would be just fine. Balza likely did more than *Nunca Más* to distance democratic rule from the dictatorship.[7]

There were other signs of a political shift on the issue of human rights in the late 1990s. New activist groups emerged, the most important of which was HIJOS (Hijos e Hijas por la Identidad y la Justicia contra el Olvido y el Silencio), a group comprised principally of children of disappeared Argentines. HIJOS focused primarily on the dictatorship and paid little attention to the smaller (though ongoing) litany of human rights abuses after 1983. But the group pioneered the *escrache*, an often impromptu mass protest in front of the home of a suspected human rights violator. In the wake of Spain's judicial investigation of and request for the extradition of Augusto Pinochet and a number of Argentine officers for crimes against Spanish citizens during the dictatorship and for crimes against humanity, a handful of Argentine federal judges also sought indictments against military officers. Their actions led to the arrest and detention of half a dozen dictatorship-era officers and soldiers.[8]

Although these moves toward a new judicial and social accounting were seen as positive developments by many, they underlined the persistent legacy of military rule. So did a variety of other problems. Through the 1980s and 1990s, human rights groups decried the ongoing viciousness of police brutality. Though they were far less serious than the systematic violence of the dictatorship, regular incidents of police brutality reminded Argentines of their unresolved authoritarian past. In 1999, for example, a homeless woman was crushed to death by a heavy mechanical gate outside the offices of the SIDE. Despite an attempted cover-up, the press learned that an officer on watch had tired of the woman's regular appearance at the entrance of the building to feed stray cats. He had deliberately lured the woman toward the building and then crushed her with the gate. The systematic breakdown of police procedure was a more troubling legacy from the time of military rule, particularly in the ranks of the *bonaerense*, the infamous Buenos Aires provincial police.[9] In February 2001, the president of the *radicales*, Leopoldo Moreau, lamented the sharp and ongoing increase in crime in Buenos Aires Province and criticized police officers who "cannot be, do not know how to be, and do not want to be police officers."[10]

Judicial and political corruption became rampant in the 1990s. The massive theft of public funds was a reminder that the country had not been able to rebuild its democratic institutions in the aftermath of military rule. In addition, Argentina's ongoing economic crisis contributed to the perseverance of decades-old rigid social divisions. This contributed to a crisis of uncertainty about how or whether problems associated with military rule would ever be set to rest. Unlike Guatemala, where military rule was characterized by an internal war that identified subaltern people of color as key enemies, in Argentina, the state terror of the dictatorship had been directed primarily against real and imagined enemies among the urban, light-skinned middle class. The search for an end to the post-1983 crisis of persistent authoritarianism belonged essentially to that group. Although some Argentines of color reviled the violence of military rule and sought a judicial and cultural accounting after 1983, for others the problem of military rule was not a problem that was crucial to their lives. For many Argentines of color, it was difficult to distinguish the brutality of the military from the so-called democratic governments that preceded and followed the dictatorship. Suburban and rural subalterns of color showed repeatedly that their quarrel was less with the military than with middle- and upper-class white Argentines.[11]

In politics, this was reflected in two important elections that many urban middle-class Argentines found difficult to grasp. In the 1990s, the people of the poor northwestern province of Tucumán elected retired (and unrepentant) General Jorge Bussi as their governor. Bussi had been governor once before, when the military had appointed him during the dictatorship. Bussi was elected in the 1990s even though human rights groups had produced evidence of his personal involvement in illegal arrests, torture, and assassinations. For many poor Argentines the problem of the legacy of militarism was far less important than the pressing everyday problems of social and economic life. The election highlighted profound social divisions in Argentina. In a similar case, cashiered colonel Aldo Rico, a leader in the 1987 Easter Weekend uprising and an outspoken defender of military atrocities between 1976 and 1983, was elected mayor of San Miguel, a town in Buenos Aires Province, in 1997. The elections of Rico and Bussi, as well as the emergence of other dictatorship figures in places of political prominence, provided evidence of the persistence of a culture of authoritarianism and the strength of the military ideologies that had been carefully constructed before 1984.

Through the late 1990s and after the collapse of the Argentine economy in December 2001, a growing chorus of Argentines singled out Carlos Menem as a villain in the national human rights narrative—a president who had watched with disinterest as the nation sank back into dictatorship-era patterns of abuse. That descent was captured in the story of Menem's ally, Alfredo Yabrán. Yabrán rose to prominence from obscure origins under the dictatorship. By the 1990s, the era of the privatized economy, he was a wealthy and powerful businessman who owned Argentina's most successful private courier service. When photographer José Luis Cabezas, who had been investigating him, was viciously murdered, a federal prosecutor issued a warrant for Yabrán's arrest on suspicion of ordering the murder. Days later, Yabrán was found dead in his ranch home, an apparent suicide.[12]

In the final stages of the Alfonsín administration, the government's ambiguous position on international human rights sharpened: the government moved away from the rhetoric of a strong pro–human rights stand in the international arena and toward a deemphasis on human rights. This change was a hallmark of Carlos Menem's domestic and foreign policies. Under Alfonsín, protocols that Argentina signed with Brazil for landmark nuclear, commercial, and diplomatic cooperation said nothing of human rights. Neither did foundational documents for Mercosur (Mercado Común del Sur), the free trade zone in the Southern Cone that was established in 1991.[13]

Following the path that Alfonsín set in the final year of his economically besieged administration, Menem set aside human rights as a foreign policy priority. In 1991, Foreign Minister Guido di Tella made no mention of human rights in a secret discussion of Argentina's international priorities during the Uruguay Round of multilateral negotiations for the General Agreement on Trade and Tariffs. On Argentina's membership in the Non-Aligned movement, di Tella said, "We're almost exclusively interested in UN votes on the Malvinas. We need to make no more than the necessary statements, so they'll vote for us on the only issue on which we need their support, and . . . for the moment they [non-aligned nations] don't represent interesting commercial markets." In 1991, Argentina left the Non-Aligned Movement.[14]

Di Tella mocked Alfonsín's break with South Africa. He claimed not to understand why it was done. While Argentina continued to take a stand against discrimination and apartheid, di Tella cynically found the rupture with South Africa so "unhinged" that it had generated no public interest, not even on "the left, to whom the gesture had been directed." Because the result was of no commercial value to Argentina, he could only conclude that the break with South Africa had been targeted at strong ties with a future "black" government there.

The new government's cynicism about international politics extended to other regions. It did nothing to solicit Latin American votes at the UN because most Latin American nations had no other diplomatic recourse than to vote with Argentina. Menem's government planned to promote a transition to democracy in Chile and Paraguay, but not for human rights reasons. Di Tella was focused on the potential for political and economic instability and saw democracy as a necessary antidote for uncertainty in the region. More important, he wanted no distractions from Argentina's priority in the region—a new commercial relationship with Brazil. Unlike Alfonsín, di Tella wanted the lowest profile possible on Nicaragua. Menem's government had no interest in the Contadora peace talks to deal with military conflicts in Nicaragua, El Salvador, and Guatemala, which di Tella felt had proposed no "realist" position. Moral questions were relegated to the back burner. Most important, di Tella wanted to avoid commercial instability in the hemisphere as a result of a U.S. invasion in Central America and "*un lío mayusculo, tipo Vietnam*" [a Vietnam-style colossal mess].[15]

The military rulers of the *proceso* had conflated pre-1976 democratic governments as incompetent and weak in their putative defense of human rights. The Alfonsín Radicals had melded military rule with Peronism as enemies of human rights. After 1990, the Menem administration fused them all together in its rejection of human rights as a key policy priority. For the new government, the period before 1990 and Menem's presidency was characterized by stages of disintegration and instability, the result of civilian governments that lacked authority and military governments that lacked legitimacy. In the *menemista* narrative of yet another new Argentina, the 1990 watermark heralded the excision of human rights as a central touchstone of modernity and democracy.[16]

Notes

Introduction

1. See, for example, Timothy Snyder, *Bloodlands: Europe between Hitler and Stalin* (New York: Basic Books, 2010); Slavko Goldstein, *1941: Godina koja se vraća* [*1941: The Year That Keeps Returning*] (Zagreb: Novi Liber, 1965); Alan Riding, *And the Show Went On: Cultural Life in Nazi-Occupied Paris* (New York: Knopf, 2010); Tina Mai Chen, "Socialism, Aestheticized Bodies, and International Circuits of Gender: Soviet Female Film Stars in the People's Republic of China, 1949–1969," *Journal of the Canadian Historical Association* 18, no. 2 (2007): 53–80; Nora Rabotnikof, "Memoria y política a treinta años del golpe," in *Argentina, 1976: Estudios en torno al golpe de estado*, edited by Clara E. Lida, Horacio Crespo, and Pablo Yankelevich (Buenos Aires: Fondo de Cultura Económica, 2008), 259–64.

2. Luisa Valenzuela, "Foreword: On Memory and Memorials," in *Accounting for Violence: Marketing Memory in Latin America*, edited by Ksenija Bilbija and Leigh A. Payne (Durham, N.C.: Duke University Press, 2011), ix. See also Elizabeth Jelin, *Monumentos, memoriales y marcas territoriales* (Madrid: Siglo XXI, 2003); Idelber Avelar, *The Untimely Present: Postdictatorial Fiction and the Task of Mourning* (Durham, N.C.: Duke

University Press, 1999); and Victoria Ruetalo, "From Penal Institution to Shopping Mecca: The Economics of Memory and the Case of Punta Carretas," *Cultural Critique* 68 (Winter 2008): 38–65.

3. See John Gray Greer, *Public Opinion and Polling around the World: A Historical Encyclopedia*, vol. 1 (Santa Barbara: ABC-CLIO, 2004), 510; José Enrique Miguens, "The Presidential Elections of 1973 and the End of Ideology," in *Juan Perón and the Reshaping of Argentina*, edited by Frederick Turner and José Enrique Miguens (Pittsburgh: University of Pittsburgh Press, 1983), 157–66; Jeane Kirkpatrick, *Leader and Vanguard in Mass Society: A Study of Peronism in Argentina* (Cambridge, Mass.: MIT Press, 1971); and Pierre Bourdieu, *Distinction: A Social Critique of the Judgement of Taste* (Cambridge, Mass.: Harvard University Press, 1973).

4. Most scholarship on the most recent Argentine dictatorship does not take into account gender, race, class, or region and continues to accept the notion that opposition to the military was widespread. On changing responses among Argentines to the dictatorship and the range of those responses, see Klaus Friedrich Veigel, *Dictatorship, Democracy, and Globalization: Argentina and the Cost of Paralysis, 1973–2001* (University Park: Pennsylvania State University Press, 2009), 124–29; Judith Noemí Freidenberg, *The Invention of the Jewish Gaucho: Villa Clara and the Construction of Argentine Identity* (Austin: University of Texas Press, 2009), 115; and Leslie Ray, *Language of the Land: The Mapuche in Argentina and Chile* (Copenhagen: International Working Group for Indigenous Affairs, 2007), 118.

5. Paul H. Lewis, *Guerrillas and Generals: The "Dirty War" in Argentina* (Westport, Conn.: Praeger, 2002), 125. See also Marguerite Feitlowitz, *A Lexicon of Terror: Argentina and the Legacies of Torture*, rev. ed. (New York: Oxford University Press, 2011), 7.

6. "Homenaje al General Enrique Mosconi," *Revista YPF* (Buenos Aires) 1, no. 1 (1977): 32–35.

7. On Guatemala, see Diane M. Nelson, *A Finger in the Wound: Body Politics in Quincentennial Guatemala* (Berkeley, Calif.: University of California Press, 1999); and Jon Schackt, "Mayahood through Beauty: Indian Beauty Pageants in Guatemala," *Bulletin of Latin American Research* 24, no. 3 (July 2005): 269–87.

8. This expression is equivalent to the expression "like selling ice to Eskimos."

9. Guido di Tella, Foreign Minister, "Hacia una realpolitik internacional argentina," 18 June 1991, 331, Argentine Government Documents (AGD). I accessed the documents I cite here as AGD at the facility at 1981 Velez Sarsfield Avenue in Buenos Aires, which is owned by the Federal Police and was managed by the Foreign Relations Ministry. Documents there included materials from a variety of federal ministries and other government agencies. In 2008, the facility closed and the Foreign Ministry transferred some of the contents to another facility. The numbers that appear before "AGD" indicate the number assigned to the packet of documents. All translations from these and other Argentine documents are mine.

10. "Charly García y los años de plomo," *Clarín*, 13 February 1999; "Charly García, irónico y testimonial," *La Nación*, 8 May 1999.

11. See, for example, "Ezequiel Demonty fue torturado antes de ser arrojado al Ria-

chuelo," *La Nación*, 8 October 2002; and "Tres ex policías pidieron que les reduzcan la pena por el crimen de Ezequiel Demonty," *Clarín*, 14 May 2007.

12. The Rosario monument constitutes a "subversive" memory in that it challenges the dominant memory of human rights abuses on the right. Despite a wealth of scholarship on memory and dictatorship in Argentina, there is no analysis of memory that does not stress opposition to military rule. See "Argentinos por la memoria completa," http://www.facebook.com/groups/13770870034/, accessed 15 March 2012.

13. Author's interview with Sergio Victor Palma, Buenos Aires, 20 February 2008; author's interview with Juan Martín Coggi, Buenos Aires, 17 July 2007; Karen Robert, "The Falcon Remembered," *NACLA: Report on the Americas* 38, no. 3 (2005): 12–15.

14. Marguerite Feitlowitz, *A Lexicon of Terror: Argentina and the Legacies of Torture* (Oxford: Oxford University Press, 1998), 59; Miguel Bonasso, "De los 'desaparecidos' a los 'chicos de la guerra,'" *Nueva Sociedad* 76 (1985): 52–61.

15. "Norma Mirta Penjerek, un asesinato que quedó impune," *Clarín*, 29 August 1999; "Penjerek: la desaparecida," *La Nación*, 26 February 2006.

Chapter 1. Dictatorship, Media, and Message

1. "La industria, el agro y el comercio enfrentan al ministro Martínez de Hoz," *Siete Dias*, 12–18 August 1977; "Roberto Campos habla del Plan Martínez de Hoz," *Gente* (Buenos Aires), 10 May 1979; "El balance de Martínez de Hoz," *Gente*, 10 November 1977; Nazareno Bravo, "El discurso de la dictadura militar argentina (1976–83). Definición del opositor político y confinamiento—'valorización' del papel de la mujer en el espacio privado," *Utopia y Praxis Latinoamericana* (Maracaibo) 8 (2003): 107–23; Horacio del Prado, "Gol Argentino," *Goles Match* (Buenos Aires), 15 October 1980.

2. Claudia Soria, "La propaganda peronista: hacía una renovación estética del Estado nacional," in *Políticas del sentimiento: el peronismo y la construcción de la Argentina moderna*, edited by Claudia Soria, Paola Cortés Rocca, and Edgardo Dieleke (Buenos Aires: Prometeo, 2010), 31–48; Natalia Milanesio, "Peronists and *Cabecitas*: Stereotypes and Anxieties at the Peak of Social Change," in *The New Cultural History of Peronism*, edited by Matthew B. Karush and Oscar Chamosa (Durham, N.C.: Duke University Press, 2010), 53–84.

3. Graciela Mochkofsky, *Timerman: El periodista que quiso ser parte del poder (1923–1999)* (Buenos Aires: Sudamericana, 2003), 94.

4. Claudia Nora Laudano, *Las mujeres en los discursos militares* (Buenos Aires: Editorial La Página, 1998), 39–42; Agustín Santella, "Workers' Mobilization and Political Violence: Conflict in Villa Constitución, Argentina, 1970–1975," *Latin American Perspectives* 35 (September 2008): 146–57; Nora R. Libertun de Duren, "Urban Planning and State Reform: From Industrial Suburbs to Gated Communities," *Journal of Planning Education and Research* 28 (2007): 312–15.

5. Inés Vázquez, "Aspectos de Memoria y Cultura en la Argentina postdictatorial," in *Un país, 30 años: el pañuelo sigue haciendo historia*, edited by Inés Vázquez and Karina Downie (Buenos Aires: Ediciones Madres de Plaza de Mayo, 2006), 201–17.

6. See Mariana Caviglia, *Dictadura, vida cotidiana y clases medias: una sociedad fracturada* (Buenos Aires: Prometeo Libros, 2006); Hugo Vezzetti, *Pasado y presente: guerra,*

dictadura y sociedad en la Argentina (Buenos Aires: Siglo XXI, 2002); Beatriz Sarlo, "Memoria e industria de la memoria," *La Nación,* 28 April 2002; Mercedes Vilanova, "Rememoración y fuentes orales," in *Historia, memoria y fuentes orales,* edited by Vera Carnovale, Federico Lorenz, and Roberto Pittaluga (Buenos Aires: Ediciones Memoria Abierta, 2006), 91–110; María Julieta Gómez, "El proceso militar de 1976–1983 en el imaginario social de San Luis, Argentina. Un estudio de casos," *Fundamentos en Humanidades* (San Luis) 3 (1998): 89–118.

7. Abel Gilbert and Miguel Vitagliano, *El terror y la gloria: la vida, el fútbol y la política en la Argentina del Mundial 78* (Buenos Aires: Grupo Editorial Norma, 1998); "Aquí están, estos son . . . ," *Goles* (Buenos Aires), 12 July 1977; "Estos serán los 24 jugadores . . . ," *Goles,* 12 July 1977.

8. Diana Taylor, *Disappearing Acts: Spectacles of Gender and Nationality in Argentina's "Dirty War"* (Durham, N.C.: Duke University Press, 1997), 1–58. See also Lauren Derby, "The Dictator's Seduction: Gender and State Spectacle during the Trujillo Dictatorship," in *Latin American Popular Culture,* edited by William H. Beezley and Linda A. Curcio (Wilmington: SR Books, 2000), 213–39.

9. "Yo? Argentino," *Goles,* 12 July 1977.

10. Felipe Martínez, Juan S. Montes Cató, Javier M. Real, and Nicolás Wachsmann, "La Revolución Libertadora y el intento por eliminar al peronismo del imaginario de los trabajadores," in *Cine e imaginario social,* edited by Fortunato Mallimacci and Irene Marrone (Buenos Aires: Oficina de Publicaciones del CBC, 1997), 269–73.

11. Gabriela Esquivada, *El diario noticias: los Montoneros en la prensa argentina* (La Plata, Argentina: Ediciones de Periodismo y Comunicación, 2004), 141–77; "Asi mataron a mi padre," *Noticias,* 9 June 1974; "Matan a villero en Plaza Mayo," *Noticias,* 26 March 1974.

12. "Tucumán: el jardín vuelve a florecer," *Siete Dias,* 17–23 December 1976.

13. Pablo Sirvén, *Quién te ha visto y quién TV* (Buenos Aires: Ediciones de la Flor, 1998), 97. On censorship, authoritarian rule, and the intersection of propaganda and the media, see also Francisco Sevillano Calero, "Cultura, propaganda y opinion en el primer franquismo," in *El primer franquismo (1936-1959),* edited by Glicerio Sánchez Recio (Madrid: Marcial Pons, 1999), 151–59; Estevao Cabral, "The Indonesian Propaganda War against East Timor," in *The East Timor Question,* edited by Paul Hainsworth and Stephen McCloskey (London: I. B. Tauris Publishers, 2000), 69–84; Marina Petrakis, *The Metaxas Myth: Dictatorship and Propaganda in Greece* (London: Tauris Academic Studies, 2006), 7–31, 64–115; Tzvi Tal, *Pantallas y revolución: una vision comparativa del cine de liberación y el cinema novo* (Buenos Aires: Ediciones Lumiere, 2005), 157–58.

14. Eduardo Blaustein and Martín Zubieta, *Decíamos ayer. La prensa argentina bajo el proceso* (Buenos Aires: Colihue, 1998), 354–66; Landrú (Juan Carlos Colombres) and Edgardo Russo, *Landrú por Landrú* (Buenos Aires: El Ateneo, 1993), 38; Carlos Ulanovsky, *Paren las rotativas* (Buenos Aires: Espasa, 1977), 175; Alejandro Lafourcade, "La revista *Humor* como medio opositor a la dictadura militar" (Licenciatura thesis, Universidad El Salvador, Buenos Aires, 2004), 18–22; "Una lección de Humor," *Siete Dias,* 17–23 December 1976; Patricia Marenghi and Laura Pérez López, "Prensa española y dictadura

argentina (1976–1983): La imagen del exilio en *ABC, El País,* y *Triunfo,*" *América Latina Hoy* (Salamanca) 34 (2003): 49–78.

15. Graciela Mochkofsky, *Timerman: el periodista que quiso ser parte del poder* (Buenos Aires: Sudamericana, 2003), 90–101; Daniel Horacio Mazzei, "Primera Plana: modernización y golpismo en los 60," in *Historia de las revistas argentinas,* edited by Asociación Argentina de Editores de Revistas (Buenos Aires: Asociación Argentina de Editores de Revistas, 1995), 13–35.

16. Eduardo Luis Duhalde, *El estado terrorista argentino. Quince años después, una mirada crítica* (Buenos Aires: EUDEBA, 1999), 245; Judith Gociol and Hernán Invernizzi, *Un golpe a los libros: represión a la cultura durante la última dictadura militar* (Buenos Aires: EUDEBA, 2002), 70–73.

17. Paula Guitelman, *La infancia en dictadura: modernidad y conservadurismo en el mundo de Billiken* (Buenos Aires: Prometeo libros, 2006), 49, 84–86; Blaustein and Zubieta, *Decíamos ayer,* 266; "Doña Pan-Cita la Panadera," *Billiken* (Buenos Aires), 2 June 1981.

18. Eduardo P. Archetti, "Estilo y virtudes masculinas en *El Gráfico*: la creación del imaginario del futbol argentino," *Desarrollo Económico* 35 (1995): 419–42.

19. "Rhodesia: La inocencia condenada a muerte," *Siete Dias,* 26 November–2 December 1976.

20. "Aerolíneas se suma al jet set del aire," *Siete Dias,* 26 November–2 December 1976.

21. "Buscado!" *Siete Dias,* 15–21 October 1976.

22. "Argentina: la agonía del terror," *Siete Dias,* 1–6 August 1976; "Pirañas: peligro en las puertas de Buenos Aires," *Siete Dias,* 31 December 1976–6 January 1977; "El miedo a este hombre dejo desierta la noche de Nueva York," *Siete Dias,* 12–18 August 1977; "Las negras dan jaque al rey, pero las blancas ganan," *Siete Dias,* 7–13 January 1977; "El asesino volvió al lugar del crimen," *Gente,* 11 November 1978; "Pero los Klein sigue de pie," *Gente,* 4 October 1979.

23. "Lo mejor de 1976," *Siete Dias,* 31 December 1976–6 January 1977; "El sueño argentino," *Satiricón,* December 1975.

24. Hugo Salas, "Operación ja ja," *Página/12,* 1 October 2006; Eduardo Jakubowicz and Laura Radetich, *La historia argentina a través del cine* (Buenos Aires: La Cruja, 2006), 139–42; "Por ahora, no habrá cambios en la conducción económica," *Siete Dias,* 10–16 November 1977; Mario Berardi, *La vida imaginada: vida cotidiana y cine argentino, 1933–1970* (Buenos Aires: Ediciones del Jilguero, 2006), 13–20; Carlos Ulanovsky, Silvia Itkin, and Pablo Sirvén, *Estamos en el aire: una historia de la television en la Argentina* (Buenos Aires: Planeta, 1999), 352–54.

25. "Punta: Enero caliente con ese delicado 'touch' de distinción," *Radiolandia 2000* (Buenos Aires), 12 January 1979. Three years later, during the Malvinas War, the media climate had changed. Magazines, newspapers, and television were less inclined to promote the military or its ideology and had begun to express more doubt about the dictatorship and the cultural and social premises that defined the *proceso.* For example, an article on Ruiz Guiñazú stressed her political toughness and even her differences with the official line of the military on disappearances and other themes. See "Magadalena Ruiz Guiñazú: El duro oficio de la verdad," *Radiolandia 2000,* 23 April 1982.

26. "Regine's o Mau-Mau?" *Gente*, 22 March 1979.

27. "La justicia merece justicia," *Gente*, 22 March 1979.

28. "Si al Viejo Almacen le pasa algo, seguro voy a llorar," *Radiolandia 2000*, 12 January 1979. See also "Del Gran Chaparral al Viejo Almacen," *Siete Dias*, 2 December 1976; "La nostalgia pide una vuelta más," *Siete Dias*, 15–21 October 1976; and "Yo, al tango, lo sigo tratando de usted," *Siete Dias*, 22–28 July 1977.

29. "Carta abierta a un político," *Gente*, 10 April 1980; Alejandro Lafourcade, "La revista *Humor*," 59–61.

30. "Argentinos . . . Asi no! Nos vamos a matar todos," *Radiolandia 2000*, 13 January 1978; Javier Lorca, "La política argentina es un espacio vacío," *Página/12*, 25 February 2008.

31. See Monzón's 1974 film *La Mary*.

32. "Si la memoria no me falla y el embrague no patina," *Siete Dias*, 7–13 January 1977; "Galería de campeones," *Radiolandia 2000*, 13 January 1978; Juan Manuel Fangio, *Fangio: My Racing Life* (London: Patrick Stephens, 1990), 283–95; Karl Ludvigsen, *Juan Manuel Fangio: Motor Racing's Grand Master* (Newbury Park, Calif.: Haynes Publishing, 1999), chapter 7; "Escribe Fangio: 'mi vida junto a los fierros,'" *Siete Dias*, 16–22 October 1976.

33. Horacio Vargas, *Reutemann: el conductor* (Rosario: Homo Sapiens Ediciones, 1997), 38–42.

34. "Vilas volvió, Vilas habló," *El Gráfico*, 12 November 1975.

35. By this time, Vilas had already earned more money than any athlete in Argentine history, with the exception of boxer Carlos Monzón.

36. "El tenis argentino en su hora más gloriosa," *Siete Dias*, 6–12 May 1977; "La leyenda de una ensaladera," *El Gráfico*, 23 September 1980.

37. "Por todo esto soy el mejor del mundo," *Siete Dias*, 15–21 September 1977.

38. Ibid.

39. "Murió el fantasma del Reutemann perdedor," *Gente*, 6 April 1978; "Porque Watson lo cerro y Lauda lo 'tocó,'" *Gente*, 11 May 1978; "Lauda, Verdugo de turno del 'Lole,'" *Goles*, 9 May 1978. See also "En la calestita de Long Beach Andretti sacó la sortija," *Goles*, 5 April 1977.

40. "El deportes es sano. El 'deportivismo' es una enfermedad," *Gente*, 6 April 1978.

41. "La vida, el peligro y la gloria a 300 kilometros por hora," *Gente*, 13 January 1977; "Reutemann sigue hacienda Milagros," *Goles*, 29 May 1979.

42. To be sure, there were irreconcilable contradictions in sport as a cultural medium for transmitting military ideologies. On the one hand, the functionality of the images of Vilas and Reutemann as men of the era depended on the distinction between the higher-class sports in which they competed and the more working-class pastimes of soccer or boxing. But the military and its allies in the media were not above investing soccer stars or boxers with traits that marked the normalizing propaganda of the dictatorship. Not only did the military government highlight the 1978 World Cup of Soccer as a showcase for Argentina, but the generals invited world champion boxers Carlos Monzón and Sergio Victor Palma to participate in highly publicized trips to entertain the troops in Tucumán, where the latter were fighting "subversion" in that province.

43. "La otra Juvenilia," *Página/12*, 17 October 2004.

44. "Cartas abiertas al Ayatollah Komeini," *Gente*, 22 March 1979.

45. "El encuentro con el Presidente Videla," *Siete Dias*, 15–21 September 1977.

46. "Vilas pierde una fortuna por los manejos sucios del tenis," *Radiolandia 2000*, 12 January 1979; "18-3-79: Compartimos la Victoria," *Siete Dias*, 21–28 March 1979.

47. "No quiero ser una máquina de jugar tenis," *Gente*, 4 May 1978.

48. "Felicitaciones, Vilas; Gracias, Alteza," *Gente*, 10 April 1980; "Carolina ya sacó los pasajes," *Gente*, 26 August 1982.

49. "No: Este público nunca tiene razón," *Gente*, 22 March 1979.

50. Laudano, *Las mujeres en los discursos militares*, 39–58.

51. "Cada piloto de Fórmula 1 se conoce a través de su mujer," *Gente*, 10 November 1977; "Horas antes de la carrera, Reutemann habla 'de todo,'" *Gente*, 10 January 1974.

52. "¿La formula uno destruye los matrimonios?" *Gente*, 8 November 1979; "Se fue tras el objetivo Kyalami," *Goles*, 8 February 1977.

53. "Todavía no sé por qué estoy en fórmula uno," *Siete Dias*, 17–23 November 1977.

54. "Detrás de la escena," *Gente*, 12 February 1976; "Juntos, felices, enamorados," *Gente*, 12 February 1976.

55. "El jet-set de las pistas se instala en Buenos Aires," *Radiolandia 2000*, 13 January 1978.

56. "Todavía no sé por qué estoy en fórmula uno," *Siete Dias*, 17–23 November 1977; "La vida, el peligro y la Gloria a 300 kilometros por hora," *Gente*, 13 January 1977; "Newman y Reutemann juntos en Italia," *Gente*, 18 November 1976; "La batalla continua en privado," *El Gráfico*, 11 August 1981; "Ligier, Ferrari . . . o una sorpresa," *El Gráfico*, 3 April 1979; "Lauda, Verdugo de turno de 'Lole,'" *Goles*, 9 March 1978.

57. "Hugo Sofovich desalojado del Shopping," *Radiolandia 2000*, 21 July 1988; "El verano de la triple p," *Siete Dias*, 25 February–2 March 1988.

58. "Ahora, el país quiere respuestas," *Gente*, 9 September 1982; "Harguindeguy y Videla tienen que ir a la cárcel," *Siete Dias*, 7–13 September 1983.

59. "Vuelve la F-1," *Goles*, 9 March 1982; "Traverso salió de paseo," *Goles*, 9 March 1982; "El Gaucho bailó en la sierra," *Goles*, 16 March 1982.

60. "Si Lole gana el título, Saluda y abandona la F-1," *Radiolandia 2000*, 25 September 1981; "Pregunto al gobierno por qué motivo se nos combate," *Radiolandia 2000*, 25 September 1981; "Quiero saber porque soy un actor prohibido," *Revista 10* (Buenos Aires), 27 July 1982.

61. "La fe sigue creciendo," *El Gráfico*, 29 April 1980; "El tenis unió al país," *El Gráfico*, 11 March 1980.

62. "El cerebro de Lafitte y el corazón de Reutemann," *El Gráfico*, 23 January 1979.

63. "Cada día estoy más contento," *El Gráfico*, 29 April 1980.

64. Y ahora, Guillermo contá todo . . . ," *El Gráfico*, 10 March 1981; "Todo lo que piensa Vilas," *El Gráfico*, 13 August 1985.

65. "'No puedo sentirme feliz,'" *El Gráfico*, 19 May 1981; "Una Victoria que hizo justicia," *El Gráfico*, 19 May 1981. Five months later, Reutemann lost the year's Formula One championship by just one point. See "Amargura, sí; drama, no," *El Gráfico*, 20 October 1981; "El dolor y la grandeza de un hombre," *El Gráfico*, 20 October 1981; "El ajedrez de

Piquet y Reutemann," *El Gráfico*, 1 September 1981; "Una batalla con dos ganadores," *El Gráfico*, 5 May 1981.

66. "Las distintas realidades de Steffi y Gaby," *El Gráfico*, 13 September 1988; "La fatiga pudo más," *El Gráfico*, 22 March 1988; "Una estrella llamada Gabriela," *El Gráfico*, 4 September 1984; "¿Cómo es tu vida en New York?" *El Gráfico*, 4 September 1984; "Nunca tan grande," *El Gráfico*, 18 April 1989.

67. "Esta vez me falto garra," *El Gráfico*, 4 August 1987; "Tres grandes del tenis mundial," *El Gráfico*, 26 July 1988; "Gaby hizo lo que debí hacer," *El Gráfico*, 8 September 1987.

68. Author's interview with Emmanuel Kahan, Tempe, Arizona, 13 June 2011.

Chapter 2. "A Correct, Hermeneutic Reading"

1. Ricardo Piglia, *Respiración artificial* (Buenos Aires: Editorial Pomaine, 1980); Idelber Avelar, "Cómo respiran los ausentes: La narrativa de Ricardo Piglia," *Modern Language Notes*, 110, no. 2 (1995): 416–32.

2. Ricardo Piglia, *Artificial Respiration*, translated by Daniel Balderston (Durham, N.C.: Duke University Press, 1994), 189; Tulio Halperín-Donghi, *The Peronist Revolution and Its Ambiguous Legacy*, Occasional Papers 17 (London: Institute of Latin American Studies, 1998), 26–28.

3. Piglia, *Respiración artificial*, 91.

4. Ministry of Foreign Relations, Argentina (hereafter MRE), "Respuesta del Gobierno de la República Argentina a la Comisión de Derechos Humanos en material de Comunicaciones sujetas al procedimiento de la Resolución 1503 (XLVIII) del ECOSOC," 28 December 1979, 123, AGD; John P. Mandler, "Habeas Corpus and the Protection of Human Rights in Argentina," *Yale Journal of International Law* 16 (1991): 3–34.

5. No. 136, Ambassador Enrique B. Vieyra, Chief, Eastern Europe Division, MRE, to Directorate General of Foreign Policy, MRE, "Actividades anti-yugoslavas de organizaciones terroristas 'Ustashas,'" 5 August 1983; Embassy of Yugoslavia, Buenos Aires, Memorandum, 5 August 1983; Inspector Laudemaro Luis Azario, Chief, Foreign Affairs Department, Federal Police, Ministry of the Interior, Argentina, 28 March 1983; No. 60, Eastern European Division to Directorate General of Foreign Policy, MRE, "Conversación con Embajador de Yugoslavia D. Zuko Kenesevic," 15 April 1983, 9, AGD; Marisol Saavedra, *La Argentina no alineada: desde la tercera posición justicialista hasta el menemismo (1973–1991)* (Buenos Aires: Biblos, 2004), 57–63.

6. Ezequiel F. Pereyra, Director of Foreign Policy, MRE, "Entrevista del Director General de Política Exterior con S.E. el Embajador de Cuba," 24 April 1976, 479 AGD; Roberto Russell, "El proceso de toma de decisiones en la política exterior argentina (1976–1989)," in *Política exterior y toma de decisiones en América Latina*, edited by Roberto Russell (Buenos Aires: Grupo Editor Latinoamericano, 1990), 13–59.

7. Author's interview with Luis García, 5 July 2004, Buenos Aires; Hugo Vezzetti, *Pasado y presente: guerra, dictadura y sociedad en la Argentina* (Buenos Aires: Siglo XXI, 2002), 147–52; No. 440/81, Gabriel Martínez, Argentine Ambassador to the Organization of American States, to Oscar Camilión, Foreign Relations Minister, "Observaciones sobre el proyecto de Convención sobre la tortura de la Comisión Jurídica Internacional," 30 April 1981, 304, AGD.

8. Grupo de Estudios en Legislación Indígena, "A Possible Indigenism: The Limits of the Constitutional Amendment in Argentina," in *Decolonizing Indigenous Rights*, edited by Adolfo de Oliveira (New York: Routledge, 2009), 122–31; Claudia Briones, *La alteridad del "Cuarto Mundo": una deconstrucción antropológica de la diferencia* (Buenos Aires: Ediciones del Sol, 1998), 179–83; Claudia Briones, "Questioning State Geographies of Inclusion in Argentina: The Cultural Politics of Organizations with Mapuche Leadership and Philosophy," in *Cultural Agency in the Americas*, edited by Doris Sommer (Durham, N.C.: Duke University Press, 2005), 248–78.

9. Ana Irma Noia, Assessor, Secretariat of Justice, Ministry of Education and Justice, Argentina, to Antonio Castagno, Director, Political and Technical Legislation, Sub-Secretariat of Legislative Affairs, Ministry of Education and Justice, 20 December 1985, 1561, AGD; Iain Guest, *Behind the Disappearances: Argentina's Dirty War against Human Rights and the United Nations* (Philadelphia: University of Pennsylvania Press, 1990), 13–15; Alison Brysk, *The Politics of Human Rights in Argentina: Protest, Change, and Democratization* (Stanford: Stanford University Press, 1994), 114.

10. MRE, "Respuesta del Gobierno de la República Argentina a la Comisión de Derechos Humanos"; Juan E. Corradi, *The Fitful Republic: Economics, Society, and Politics in Argentina* (Boulder, Colo.: Westview Press, 1985), 117–23.

11. Marcelo Larraquy and Roberto Caballero, *Galimberti: De Perón a Susana, de Montoneros a la CIA* (Buenos Aires: Norma, 2000), 141–56; Deborah Lee Norden, *Military Rebellion in Argentina: Between Coups and Consolidation* (Lincoln: University of Nebraska Press, 1996), 45–47; Carlos Escudé, "From Captive to Failed State: Argentina under Systemic Populism, 1975–2006," *The Fletcher Forum of World Affairs* 30 (Summer 2006): 125–47; José Amorín, *Montoneros: La buena historia* (Buenos Aires: Catálogos, 2005), 271–97.

12. MRE, "Respuesta del Gobierno de la República Argentina a la Comisión de Derechos Humanos en material de Comunicaciones"; Luis Roniger and Mario Sznajder, *The Legacy of Human Rights Violations in the Southern Cone: Argentina, Chile, and Uruguay* (Oxford: Oxford University Press, 1999), 16.

13. Pablo A. Pozzi, *El PRT-ERP: La guerrilla marxista* (Buenos Aires: EUDEBA, 2001), 4–35; Ariel C. Armony, "Transnationalizing the Dirty War," in *In from the Cold: Latin America's New Encounter with the Cold War*, edited by Gilbert M. Joseph and Daniela Spenser (Durham: Duke University Press, 2008), 140.

14. Laudano, *Las mujeres en los discursos*, 57.

15. Horacio Verbitsky, *Ezeiza* (Buenos Aires: Contrapunto, 1985), 53–57; Ignacio González Janzen, *La triple-A* (Buenos Aires: Contrapunto, 1986); José Pablo Feinmann, *López Rega: la cara oscura de Perón* (Buenos Aires: Legasa, 1987), 64–74; Ricardo Canaletti and Rolando Barbano, *Todos mataron: génesis de la Triple A (el pacto siniestro entre la federal, el gobierno y la muerte)* (Buenos Aires: Planeta, 2009).

16. MRE, "Respuesta del Gobierno de la República Argentina a la Comisión de Derechos Humanos en material de Comunicaciones."

17. Ibid.

18. Victoria Crespo, "Legalidad y dictadura," in *Argentina, 1976: Estudios en torno al*

golpe de estado, edited by Clara E. Lida, Horacio Crespo, and Pablo Yankelevich (Buenos Aires: Fondo de Cultura Económica, 2008), 165–79.

19. James Scorer, "From la *guerra sucia* to 'A Gentleman's Fight': War, Disappearance and Nation in the 1976–1983 Argentine Dictatorship," *Bulletin of Latin American Research* 27 (2008): 46–47; Lucas M. Bietti, "'Piercing Memories': Empty Spaces in the Histories of Argentinean Families—Personal Reflections," *Memory Studies* 4, no. 1 (January 2011): 83–87.

20. "Movimiento Peronista Montonero," broadside, April 1978, 1561, AGD.

21. "Daniel Viglietti in Concert," broadside, 26 March 1978, 1561, AGD.; "Tribute to the Argentine Resistance," broadside, 25 March 1978, 1561, AGD.; Daniel Viglietti, "Reflexiones en torno al exilio desde el ámbito cultural e intelectual," in *Memorias de la violencia en Uruguay y Argentina: golpes, dictaduras, exilios (1973–2006)*, edited by Eduardo Rey Tristán (Santiago de Compostela: Universidad de Santiago de Compostela, 2007), 259–70.

22. Chilean Refugee Committee et al., "Argentina: Two Years of Fascist Military Dictatorship," broadside, n.d. [1978], 1561, AGD.

23. No. 199, Rafael M. Gowland, Argentine Minister in London, to Subsecretary of Foreign Relations, 16 March 1978; British Broadcasting Corporation, *Tonight*, 1 March 1978, Transcript, 1561, AGD; Pablo Alabarces and Carolina Duek, "Fútbol (argentino) por TV: entre el espectáculo de masas, el monopolio y el estado," *Logos* 17 (2010): 20–22.

24. Argentine Support Movement (London), "Support the Argentine Resistance," broadside, n.d. [1978], 1561, AGD.

25. Amnesty International USA, "Visit Beautiful Argentina, but Remember the Forgotten Prisoners," n.d. [1978]; Amnesty International (London), "Carta abierta de Amnistía Internacional a los Jefes de Delegación participantes en la XII Sesión Ordinaria de la Asamblea General de la Organización de los Estados Americanos," 21 October 1982; Ann Marie Clark, *Diplomacy of Conscience: Amnesty International and Changing Human Rights Norms* (Princeton, N.J.: Princeton University Press, 2001), 75–81; Steven C. Poe, Sabine C. Carey, and Tanya C. Vazquez, "How Are These Pictures Different? A Quantitative Comparison of the US State Department and Amnesty International Human Rights Reports, 1976–1995," *Human Rights Quarterly* 23, no. 3 (2001): 650–77.

26. Ambassador Carlos A. Delia to Oscar A. Montes, Argentine Foreign Minister, 4 April 1978, 1561, AGD; Marina Franco and Pilar González Bernaldo, "Cuando el sujeto deviene objeto: La construcción del exilio argentino en Francia," in *Represión y destierro: Itinerarios del exilio argentino*, edited by Pablo Yankelevich (La Plata: Ediciones Al Margen, 2004), 17–48.

27. Larraquy and Caballero, *Galimberti*, 321–35.

28. Delia to Montes, 4 April 1978.

29. SIDE, "Informe Especial: Conexiones entre la BDS Montoneros y la Agencia Noticiosa I.P.S.," May 1978, 1561, AGD; María Seoane, *El burgués maldito* (Buenos Aires: Planeta, 1998), 241–43. This anti-Semitic component of military anti-communist ideology was exercised at precisely the time that high-level Argentine naval and air force officers were purchasing war matériel from Israel. See Hernán Dobry, *Operación Israel: El rearme argentino durante la dictadura (1976–1983)* (Buenos Aires: Lumiere, 2011), 255.

30. MRE, "Respuesta del Gobierno de la República Argentina a la Comisión de Derechos Humanos en material de Comunicaciones."

31. Ibid.

32. David Pion-Berlin, "Between Confrontation and Accommodation: Military and Government Policy in Democratic Argentina," *Journal of Latin American Studies* 23, no. 3 (1991): 543–71.

33. Inter-American Commission on Human Rights, *Annual Report of the Inter-American Commission on Human Rights, 1979–1980*, OEA/Ser. L/V/II.50, Doc. 13, rev. 1, 2 October 1980.

34. Ibid.

35. Marina Franco, "Between Urgency and Strategy: Argentine Exiles in Paris, 1976–1983," *Latin American Perspectives* 34, no. 4 (2007): 50–67.

36. MRE, "Respuesta del Gobierno de la República Argentina a la Comisión de Derechos Humanos en material de Comunicaciones."

37. Jorge Saborido, "El antisemitismo en la historia argentina reciente," *Revista complutense de historia de América* 30 (2004): 209–23.

38. Inter-American Commission on Human Rights, *Annual Report of the Inter-American Commission on Human Rights, 1979–1980*.

39. "La carcel de Caseros y una historia negra que pronto quedará reducida a escombros," *Hoy*, 22 August 2000.

40. UN Economic and Social Council Resolutions 663 C (XXIV) (31 July 1957) and 2076 (LXII) (13 May 1977).

41. Office of the United Nations High Commission on Human Rights, *Human Rights and Prisons: A Compilation of International Human Rights Instruments Concerning the Administration of Justice* (New York: UN Publications, 2005), 167; Graham Zellick, "Prison Offences," *British Journal of Criminology* 20, no. 4 (2004): 377–84; Dirk van Zyl Smit, "Punishment and Human Rights in International Criminal Justice," *Human Rights Law Review* 2, no. 1 (2002): 1–17.

42. Ana Guglielmucci, "Visibilidad e invisibilidad de la prisión política en Argentina: La 'cárcel vidriera' de Villa Devoto (1974–1983)," *A contracorriente* 4 (2007): 86–136; Santiago Garaño and Werner Pertot, *Detenidos-aparecidos: presas y presos políticos desde Trelew a la dictadura* (Buenos Aires: Biblos, 2007), 114–18.

43. Pilar Calveiro, *Poder y desaparición: los campos de concentración en la Argentina* (Buenos Aires: Colihue, 2008), 39–43. How the Montoneros are understood in Argentine popular culture is still a problem. See María Verónica Elizondo, "La construcción/deconstrucción de la memoria nacional a través de la cultura popular: El caso del programa argentino, *Peter Capusotto y sus videos* y del músico apócrifo, *Bombita Rodríguez, el Palito Ortega Montonero*," *452°F. Revista de teoría de la literatura y literatura comparada* 3 (2010): 102–14.

44. MRE, "Respuesta del Gobierno de la República Argentina a la Comisión de Derechos Humanos en material de Comunicaciones."

45. Ibid.; Jennifer G. Schirmer, "'Those Who Die for Life Cannot Be Called Dead': Women and Human Rights Protest in Latin America," *Feminist Review* 32 (1989): 3–29;

Hernán Felipe Corral Talciani, *Desaparición de personas y presunción de muerte en el derecho civil chileno* (Santiago de Chile: Editorial Jurídica de Chile, 2000), 467–69.

46. Gerardo L. Munck, *Authoritarianism and Democratization: Soldiers and Workers in Argentina* (Philadelphia: University of Pennsylvania Press, 1998), 81; James P. Brennan, "Industrial Sectors and Union Politics in Latin American Labor Movements: Light and Power Workers in Argentina and Mexico," *Latin American Research Review* 30, no. 1 (1995): 39–68.

47. Pablo A. Pozzi, *La oposición obrera a la dictadura (1976–1982)* (Buenos Aires: Imago Mundi, (March 2008), 1–10.

48. Walter Delrio, "Mecanismos de tribalización en la Patagonia. Desde la gran crisis al primer gobierno peronista," *Memoria Americana. Cuadernos de Etnohistoria* 13 (2006): 209–42; Walter Delrio, Diana Lenton, Marcelo Musante, Mariano Nagy, Alexis Papazian, and Pilar Pérez, "Discussing Indigenous Genocide in Argentina: Past, Present, and Consequences of Argentinean State Police Policies toward Native Peoples," *Genocide Studies and Prevention* 5, no. 2 (2010): 139–59.

49. Morita Carrasco, *Los derechos de los pueblos indígenas en Argentina* (Buenos Aires: Vinciguerra, 2000), 31–32; Pablo G. Wright, "Colonización del espacio, la palabra y el cuerpo en el Chaco argentino," *Horizontes Antropológicos* 9 (2003): 137–52.

50. Ana Richter, Counselor, Comisión Nacional de la Política Aborígena, to Héctor Mendizabal Nougues, Delegate, Comisión Nacional, "Reunión sobre política aborigen (19 August 1982)," 20 August 1982, 105, AGD.

51. No. 39, Richter to Mendizabal Nougues, 23 November 1982, 105, AGD.

52. Argentina, Ministry of Social Welfare, Memorandum, 1982, 311, AGD.

53. Hugo Gaggiotti, "La pampa rioplatense: un espacio degradado en el imaginario hispano-criollo," *Scripta Nova: Revista electronic de geografía y ciencias sociales* 17 (1 March 1998): 14–31; Ana Carolina Hecht, "Pueblos indígenas y escuela. Políticas homogeneizadoras y políticas focalizadas en la educación argentina," *Políticas Educativas* 1 (2007): 183–94.

54. María Luz Endere, "The Reburial Issue in Argentina: A Growing Conflict," in *The Dead and Their Possessions: Repatriation in Principle, Policy and Practice*, edited by Cressida Fforde, Jane Hubert, and Paul Turnbull (New York: Routledge, 2002), 267.

55. Richter to Nougues, 23 November 1982.

56. Florencia Alam, "Civilización/barbarie en los manuales de historia secundario," *Nómadas. Revista Crítica de Ciencias Sociales y Juridicas* 16 (2007): 393–401; Roberto Morales Urra, "Cultura Mapuche y Represión en Dictadura," *Revista Austral de Ciencias Sociales* 3 (1999): 81–108.

57. María Felicitas Elías, "Derechos humanos, salud y trabajo social," in *Anales: Primeras Jornadas Sobre Salud y Trabajo Social* (La Plata, Argentina: Universidad Nacional de La Plata, 1999): 1–4; Marcela Mendoza, "Western Toba Messianism and Resistance to Colonialism, 1915–1918," *Ethnohistory* 51, no. 2 (2004): 293–316.

58. Richter to Nougues, 23 November 1982.

59. Ibid.

60. Authorities were influenced by an August 1978 episode in Neuquén Province in which Pentecostal missionaries encouraged a trance-like ritual among indigenous

peoples that led to four deaths. "El trágico ayuno," *Diario la mañana Neuquén* (Neuquén), 31 January 2010; "La matanza de Lonco Luan," *Clarín*, 29 March 2000; Andrea N. Lombraña, "Análisis sobre la eficacia de la construcción de inimputabilidad en La Matanza de Lonco Luán: el poder de 'perdonar,'" *Horizontes y convergencias* (Córdoba), 29 March 2010.

61. No. 39, Richter to Mendizabal Nougues, 23 November 1982, 105, AGD.

62. In 1982, 700 Vietnamese refugees from the southern city of Rio Negro sought refugee status in France. See Chief, Division of Special Social Affairs (DASE), MRE, to Enrique Ros, Sub-Secretary of Foreign Relations, "Refugiados indochinos en la Argentina," 6 July 1982; No. 6, DASE to Ros, 29 March 1982, 202, AGD; Armando M. Listre, MRE, "Informe de la conferencia sobre la reafirmación y el desarrollo del derecho humanitario aplicable a los conflictos armados," 6 June 1974, 228, AGD.

63. Eastern Europe Division, MRE, to Director General, Foreign Relations, MRE, "Relaciones de la República con los países de Europa Oriental al finalizar el año 1980," 30 November 1980, 140–208, AGD.

64. "L'Union soviétique s'opposerait à tout débat sur l'Argentine à la sous-commission des droits de l'homme," *Le Monde*, 13 September 1978.

65. Martínez, "Informe Especial sobre el 'caso Argentina' ante la subcomisión de prevención de discriminaciones y protección de minorias," 21 September 1976, 3132, AGD.

66. Martínez to César A. Guzzetti, Argentine Foreign Minister, 4 August 1976; Martínez to Secretary-General, United Nations, 29 July 1977, 3132, AGD.

67. Martínez, "Consideración del 'caso sobre Argentina' en la 31a. reunión de la subcomisión de prevención de las discriminaciones y protección a las minorias (agosto/septiembre de 1978)," 19 September 1978; Martínez to UN Secretary-General, 10 August 1978; MRE, "Ayuda Memoria, Anexo III," September 1978; Women's International Democratic Federation to Theodor van Boven, Director, Human Rights Division, UN, 20 February 1978, 3132, AGD; Amnesty International, *Argentina: Further Evidence of Violations of Human Rights since the Military Coup of 24 March 1976* (London: Amnesty International, 1978).

68. Martínez to UN Secretary-General, 7 August 1978, 3132, AGD.

69. Rosana Gruber, "Las manos de la memoria," *Desarrollo Económico* 36 (1996): 423–42; Juan Alonso, *¿Quién mató a Aramburu?* (Buenos Aires: Sudamericana, 2005), 56–70; Aldo Luis Molinari, *Aramburu: La verdad sobre su muerte* (Buenos Aires: Talleres Gráficos Valdez, 1993), 109–17.

70. Martínez to UN Secretary-General, 7 August 1978.

71. UN Committee on the Elimination of Racial Discrimination, 22nd session, Provisional Summary Record of the 479th Meeting, 5 August 1980, CERD/C/SR.479/7, August 1980; No. 1209/80/311, Argentine Permanent Mission, United Nations, to MRE, "Preparación del séptimo informe argentino sobre discriminacion racial," 27 August 1980, 311, AGD.

72. Juan Carlos Beltramino, "Informe del miembro argentine de la subcomision sobre prevención de discriminaciones y protección a las minorias sobre las sessions celebradas entre el 1 y el 11 de setiembre de 1982," 1561; UN, "Informe del Grupo de Trabajo sobre Comunicaciones," EC/CN.4/Sub.2/R. 45, 1982; No. 104/82, Carlos Alberto Lacoste,

Minister of Social Action, to Nicanor Costa Mendez, Foreign Minister, 9 February 1982, 311, AGD.

73. Author's interview with Juan Carlos Beltramino, Buenos Aires, 28 July 2003.

74. UN, "Comunicaciones relativas a la Argentina," E/CN.4/GR.82/1 and 8, 1982; Roniger and Sznajder, *Legacy of Human Rights Violations in the Southern Cone.*

75. Author's interview with Juan Carlos Beltramino.

76. No. 11, Argentine Permanent Mission, UN, to UN Secretary-General, 14 September 1982, 311, AGD.

77. Ibid.

78. MRE, "Organización de las Naciones Unidas: Síntesis de la actuación argentina durante 1979," n.d. [1979], 760–820, AGD.

79. MRE, "Órganos y comisiones del sistema de las naciones Unidas de Composición Limitada de los que Argentina es miembro," 6 December 1979, 311, AGD; MRE, "Argentinos que ocupan cargos en organismos de Naciones Unidas a título personal o elegidos en representación del País, 6 December 1979, 311, AGD.

Chapter 3. The Frank War, the Fabrication of an Ongoing Menace, and the Jews

1. MRE, "Prensa," April 1978, 760–820, AGD.

2. No. 81–1404, SIDE, "Informe de Inteligencia Periódico," July–September 1981, 12186, AGD.

3. Ibid.

4. Susana Sosenski, "Guardianes de la memoria. La conmemoración del golpe militar entre los exiliados argentinos en México," *Economía, Sociedad y Territorio* 5 (2005): 379–81; Clara Lida, "Enfoques comparativos sobre los exilios en México: España y Argentina en el siglo XX," in *México, país refugio. La experiencia de los exilios en el siglo XX*, edited by Pablo Yankelevich (Mexico City: Plaza y Valdes, 2002), 205–17.

5. Miguel Angel Estrella v. Uruguay, Communication No. 74/1980, U.N. Doc. Supp. No. 40 (A/38/40) at 150 (1983), available at http://www1.umn.edu/humanrts/undocs/session38/74-1980.htm; Inés Rojkind, "La revista *Controversia*: reflexión y polémica entre los argentinos exiliados en México," in *Represión y destierro: Itinerarios del exilio argentino*, edited by Pablo Yankelevich (La Plata: Ediciones Al Margen, 2004), 223–52.

6. Paul H. Lewis, *Guerrillas and Generals: The Dirty War in Argentina* (Westport, Conn.: Praeger, 2002), 84–85, 100.

7. No. 81–1404, SIDE, "Informede Inteligencia Periodico," July–September 1981, 12186, AGD.

8. SIDE, "Guatemala: Reunión de Embajadores Centroamerica y Caribe, marzo 1980," March 1980, 371, AGD; "Argentina: dura labor para Comisión interamericana de derechos humanos," *Prensa Libre*, 8 September 1979. See also Ariel C. Armony, *Argentina, the United States, and the Anti-Communist Crusade in Central America, 1977–1984* (Athens: Ohio University Press, 1997).

9. Roberto H. Tiscornia, Argentine Ambassador to Guatemala, to Argentine Foreign Minister, "Pautas a seguir en Guatemala para afianzar la presencia argentina," 12 March 1980; Tiscornia to Foreign Minister, "Invitación a la República Argentina de Cancilleres de países de América Central y Panamá," 24 March 1980, 371, AGD; "Noticias Diversas

desde Argentina," *La Hora de Guatemala*, 22 February 1980; "Peronismo en guerra abierta contra gobierno argentino," *Prensa Libre*, September 1979.

10. Arturo Ossorio Arana, Argentine Ambassador to Honduras, to Argentine Foreign Minister, 21 March 1980, 371, AGD; "Comisión de derechos humanos concluyó misión en Argentina," *Prensa Libre*, 21 September 1979; "Derechos Humanos en Argentina: un diálogo de sordos," *Prensa libre*, 24 September 1979.

11. No. 65/8, Directive, Executive Office (President), "Estructurar los actos destinados a afirmar la presencia argentina en el exterior. Adoptar una política agresiva sobre derechos humanos, atacar y no defendernos," 30 March 1981, 202, AGD.

12. MRE, "José Siderman," 1 July 1981, 202, AGD; Provincia de Tucumán, causa no. 1977/77, Juzgado de Primera Instancia en lo Federal no. 1, Cámara Federal de Tucumán (Tucumán Federal Court), Poder Judicial de la Nación (National Judicial Authority), Argentina; Gobierno de la Provincia de Tucumán c/Siderman José s/acción de lesividad, expte 2007/77, Cámara Federal de Tucumán (Tucumán Federal Court), Poder Judicial de la Nación (National Judicial Authority), Argentina.

13. Author's interview with Rosita Levin, Buenos Aires, 14 July 2004.

14. Marguerite Feitlowitz, *A Lexicon of Terror: Argentina and the Legacies of Torture* (New York: Oxford University Press, 1998), 90.

15. Edy Kaufman, "Jewish Victims of Repression in Argentina under Military Rule (1976–1983)," *Holocaust and Genocide Studies* 4, no. 4 (Fall 1989): 483.

16. Jacobo Timerman, *Prisoner without a Name, Cell without a Number* (New York: Alfred A. Knopf, 1981), 55. See also Federico Rivanera Carles, *Las escuelas judías comunistas en Argentina* (Buenos Aires: Biblioteca de formación política, 1986); and Matilde Mellibovsky, *Circle of Love over Death: Testimonies of the Mothers of the Plaza de Mayo* (Willimantic: Curbstone Press, 1997).

17. Timerman, *Prisoner without a Name, Cell without a Number*, 73–74; Diana Taylor, *Disappearing Acts: Spectacles of Gender and Nationalism in Argentina's "Dirty War"* (Durham, N.C.: Duke University Press, 1997), 61–62. See also Ricardo Feierstein, *Contraexilio y mestizaje: ser judío en la Argentina* (Buenos Aires: Editorial Milá, 1996); and Jorge Saborido, "El antisemitismo en la historia argentina reciente: La revista *Cabildo* y la conspiración judía," *Revista Complutense de Historia de América* 30 (2004): 209–23.

18. Timerman, *Prisoner without a Name, Cell without a Number*, 78.

19. Genaro R. Carrió, *El caso Timerman: materiales para el estudio de un "habeas corpus"* (Buenos Aires: EUDEBA, 1987), 137; Ramón J. A. Camps, *Caso Timerman: Punto Final* (Buenos Aires: Tribuna Abierta, 1982), 26–29; Feitlowitz, *A Lexicon of Terror*, 97.

20. Alicia Partnoy, *The Little School: Tales of Disappearance & Survival in Argentina* (Pittsburgh: Cleis Press, 1986), 63.

21. Kaufman, "Jewish Victims of Repression in Argentina," 486–87.

22. Mariano Ben Plotkin, *Freud in the Pampas: The Emergence and Development of a Psychoanalytic Culture in Argentina* (Stanford, Calif.: Stanford University Press, 2001), 219.

23. Feitlowitz, *A Lexicon of Terror*, 100.

24. Ricardo D. Salvatore, *Imágenes de un imperio: Estados Unidos y las formas de representación de América Latina* (Buenos Aires: Sudamericana, 2006), 10.

25. Rosenthal to Aja Espil, 14 April 1978, 1561, AGD.

26. Ibid.

27. Rosenthal to ADL Regional Offices, 17 March 1982; Rosa Mery Riveros to Comisión Encargada de Pedir por los Presos Políticos Judíos, collection of Paulina Maciulis, Toronto; "Argentina's Jews: Days of Uncertainty," *Boston Globe Magazine*, 29 November 1981.

28. J. L. García et al., *Fuerzas armadas argentinas: el cambio necesario* (Buenos Aires: Galerna, 1987), 45–53; Ernesto López, *Seguridad nacional y sedición militar* (Buenos Aires: Editorial Legasa, 1987), 55–77; Horacio Verbitsky, *La última batalla de la tercera guerra mundial* (Buenos Aires: Legasa, 1987); "Buenos Aires Is the Capital of the Aryan World," *Canada Argentina Bulletin* (January–February 1981), 3.

29. Morton M. Rosenthal, "Headlines and Footnotes: Free Timerman!" *National Jewish Monthly*, April 1979, 1–3; Abraham H. Foxman to President Roberto Eduardo Viola, 18 November 1981, 413, AGD; Joel Barromi, "Israeli Policies toward Argentina and Argentinian Jewry during the Military Junta, 1977–1983," *Israel Affairs* 5, no. 1 (Autumn 1998): 27–44.

30. CIDH, *Informe, 1976*, doc. OEA, Ser. L/V/II 40 doc. 5 del 11 de febrero 1977; Alberto R. Jordán, *El proceso, 1976–1983* (Buenos Aires: Emecé, 1993), 167; Emilio F. Mignone, *Iglesia y dictadura: el papel de la Iglesia a la luz de sus relaciones con el régimen militar* (Buenos Aires: Colihue, 2006), 116–19.

31. Santiago Mellibovsky to United Nations Commission on Human Rights, 21 July 1979; General Administration Division, Interior Ministry, to Santiago Mellibovsky, 6 February 1978; Santiago Mellibovsky to Secretary General, United Nations, 21 July 1979; Justice Department, "Interpone recurso de habeas corpus por persona desaparecida plantea caso federal, Graciela Mellibovsky," n.d.; Rodolfo E. Madariaca, Secretary, Department of Justice, to Santiago Mellibovsky, 20 July 1977, 16, AGD; Madres de Plaza de Mayo—Línea Fundadora, *¡Presentes! ¡Ahora y Siempre!* (Buenos Aires: Colihue, 2007), 12.

32. Ministry of the Interior, Argentina, Memorandum, 1979, 411, AGD; Marcos Novaro and Alejandro Avenburg, "La CIDH en Argentina: Entre la democratización y los derechos humanos," *Desarrollo Economico* 49 (2009): 61–90; Beira Aguilar Rubiano and Angela Milena Salas Garcia, "Dictadura, transición, y experiencias locales de reparación: el caso argentino," in *El tránsito hacía la paz: de las herramientas nacionales a las locales*, edited by Camila de Gamboa Tapias (Bogotá: Editorial Universidad del Rosario, 2010), 36–37.

33. Ministry of the Interior, Argentina, "Aspectos Básicos para la Visita de la Comisión Interamericana para los Derechos Humanos," August 1979, 411, AGD; Elizabeth Jelin, "The Politics of Memory: The Human Rights Movement and the Construction of Democracy in Argentina," *Latin American Perspectives* 21, no. 2 (1994): 38–58.

34. MRE, "Consideraciones del Gobierno Argentino con respecto a las recomendaciones preliminaries formuladas por la Comisión Interamericana de Derechos Humanos con motivo de la finalización de su visita *in loco*," n.d. [1980], 426, AGD.

35. Ibid.; Marcelo Borreli and Jorge Saborido, "La prensa del 'Proceso.' El diario *Con-*

vicción durante la dictadura militar argentina (1976–1983)," *Estudios sobre el Mensaje Periodistico* 14 (2008): 49–78.

36. SIDE, No. 205, Memorandum, 16 January 1979, 411, AGD.

37. MRE, Memorandum No. 8, 14–20 May 1981, 3, AGD.

38. Ibid.

39. MRE, Memorandum No. 23, 26 August–1 September 1981, 3, AGD.

40. David Sheinin, *Argentina and the United States: An Alliance Contained* (Athens: University of Georgia Press, 2006), chapters 5 and 6.

41. MRE, Memorandum No. 17, 16–21 July 1981, 3, AGD.

42. MRE, Memorandum No. 16, 8–15 July 1981, 3, AGD.

43. MRE, Memorandum No. 17, 16–21 July 1981.

44. MRE, Memorandum No. 18, 22–28 July 1981, 3, AGD.

45. MRE, Memorandum No. 23, 26 August–1 September 1981, 3, AGD.

46. Diego Hurtado de Mendoza, "De átomos para la paz a los reactores de potencia. Tecnología y política nuclear en la Argentina (1955–1976)," *Revista Iberoamericana de Ciencia, Tecnología y Sociedad* 4 (2005): 41–66; David Sheinin, "Nuclear Development and the Shaping of an Independent Argentine Foreign Policy, 1950–1990," *Estudios Interdiciplinarios de América Latina y el Caribe* 16 (December 2005): 37–62. For Operation Charly, see Maria Seoane, "Los secretos de la guerra sucia continental de la dictadura," *Clarin*, 24 March 2006.

47. MRE, Memorandum No. 26, 7–13 October 1981, 3, AGD.

48. MRE, Memorandum No. 24, 2–8 September 1981, 3 AGD; Armony, *Argentina, the United States, and the Anti-Communist Crusade*, 88–89.

49. MRE, Memorandum No. 10, 28 May–2 June 1981, 3, AGD; Marisol Touraine, "La représentation de l'adversaire dans la politique extérieure française depuis 1981," *Revue française de science politique* 43 (1993): 807–22.

50. Jolyon Howorth, "Consensus of Silence: The French Socialist Party and Defense Policy under François Mitterand," *International Affairs* 60, no. 4 (1984): 579–600; Pierre Lelouche, "France and the Euromissiles: The Limits of Immunity," *Foreign Affairs* 62, no. 2 (1983): 318–34; "An Interview with Mitterand," *Time*, 25 May 1981.

51. MRE, Memorandum No. 16, 8–15 July 1981.

52. MRE, Memorandum No. 10, 31 May–2 June 1981, 3, AGD; Sheinin, *Argentina and the United States*.

53. MRE, Memorandum No. 11, 3–9 June 1981, 3, AGD.

54. Patricia Blake and Dean Brelis, "Now, the Timerman Affair," *Time*, 22 June 1981; Richard M. Cook, *Alfred Kazin: A Biography* (New Haven, Conn.: Yale University Press, 2008), 362–63.

55. MRE, Memorandum No. 11, 3–9 June 1981.

56. Blake and Brelis "Now, the Timerman Affair."

57. "US Legislator Predicts Softer Human-Rights Line," *New York Times*, 13 January 1981; Feitlowitz, *A Lexicon of Terror*, 103–8; MRE, Memorandum No. 9, 21–27 May 1981, 3, AGD; Cynthia J. Arnson, "The U.S. Congress and Argentina: Human Rights and Military Aid," in *Argentina-United States Bilateral Relations*, edited by Cynthia J. Arnson (Washington, D.C.: Woodrow Wilson International Center for Scholars, 2003), 88–89.

58. MRE, Memorandum No. 14, 24–30 June 1981, 3, AGD; Patricia Derian, "Some of Our Best Friends Are Authoritarians," *The Nation*, 7 November 1981; Walter Isaacson, Laurence I. Barrett, and Gregory H. Wierzynski, "Fighting the Backbiting," *Time*, 15 November 1981.

59. MRE, Memorandum No. 14, 24–30 June 1981; "Argentina Complains on Timerman Debate," *New York Times*, 29 June 1981.

60. MRE, Memorandum No. 15, 1–7 July 1981, 3, AGD.

61. MRE, Memorandum No. 16, 8–15 July 1981.

62. Ibid.

63. MRE, Memorandum No. 22, 20–25 August 1981, 3, AGD.

64. MRE, Memorandum No. 20, 5–11 August 1981, 3, AGD.

65. Mark. B. Baker, "The South American Legal Response to Terrorism," *Boston University International Law Journal* 67 (1985): 67–74.

66. Central Nacional de Inteligencia, Secretaria General, "Informe sobre la campaña que utiliza los derechos humanos (período del 21 dic al 30 abr 82)," 413, AGD.

67. Jacobo Timerman, *The Longest War* (London: Chatto and Windus, 1982); Mark A. Bruzonsky and Dale Gavlak, "Israel's War in Lebanon," *Middle East Journal* 38 (Winter 1984): 115–20; "Conversation: Jacobo Timerman and Stanley Diamond," *Dialectical Anthropology* 8 (October 1983): 129–60; Raanan Rein and Efraim David, "'Exile of the World': Israeli Perceptions of Jacobo Timerman," *Jewish Social Studies: History, Culture, Society* 16, no. 3 (2010): 1–31.

68. "Timerman, el 'sherpa' de Cristina," *Cronista Comercial*, 5 March 2010; "Héctor Timerman dirigía un diario que elogiaba a Videla," *Diario Perfil*, 3 November 2007.

69. Bridget Kevane, "Diplomatic Immunity: Jacobo Timerman's Son Héctor Says There's No Such Thing as an Anti-Semitic Country," *Tablet Magazine*, 29 January 2010.

70. Ironically, in response to policy shifts in the Reagan administration, the Chilean government began lobbying political and military leaders in Washington about what they viewed as a potential imbalance in U.S. policy in regard to Humphrey-Kennedy. The Reagan administration's potential abrogation of the amendment would allow arms sales to Argentina but not to Chile. Argentine authorities perceived Washington's distinction here between Argentina and Chile as a policy success of their own; since 1976, the dictatorship had tried wherever possible to distance Argentine military rule from that of Chile, which was cast by the Argentines in diplomatic circles as the key author of state-sponsored terror in South America. MRE, Memorandum No. 10, 28 May–2 June 1981.

71. Kevane, "Diplomatic Immunity"; Iain Guest, *Beyond the Disappearances: Argentina's Dirty War against Human Rights and the United Nations* (Philadelphia: University of Pennsylvania Press, 2000), 248; MRE, Memorandum No. 26, 7–13 October 1981; MRE, Memorandum No. 20, 5–11 August 1981.

Chapter 4. Democracy and the (Re)Shaping of Human Rights Politics

1. SG 120, Raúl A. Quijano, Argentine Ambassador, Organization of American States, to Marco Gerardo Monroy Cabra, President, Inter-American Human Rights Commission, 7 April 1983, 432, AGD; Leonidas F. Ceruti, *Cultura y dictadura en Rosario: 1976–1983* (Rosario: Ediciones del Castillo, 2010), 260–71.

2. Carlos J. Moneta, "El conflicto de las Islas Malvinas en el contexto de la política exterior argentina," in *América Latina y la guerra del Atlántico sur: experiencias y desafíos*, edited by Roberto Russell (Buenos Aires: Editorial de Belgrano, 1984), 1–59; J. Patrice McSherry, *Incomplete Transition: Military Power and Democracy in Argentina* (New York: St. Martin's Press, 1997), 106–7.

3. Carlos Quirós, *Guia Radical* (Buenos Aires: Editorial Galerna, 1986), 13–15.

4. MRE, "Informe sobre las medidas adoptadas de conformidad con el programa de acción para el 2 decenio de la lucha contra el racismo y la discriminación racial," 28 April 1987, 432, AGD.

5. "Documento secreto del Ejercito: 'Con la democracia avanza la subversión,'" *El Periodista* (Buenos Aires), 13–19 January 1989; Ejército Argentino, "XIV Conferencia Bilateral de Inteligencia: Bolivia-Argentina," 1988, 411, AGD.

6. MRE, No. 2, "Política exterior argentina y derechos humanos," 19 February 1987, 179, AGD.

7. Michelle D. Bonner, "Defining Rights in Democratization: The Argentine Government and Human Rights Organizations, 1983–2003," *Latin American Politics & Society* 47, no. 4 (2005): 59; Virgilio R. Beltrán, "Political Transition in Argentina: 1982–1985," *Armed Forces & Society* 13, no. 2 (1987): 218–21.

8. Joel Horowitz, *Argentina's Radical Party and Popular Mobilization, 1916–1930* (State College: Pennsylvania University Press, 2008), 6–7.

9. Marcela Ferrari, "Les préférences politiques et électorales des Argentins: mémoires des votes (1946–2001)," *Social Science Information* 48, no. 4 (2009): 685–88.

10. MRE, "Política exterior argentina y derechos humanos."

11. Dominique Fournier, "The Alfonsín Administration and the Promotion of Democratic Values in the Southern Cone and the Andes," *Journal of Latin American Studies* 31, no. 1 (1999): 39–74.

12. SIDE, "Deterioro de los derechos humanos: Ecuador," 16 January 1987, 179, AGD.

13. An arm of the Chilean Catholic Church, the Vicariate of Solidarity was established in 1976 by Pope Paul VI to document and to fight human rights abuses in Chile.

14. No. 156, María Teresa M. de Morini, Director, Human Rights Office, Foreign Relations Ministry, to Evaristo Iglesias, President of the Committee on Refugee Eligibility, Argentina, 5 March 1987, 179, AGD; Silvia Dutrénit Bielous, "Represión política y asilo diplomático en el Cono Sur," in *El presente de la dictadura: Estudios y revlexiones a 30 años del golpe de Estado en Uruguay*, edited by Aldo Marchesi, Vania Markarian, Alvaro Rico, and Jaime Yaffé (Montevideo: Ediciones Trilce, 2004), 109–26.

15. No. 156, Morini to Evaristo Iglesias, President of the Committee on Refugee Eligibility, Argentina, 5 March 1987, 179, AGD.

16. Morini to Iglesias, 5 March 1987.

17. Paige Arthur, "How 'Transitions' Reshaped Human Rights: A Conceptual History of Transitional Justice," *Human Rights Quarterly* 31, no. 2 (2009): 334–40.

18. Morini to Evaristo Iglesias, 5 March 1987.

19. "Discurso pronunciado por el ministro de relaciones exteriores y culto, Licenciado Dante Caputo ante la commission de Derechos Humanos en Ginebra, el 27 de Febrero de 1984," 28, AGD.

20. MRE, "Consecuencias adversas que tiene para el disfrute de los derechos humanos la asistencia política, económica y de otra indole que se presta al régimen racista y colonialista de Sudafrica," 19 June 1987; MRE, "Aplicación de la Convención Internacional sobre la represión y el castigo del crimen del apartheid," 5 November 1987, 432, AGD.

21. "Reuniones mantenidas con funcionarios del consejo de planeamiento político del Departamento de Estado los dias 9 y 10 de mayo del corriente año," May 1985, 199, AGD.

22. Rut Diamint, "La historia sin fin: el control civil de los militares en Argentina," *Nueva Sociedad* 213 (2008): 95–111; Diego Buffa, *El Africa subsahariana en la política exterior argentina: Las presidencias de Alfonsín y Menem* (Córdoba: Centro de Estudios Avanzados, Universidad Nacional de Córdoba, 2006).

23. Raúl Alfonsín, Decree 187, 15 December 1983, in Congreso Nacional Argentina, *Anales de la Legislación Argentina*, vol. XLIV-A (Buenos Aires: Ediciones La Ley, 1984), 137–138.

24. Eduardo Rabossi, National Commission on the Disappeared, to Horacio R. Ravenna, Director, Human Rights Division, MRE, 7 June 1984; "Breve información básica sobre lo actuado por la Comisión Nacional hasta la fecha," 7 June 1984; Ravenna to Antoine Van Dongen, President, Working Group on Forced and Involuntary Disappearances, United Nations, 21 June 1984, 36, AGD.

25. Alipio Paoletti, *Como los Nazis, como en Vietnam* (Buenos Aires: Contrapunto, 1987), 143–60.

26. Ministry of Foreign Relations, "Presentación del gobierno argentino ante el XXVI período de sesiones del Grupo de Trabajo sobre Desaparaciones forzadas o involuntarias de Personas," 1 December 1988, 36, AGD.

27. Carlos Nino, *Juicio al mal absoluto. Los fundamentos y la historia del juicio a las juntas del proceso* (Buenos Aires: Emecé, 1997), 117–19.

28. Director General, Human Rights Division, MRE, "Solicitud del relator especial sobre tortura y otros tratos y penas crueles, inhumanas o degradantes de la Comisión de DH, Profesor E. Kooijmans para visitar la República," 14 July 1987, 416–18; No. 504, Leopoldo H. Tettamanti, Argentine Permanent Representative, UN, to Sub-Secretariat, Human Rights, MRE, 7 July 1987, 416–8, AGD.

29. Ministry of the Interior, Centro de Desarrollo Social y Asuntos Humanitarios, Subdivisión de Prevención del Delito y Justicia Penal, "Encuesta sobre la aplicación de las reglas minimas de las Naciones Unidas para el Tratamiento de los Reclusos y Recomendaciones Conexas," 1984, 426, AGD; Comisión Nacional Sobre la Desaparición de Personas, *Nunca Más: Informe de la CONADEP* (Buenos Aires: EUDEBA, 1985); Jorge L. Ubertalli et al., *El complot militar: un país en obediencia debida* (Buenos Aires: Ediciones Dialéctica, 1987), 54–55.

30. Maria Teresa M. de Morini, "Situación actual de los detenidos en el regimen de facto," March 1987, 292, AGD; Inter-American Commission on Human Rights, *Inter-American Yearbook on Human Rights* (Amsterdam: Martinus Nijhoff, 1997), 637; Brian Loveman, "'Protected Democracies' and Military Guardianship: Political Transitions in Latin America, 1978–1983," *Journal of Inter-American Studies and World Affairs* 36, no. 2 (1994): 130–33; Andrés Cisneros and Carlos Escudé, *Historia General de las Relaciones*

Exteriores Argentinas, vol. 14 (Buenos Aires: Grupo Editor Latinoamericano, 1999), chapter 69; Cristina Basombrío, "Estudiantes universitarios y esfera pública: la influencia del grupo de niño en el gobierno de Alfonsín," *Modernidades* 3 (December 2007), http://www.ffyh.unc.edu.ar/archivos/modernidades_a/VII/DEFINITIVOS/Brasombrio.htm.

31. No. 186, Maria Teresa M. de Morini to Foreign Minister, 17 March 1987, 292, AGD.

32. Alberto Gustavo Ramallo, Director General, Ministry of the Interior, Informe, 15 January 1986, 199, AGD.

33. The CONADEP report not only became a cause célèbre but helped promote the publication and dissemination of dozens of similar reports, including Federico Mittlebach, *Informe sobre desaparecedores* (Buenos Aires: Ediciones de Urraca, 1986). A renegade military officer who opposed dictatorship-era human rights violations, Mittlebach was one of several post-dictatorship figures who became minor celebrities during the period of Radical government of the 1980s.

34. Sub-Secretariat of Human Rights, Ministry of the Interior, "La Subsecretaria de Derechos Humanos y la CONADEP," March 1987, 416–9, AGD.

35. Graciela Fernández Meijide, "¿Valió la pena la CONADEP?, si, volvería a hacerlo," *Derechos humanos: revista de la Asamblea Permanente por los Derechos Humanos* 21 (1989): 10; Emilio Crenzel, *La historia política del Nunca Más. La memoria de las desapariciones en la Argentina* (Buenos Aires: Siglo XXI, 2008).

36. The nine were Abuelas de Plaza de Mayo, Asamblea Permanente por los Derechos Humanos, Asociación de Ex-Detenidos Desaparecidos, Centro de Estudios Legales y Sociales, Familiares de Desaparecidos y Detenidos por Razones Políticas, Liga Argentina por los Derechos del Hombre, Madres de Plaza de Mayo, Movimiento Ecuménico por los Derechos Humanos, and Servicio de Paz y Justicia.

37. Ana Irma Noia, Assessor, Secretariat of Justice, Ministry of Education and Justice, to Antonio Castagno, Director, Political and Technical Legislation, Sub-Secretariat of Legislative Affairs, Ministry of Education and Justice, 20 December 1985; Ricardo P. Ottonello, Secretariat of Justice, Ministry of Education and Justice, to Carlos Suarez Anzorena, Sub-Secretariat of Legislative Affairs, Ministry of Education and Justice, 1 August 1985, 1561, AGD.

38. MRE, "Subsecretaria de Derechos Humanos," 1986, 1398, AGD.

39. Andrés Alberto Masi Rius and Eduardo Aníbal Pretel Eraso, "Fuerzas armadas y transición democrática argentina, 1983–1989," *Historia Actual Online*, 13 (2007): 89–97; Pablo Baisotti, "La política de distensión a partir de los años 80 y el resurgimiento de la sociedad civil en Argentina," *Investigaciones Sociales* 10 (2006): 505–22.

40. No. 1127, Ravenna to Sábato, 30 May 1984, 36, AGD.

41. MRE, "Proyecto de informe del gobierno argentino al grupo de trabajo sobre desapariciones forzadas o involuntarias," 1988, 36, AGD.

42. Jacobo Timerman, "Preface," in *With Friends Like These: The Americas Watch Report on Human Rights and U.S. Policy in Latin America*, edited by Cynthia Brown (New York: Pantheon, 1985), xi–xiv.

43. Terence Roehrig, *The Prosecution of Former Military Leaders in Newly Democratic Nations* (Jefferson, N.C.: McFarland, 2002), 58–83; Alison Brysk, "The Politics of

Measurement: The Contested Count of the Disappeared in Argentina," *Human Rights Quarterly* 16, no. 4 (1994): 676–92.

44. MRE, "Observaciones del gobierno argentino respecto 'la participación popular en sus diversas formas como factor importante del desarrollo y de la plena realización de todos los derechos humanos' (Resolución 1987/21 de la Comisión de Derechos Humanos," 23 November 1987, 432, AGD.

45. Ana M. Mustapic and Mateo Goretti, "Gobierno y oposición en el Congreso: La práctica de la cohabitación durante la presidencia de Alfonsín (1983–1989)," *Desarrollo Económico* 32 (1992): 251–69.

46. Adriana Chiroleu, "La política universitaria de Alfonsín y Menem: Entre la democracia y la equidad," *Revista del Instituto de Investigaciones en Ciencias de la Educación* 15 (1999): 21–32.

47. Juan Carlos Portantiero and Germán Bidart Campos, "La cuestión social en la transición a la democracia," in *Política social y democracia*, edited by Raúl Alfonsín et al. (Quilmes: Universidad Nacional de Quilmes, 1997), 13–24; María de Monserrat Llairó, "La crisis del Estado Benefactor y la Imposición Neoliberal en la Argentina de Alfonsín y Menem," *Aldea Mundo. Revista sobre Fronteras e Integración* 11 (2006): 57–64.

48. Luis Alberto Romero, "La democracia y la sombra del *Proceso*," in *Argentina 1976–2006: Entre la sombra de la dictadura y el futuro de la democracia*, edited by Hugo Quiroga and César Tcach (Rosario: Homo Sapiens, 2006), 15–30.

49. MRE, Subsecretaría de Derechos Humanos en el Orden Internacional, "Informe argentino al comité para la eliminación de la discriminación racial," 2 August 1988, 49, AGD.

50. "Autodeterminación y desarrollo para los indígenas de Río Negro que tendrán su propia ley integral," *La Razón*, 28 November 1988.

51. MRE, "Medidas para promover y proteger los derechos humanos pertenecientes a pueblos indígenas," 3 June 1987, 432, AGD.

52. MRE, "Informe sobre las medidas adoptadas de conformidad con el programa de acción para el 2 decenio de la lucha contra el racismo y la discriminación racial," 1987, 416–9, AGD.

53. Victor Bazan, "La problemática indígena y sus mutaciones constitucionales en Argentina," *Revista de Derecho Constitucional Latinoamericano* 8 (2004): 1–29.

54. MRE, "Proyecto de informe del gobierno argentino al grupo de trabajo sobre desapariciones forzadas o involuntarias"; Cecilia N. Lesgart, "Luchas por los sentidos del pasado y el presente: Notas sobre la reconsideración actual de los años '70 y '80," in *Argentina 1976–2006: Entre la sombra de la dictadura y el futuro de la democracia*, edited by Hugo Quiroga and César Tcach (Rosario: Homo Sapiens, 2006), 196.

55. Argentina, Congress, *Tramite parlamentario No. 2*, 4 June 1986, 501–2, AGD; Morini, "Derogación de la Ley 22.546," 14 July 1986, 179, AGD; No. 734, Ruiz Cerrutti, "Rem. Proyecto de ley C. Diputados derogando ley 22546 aprobatoria convenio argentino-uruguayo s/protección int. de menores," 5 August 1986, 179, AGD.

56. Daniel Levy, "Recursive Cosmopolitization: Argentina and the Global Human Rights Regime," *British Journal of Sociology* 61, no. 3 (2010): 579–96.

57. Ironically, that failing allowed for prosecutions of military officials in the 1990s. The pardons that Carlos Menem issued to those convicted under Alfonsín did not include those who had kidnapped children since there were never any charges or convictions related to those cases. See Eglise Nationale Protestante de Geneve, Paroisse de Montbrillant, to Argentine Ambassador, Switzerland, 28 May 1986, 523, AGD; Groupe d'action a faveur de prisonniers d'opinion (Winterthur, Switzerland) to Argentine Ambassador, Switzerland, 1 June 1986, 523, AGD; J. Gesell (Bottmingen, Switzerland) to Alfonsín, 28 May 1986, 523, AGD; Laurent Joseph (La Chaux-de-Fonds, Switzerland) to Argentine Ambassador to Switzerland, 26 May 1986, 523, AGD; Eglise Nationale Protestante de Geneve, Paroissede Pregny-Chambésy-Grand-Saconnex to Argentine Ambassador, Switzerland, 1 June 1986, 523, AGD.

58. No. 893, Italian Embassy, Buenos Aires, to Foreign Minister, Argentina, 6 November 1985, 523, AGD.

59. No. 1597, Human Rights Directorate, MRE, "Visita Jefe del Departamento de Asuntos Extranjeros de Suiza," 12 September 1984, 523, AGD; Alberto Gustavo Ramallo, Director General de Promoción, Interior Ministry, to Leandro O. Despouy, Director General, Human Rights Office, MRE, 19 May 1987, 523, AGD.

60. Argentine Embassy, Tel Aviv, to Subsecretary of Human Rights, MRE, 9 June 1987; Morton M. Rosenthal, Director, Department of Latin American Affairs, Anti-Defamation League of B'nai B'rith, to Enrique J. A. Candioti, Argentine Ambassador to Washington, 6 March 1987; No. 3623, Mariano Maciel to General Directorate of Human Rights, 29 June 1987; SIDE, "Complementar Informe S/detención de possible Agente Adscripto al Servicio Secreto Israeli," 9 July 1976, 416–8, AGD; "Joven cumple larga condena en Argentina por ser 'espia israelí,'" *Aurora*, 16 July 1987; "Encarcelado durante 11 años, acusado de haber sido agente del 'Mosad,'" *Al Hamishar*, 12 July 1987.

61. Grossman was released in 1991 after an amnesty proclaimed by Alfonsín's successor, Carlos Menem. There seems little doubt that he was an active Montonero in the 1970s who was involved in extortion and kidnapping and that he may have worked closely with Israeli intelligence. "Genera controversias el pasado de un socio y asesor de Zaffaroni," *La Nacion*, 9 October 2003.

62. Morton M. Rosenthal, Director, Department of Latin American Affairs, Anti-Defamation League of B'nai B'rith, to Enrique J. A. Candioti, Argentine Ambassador to Washington, 6 March 1987, 416–8, AGD.

63. No. 3623, Mariano Maciel, Director General, Judicial Affairs, MRE, to Human Rights Office, 29 June 1987, 416–8, AGD.

64. No. 325, Argentine Embassy, Israel, to MRE, 9 June 1987; Argentine Armed Forces, Encargado Grupo 6 del 220 Seguridad y Vigilancia, "Para Conocimiento del Jefe de Batallon 601," 9 July 1976, 416–8, AGD; Marcos Novaro and Vicente Palermo, *La dictadura militar (1976–1983): Del golpe de Estado a la restauración democrática* (Buenos Aires: Paidós, 2003), 68–73.

65. No. 883, Horacio Ricardo Ravenna, "Visita del Grupo de Trabajo Sobre Desapariciones Forzadas o Involuntarias," 16 April 1984, AGD; No. 1091, Horacio Ricardo Ravenna, Director General of Human Rights, Ministry of Foreign Relations, to Minister of Foreign Relations, 28 May 1984, AGD; No. 883, Ravenna to Minister of Foreign

Relations, 8 May 1985, 36, AGD; José Paradiso, *Debates y trayectoria de la política exterior argentina* (Buenos Aires: Grupo Editor Latinoamericano, 1993), 192–93.

66. No. 1556, Human Rights Division, MRE, to National Commission on Disappearances, 3 September 1984, 36, AGD.

67. Human Rights Division, MRE, to Secretariat of Foreign Relations and Worship, "Sesión en la Argentina del Grupo de Trabajo de Desapariciones Forzadas de Naciones Unidas," 8 May 1985, 36, AGD.

68. Ivan Tosevski, Chair, Working Group on Forced Disappearances, UN, to Osvaldo López Noguerol, Argentine Representative to the United Nations in Geneva, 8 August 1985, GSO 217/1 ARG, 36, AGD.

69. No. 51701, Tettamanti to Foreign Ministry, 18 September 1987, 36, AGD.

70. No. 1674, Tettamanti to Foreign Ministry, 27 November 1987; No. 1683, Tettamanti to Foreign Ministry, 27 November 1987, 36, AGD. In the aftermath of the 1987 Semana Santa (Easter Week) military uprising, the federal government effectively ended the prosecution of dictatorship human rights violators. That change was made possible by the Law of Due Obedience, which ended prosecutions against most military personnel. See Chapter 5.

71. Ramos to President, Colegio de Geólogos de Chile, 13 October 1987, 522, AGD.

72. Reich to Alfonsín, 3 November 1987, 522, AGD.

73. Elizabeth Jelin, "La matriz cultural argentina, el peronismo y la cotidianidad," in *Vida cotidiana y control institucional en la Argentina de los '90*, edited by Elizabeth Jelin et al. (Buenos Aires: Nuevohacer, 1996), 38–39.

74. Christopher Mitchell to Carlos Nino, Coordinator, Consejo para la Consolidación de la Democracia, Buenos Aires, 24 November 1986, 292, AGD; John G. Healey to Alfonsín, 14 November 1986, 292, AGD.

75. MRE to Secretario Ejecutivo de la Comité Interamericana de Derechos Humanos, n.d. [1987], 523, AGD.

76. After launching appeals in federal court and before the Supreme Court without success, López cited the Argentine state for violations of articles 7, 8, 9, 24, and 25 of the Inter-American Human Rights Convention, without distinguishing between the dictatorship and the Alfonsín government.

77. Jorge Sabato to José Severo Caballero, President, Argentine Supreme Court, n.d. [1987]; No. 243, Morini to Ideler Tonelli, Secretary of Justice, Argumenos a tener en cuenta ante posibles consultas de la prensa sobre el caso Osvaldo A. López," n.d. [1987], 416–8, AGD.

78. Sabato to Caballero, n.d. [1987]; No. 243, Morini to Ideler Tonelli, Secretary of Justice, "Argumenos a tener en cuenta ante posibles consultas de la prensa sobre el caso Osvaldo A. López," n.d. [1987], 416–8, AGD.

79. Sabato to Caballero, n.d. [1987]; Morini to Tonelli, "Argumenos a tener en cuenta ante posibles consultas de la prensa sobre el caso Osvaldo A. López."

80. Sabato to Caballero, n.d. [1987]; Morini to Tonelli, "Argumenos a tener en cuenta ante posibles consultas de la prensa sobre el caso Osvaldo A. López."

81. Eugenio Raúl Zaffaroni and Ricardo Juan Cavallero, *Derecho Penal Militar* (Buenos Aires: Editorial Ariel, 1980), 523.

82. Osvaldo Antonio López, Case 9635, Inter-American Commission on Human Rights, 32, OEA/ser. L/V/II.71, doc. 9, rev 1 (1987).

83. "Observaciones del gobierno argentino respeto la participación popular en sus diversas formas como factor importante del desarrollo y de la plena realización de todos los derechos humanos (Resolucion 1987/21 de la comisión de derechos humanos)," 23 November 1987, 416–8, AGD; Gastón J. Beltrán, "Acción empresaria e ideología. La génesis de las reformas estructurales," in *Los años de Alfonsín ¿El poder de la democracia o la democracia del poder?* edited by Alfredo Pucciarelli (Buenos Aires: Siglo Veintiuno, 2006), 218–30.

84. Julio Montero, "Derechos humanos y democracia: Un cambio de paradigmo a dos décadas de distancia," in *Pensar la democracia, imaginar la transición (1976/2006)*, edited by Cecilia Macón (Buenos Aires: Ladosur, 2006), 52–60.

85. "Killings, Torture Still Taking Place in Argentina, Nobel Laureate Says," *Globe and Mail*, 21 October 1987.

86. No. 264, Argentine Embassy to Subsecretariat of Human Rights, Foreign Relations Ministry, 20 October 1987, 522, AGD.

87. No. 21/86, Eduardo A. Rabossi, Subsecretary of human Rights, Ministry of the Interior, to Morini, 17 November 1986; No. 124, Morini to Argentine Embassy, Copenhagen, 24 February 1987, 179, AGD.

Chapter 5. Finding a Cynical Center

1. Kathryn Lee Crawford, "Due Obedience and the Rights of Victims: Argentina's Transition to Democracy," *Human Rights Quarterly* 12, no. 1 (1990): 17–52; Elizabeth Jelin, "The Politics of Memory: The Human Rights Movement and the Construction of Democracy in Argentina," *Latin American Perspectives* 21, no. 2 (1994): 38–58.

2. Amnesty International, *Argentina: The Military Juntas and Human Rights* (London: Amnesty International, 1987); Amnesty International, "Argentina: Amnesty Report on Junta Trials Published," Press Release, 18 November 1987, 522, AGD; Ian Martin, Secretary General, Amnesty International, to Dante Caputo, Minister of Foreign Relations, 29 October 1987, 522, AGD; Fernand Walch, Amnesty International Luxembourg, to Gabriel Matzkin, Argentine Ambassador, Luxembourg/Belgium, 18 November 1987, 522, AGD; Americas Watch, Press Release, 13 August 1987, 416–8, AGD; Sylvia Estrada-Claudio, Programme Coordinator, Philippine Action Concerning Torture, Medical Action Group, to Alfonsín, 21 May 1987, 416–8, AGD.

3. Morini to Argentine Embassy, Denmark, 1 April 1987, 292, AGD; Eduardo Luis Duhalde, *El estado terrorista argentino. Quince años después, una mirada crítica* (Buenos Aires: EUDEBA, 1999), 157–60.

4. "Liv Ullman y Sting apoyan en Argentina a las madres de los desaparecidos," *El País*, 14 December 1987; Francisco Javier Garay Ruiz-Tagle, "Derechos humanos, dictadura y democracia," *Ya*, 13 December 1987; Raymonde Dury and Didier Motchane, European Parliament, to Alfonsín, 11 March 1987; Adolphe Proulx, Bishop of Gatineau Hull and President of the Inter-Church Committee on Human Rights in Latin America, to Alfonsín, 4 May 1987; J. Westercamp, President of Action des Chrétiens pour l'Abolition de la Torture, to Alfonsín, 15 May 1987, 416–8, AGD.

5. Directorate General of Human Rights, MRE, to Foreign Minister, "Respuesta a posibles alegaciones a la ley de 'od,'" 29 May 1987, 523, AGD; No. 327, Despouy to Foreign Minister, 19 May 1987, 523, AGD; "Torture: un pas en avant un pas en arrière," *Journal de Genève*, 15 July 1987.

6. Leigh A. Payne, "Perpetrators' Confessions: Truth, Reconciliation, and Justice in Argentina," in *What Justice? Whose Justice? Fighting for Fairness in Latin America*, edited by Susan Eva Eckstein and Timothy P. Wickham-Crowley (Berkeley: University of California Press, 2003), 169–72.

7. "Informe del Señor Emajador D. Leandro Despouy—Director General de Derechos Humanos—sobre su participación en el 43 periodo de sesiones de la Comité de Derechos Humanos de las Naciones Unidas (Ginebra-26 de enero al 13 marzo de 1987)," 13 March 1987, 523, AGD.

8. Raymond Dury, Deputy, European Parliament, to Alfonsín, 11 March 1987; MRE to Raymond Dury, 3 August 1987; Proulx to Alfonsín, 4 May 1987; Westercamp to Alfonsín, 15 May 1987; No. 571, Morini to MRE, 29 July 1987, 416–8, AGD.

9. Human Rights Watch, Press Release, 13 August 1987, 416–8, AGD.

10. Sylvia Estrada-Claudio to Alfonsín, 21 May 1987, 416–8, AGD.

11. MRE to Sylvia Estrada-Claudio, August 1987, 416–8, AGD. Morini's language became a template for the Argentine government's response to criticisms from overseas, as is evident in a July 1987 letter from Jaime E. Malamud Goti, advisor to Alfonsín. See Jaime E. Malamud Goti to Leandro Despouy, 22 July 1987, 416–8, AGD; Camila de Gamboa, "Entrevista a Jaime Malamud," *Semana*, 14–21 August 2005; Marcela Madero and Egie Piedrafita, "La prensa: Los Derechos humanos en noticias," in *Los derechos humanos en la Argentina: Del ocultamiento a la interpelación política*, edited by Norma Fóscolo (Buenos Aires: Editorial de la Universidad Nacional de Cuyo, 2000), 63–64.

12. Alfonsín to Westercamp, n.d. [1987], 416–8, AGD.

13. Livia Cecilia Pombo, Federal Attorney, National Judiciary, to Comisión de Apoyo a la Subsecretaría de Derechos Humanos en el Orden Internacional, 19 August 1986, 369, AGD.

14. David Weissbrodt, "Country-Related and Thematic Developments at the 1988 Session of the UN Commission on Human Rights," *Human Rights Quarterly* 10, no. 4 (1988): 544–58; Deborah Lee Norden, *Military Rebellion in Argentina: Between Coups and Consolidation* (Lincoln: University of Nebraska Press, 1996), 103–5; Gerardo Aboy Carlés, *Las dos fronteras de la democracia argentina: La reformulación de las identidades políticas de Alfonsín a Menem* (Rosario: Homosapiens, 2001), 256.

15. Carlos A. Gonzalez Gartland (lawyer for Graciela Beatriz Daleo) to UN Working Group on Forced and Involuntary Disappearances, n.d. [1988]; Executive Authority, Argentina, "Para resolver la situación procesal de Raúl José Melchor Magario y Graciela Beatriz Dal, esta Causa No. 41.811 del registro de la Secretaría No. 1," 2 September 1988, 523, AGD.

16. See Americas Watch and Centro de Estudios Legales y Sociales, *Police Violence in Argentina: Torture and Police Killings in Buenos Aires* (New York: Human Rights Watch, 1991); "Caso Budge: el fiscal pidió que se procese a un testigo," *Clarín*, 17 May 1990; Laura

Gringold, *Memoria, moral y derecho: el caso de Ingeniero Budge (1987–1994)* (Mexico, DF: Juan Pablos Editor, S.A., 1997), 124–29.

17. "La orden que dio la dictadura para la compra de Falcon verdes sin patentes," *Clarin*, 23 March 2006; "Ford Falcon, modelo 76," *Página/12*, 26 February 2006; Kelly Hearn, "Ford's Past in Argentina," *The Nation*, 8 May 2006.

18. Declaration of Noemí Alicia Diaz de Rivas (Banfield), 19 June 1988; Francisco Soberon Garrido, Coordinador, Asociación Pro-Derechos Humanos, Lima, Peru, to Argentine Ambassador, Peru, 26 June 1988, 523, AGD.

19. UN Economic and Social Council, "Lista Confidencial de Comunicaciones Relativas a los derechos humanos transmitidas en agosto de 1987," 25 September 1987, E/CN.4/CCR/87/8; Inés Vázquez, "Aspectos de Memoria y Cultura en la Argentina postdictatorial," in *Un país, 30 años, el pañuelo sigue haciendo historia*, edited by Inés Vázquez and Karina Downie (Buenos Aires: Ediciones Madres de Plaza de Mayo, 2006), 201–6.

20. Lars Jönsson to Mikulski, 24 March 1987, 416–9 AGD; Mikulski to Enrique José Candioti, Argentine Ambassador to Washington, 6 April 1987, 416–9, AGD; No. 297, Morini to Argentine Embassy, Washington, 18 November 1986, 416–9, AGD.

21. Duane Bratt, *The Politics of CANDU Exports* (Toronto: University of Toronto Press, 2006), 131–37.

22. MRE, "Estado actual y posible evolución de la situación política interna canadiense," n.d. [1984], 473, AGD.

23. Ibid.

24. Ibid.

25. Hal Klepak, "The Inter-American Dimension of Future Canadian Security Policy," *Canadian Foreign Policy Journal* 5, no. 2 (1998): 107–28.

26. Ibid.

27. Etel Solingen, *Industrial Policy, Technology, and International Bargaining: Designing Nuclear Industries in Argentina and Brazil* (Stanford, Calif.: Stanford University Press, 1996), 71; David Sheinin, "Nuclear Development and the Shaping of an Independent Argentine Foreign Policy, 1950–1990," *Estudios Interdisciplinarios de America Latina* 16 (2005): 37–62.

28. Joseph S. Nye, "New Approaches to Nuclear Proliferation Policy," *Science* 256, no. 5061 (26 May 1992): 1293–97.

29. MRE, "Estado actual y posible evolución de la situación política interna canadiense," n.d. [1984], 473, AGD.

30. Morini to Catherine Kellvick, 13 November 1986; Secretaría de Desarrollo Humano y Familia, Ministry of Health and Social Action to MRE, 26 November 1986, 523, AGD; Michiel Baud, *El padre de la novia: Jorge Zorreguieta, la sociedad argentina y el régimen militar* (Buenos Aires: Fondo de Cultura Económica, 2001), 148–49.

31. Col. Timoteo Gordillo, Chief of Military Instruction, Argentine Armed Forces, to Morini, 19 June 1986, 523, AGD; Gordillo to Morini, 21 July 1986, 523, AGD; Morini to Gordillo, 22 September 1986, 523, AGD; Gordillo to Morini, 17 October 1986, 523, AGD.

32. Morini, Informe Técnico, 19 May 1988, 400, AGD.

33. Ministerio del Interior, "Eliminación de la discriminación en la espera de la enseñanza," 7 June 1988, 49, AGD.

34. Pablo Gabriel Tonelli, Chief of Cabinet Advisors, Secretariat of Justice, Ministry of Education and Justice, "Información solicitada a la República Argentina en relación con la resolución 1984/4 del Consejo Económico y Social de las Naciones Unidas relativa a 'Medidas para combater el racismo y la discriminación racial,'" 7 June 1988, 49, AGD.

35. Ibid.

36. Eugenia Aruguete, "Lucha política y conflicto de clases en la posdictadura. Límites a la constitución de alianzas políticas durante la administración Alfonsín," in *Los años de Alfonsín ¿El poder de la democracia o la democracia del poder?* edited by Alfredo Pucciarelli (Buenos Aires: Siglo Veintiuno, 2006), 413–60.

37. Ministry of the Interior, "Informe Respecto a Medidas Adoptadas para Asegurar el Derecho a Reparación por Daños Causados por Discriminación Racial," 7 June 1988, 49, AGD.

38. Roberto Mazal Nuthes, "La libertad religiosa y el derecho migratorio," presentación en el IX Coloquio Anual del Consorcio Latino Americano de Libertad Religiosa de Septiembre de 2009, Montevideo, Uruguay; "Testigos de Jehová, testigos del horror," *Página/12* (Buenos Aires), 11 de mayo 2006.

39. MRE, "Medidas adoptadas por parte del gobierno argentino en contra de la discriminación racial en Sudáfrica," November 1987, 28, AGD; Guillermo Miguel Figari, *De Alfonsín a Menem: Política exterior y globalización* (Buenos Aires: Memphis, 1997), 141.

40. Morini, "Consecuencias adversas que tiene para el disfrute de los derechos humanos la asistencia política, militar, económica y de otra índole que se presta al régimen racista y colonialista de Sudáfrica," 19 June 1987, 447, AGD.

41. Ibid.

42. Morini, "Informe de la Señora Subsecretaria de Derechos Humanos en el Orden Internacional, Doctora María Teresa Merciadri de Morini, sobre su participación en la conferencia Internacional de la Cruz Roja (Ginebra)," 1986, 523, AGD.

43. Morini to Evaristo Iglesias, Immigration Directorate, 27 October 1986; Espeche Gil, "Informe," 18 August, 1986; Morini, "Socitud Ingreso al país refugiado iraquí," 16 July 1986, 523, AGD.

44. No. 383, International Relations Secretariat, MRE, to Human Rights Sub-Secretariat, MRE, 6 October 1986, 523, AGD.

45. No. 418/86, Central America, Mexico, and Caribbean Division, MRE, "Visita del Presidente de Guatemala (Derechos Humanos)," 15 October 1986, 523, AGD.

46. MRE, "Reuniones mantenidas con funcionarios del consejo de planeamiento político del Departamento de Estado los dias 9 y 10 de mayo del corriente año," May 1985, 199, AGD.

47. Subsecretariat of Human Rights (International), MRE, "Visita canciller de Israel a Argentina (Memorandum No. 133)," 5 May 1987; Gustavo A. Matzkin, Secretary General, Consejo Juvenil Sionista Argentino, to Alfonsín, 27 November 1986; No. 127, General Directorate of International Bodies, MRE, "Solicitud del Consejo Juvenil Sionista Argentino para que el gobierno nacional emita una declaración descalificando la resolución 3379 adoptada por la AGNU el 10-XI-75 que declara al sionismo como una forma de racismo," 13 February 1987, AGD; No. 375, MRE, Sub-Secretariat of Human

Rights, "Inclusión del término 'sionismo' en los proyectos de resolución de la comisión de derechos humanos," 9 September 1986, 199, AGD; Gustavo A. Matzkin, Secretario General, Consejo Juvenil Sionista Argentina, to Alfonsín, 27 November 1986, 292, AGD.

48. Several months before, when the Argentine Zionist Youth Council protested Argentina's previous, more ambivalent stand on Zionism and racism, Raúl Medina Muñoz, director of international organizations in the Argentine foreign ministry, had responded by advising against a substantive shift in Argentine policy. Medina Muñoz noted that there had been a similar campaign among Jewish groups in the United States, suggesting an "international" Jewish component to the position of the Argentine Zionist Youth Council. As had the dictatorship, some in the Alfonsín administration continued to believe in an elusive international Jewish conspiracy. Javier Pelacoff, "La identidad como paradoja, o del remozado sentido de la figura del judío errante," in *La cultura en la Argentina de fin de siglo: Ensayos sobre la dimensión cultural*, edited by Mario Margulis and Marcelo Urresti (Buenos Aires: Oficina de Publicaciones del CBC, Universidad de Buenos Aires, 1997), 83–94.

49. No. 403/86, MRE, International Relations Secretariat, "Extensión del campo de aplicación de la Convención Europea de Derechos Humanos a las Islas Malvinas, Georgias del Sur y Sandwich del Sur. Nota Argentina," 13 October 1986, 523, AGD.

50. No. 366, Sub-Secretariat of Latin American Affairs, MRE, "Cuestión Cuba," 19 May 1987; MRE, "Reunión entre el Subsecretario de Asuntos Latinoamericanos, Embajador Raúl Alconada Sempé, y el Director de Organismos Internacionales del Departamento de Estado, Embajador Alan Keyes, Washington, DC, 6 de mayo de 1987," 6 May 1987, 416–9, AGD; author's interview with Raúl Alconada Sempé, Buenos Aires, 30 July 2004.

51. MRE, Human Rights Directorate, "Cuestión Cuba," 29 May 1987, 523, AGD; Carlos Escudé, *Realismo periférico: Fundamentos para la nueva política exterior argentina* (Buenos Aires: Planeta, 1992), 116–17.

52. MRE, Human Rights Directorate, "Cuestión Cuba," 29 May 1987, 523, AGD.

53. "Reunión entre el Subsecretario de Asuntos Latinoamericanos, Embajador Raúl Alconada Sempé, y el Director de Organismos Internacionales del Departamento de Estado, Embajador Alan Keyes, Washington, DC, 6 de mayo de 1987," 416–9, AGD.

54. No. 366, Despouy, Human Rights Division, MRE, "Cuestión Cuba," 28 May 1987, 416–9, AGD.

55. Raúl Alfonsín, Decree 768-M.87, 22 August 1986; Raúl Alfonsín, Decree 2007-M.282, 14 October 1985.

56. Morini to MRE, 7 July 1987, 416–8, AGD.

57. No. 475, Morini, "Observaciones de la RA al proyecto de Protocolo Adicional a la CADH," 3 July 1987, 416–8, AGD.

58. Malamud Goti to Leandro Despouy, 22 July 1987, 416–8, AGD; Christian Vogt, "Torture: un pas en avant un pas en arrière," *Journal de Genève*, 15 July 1987.

59. UN Working Group on Forced Disappearances, "Argentina: Information Reviewed and Transmitted to the Government," January 1989, E/CN.4/1989/18, 416–8, AGD.

Epilogue: Saving Jorge Omar Merengo

1. "El argentino que zafó la pena de muerte," *Hoy*, 17 January 2004.

2. Claudia Nora Laudano, *Las mujeres en los discursos militares* (Buenos Aires: Editorial La Página, 1998), 24–42; Lea Fletcher, "El sexismo lingüístico y el uso acerca de la mujer," *Feminaria* 1 (1988): 29–31; Judith Filc, *Entre el parentesco y la política: Familia y dictadura 1976–1983* (Buenos Aires: Biblos, 1997); "El albañil," *Billiken*, 2 June 1981.

3. Marta Flores, *La música popular en el Gran Buenos Aires* (Buenos Aires: Centro Editor de América Latina, 1993), 13–33.

4. Andreas Huyssen, "The Mnemonic Art of Marcelo Brodsky," in *Nexo. Un ensayo fotográfico/A Photographic Essay by Marcelo Brodsky*, edited by Marcelo Brodsky (Buenos Aires: La Marca Editora, 2001), 7–11.

5. Marguerite Feitlowitz, *A Lexicon of Terror: Argentina and the Legacies of Torture*, rev. ed. (New York: Oxford University Press, 2011), 209–13; Luis Roniger and Mario Sznajder, *The Legacy of Human Rights Violations in the Southern Cone: Argentina, Chile, and Uruguay* (Oxford: Oxford University Press, 1999), 270.

6. Jorge Rial, *El intruso: Todo lo que usted quiere saber sobre la farándula, el deporte y la política* (Buenos Aires: Planeta, 2001), 39–46; Marta Gordillo and Víctor Lavagno, *Los hombres de Perón* (Buenos Aires: Puntosur, 1987), 52–53; Christopher Larkins, "The Judiciary and Delegative Democracy in Argentina," *Comparative Politics* 30, no. 4 (1998): 423–42; Carlos Escudé, *El realismo de los estados débiles* (Buenos Aires: Grupo Editor Latinoamericano, 1995), 207–11.

7. "Martín Balza, ex jefe del Ejército," *Clarín*, 27 December 2000.

8. "Un ex represor podrá ser juzgado en España," *Clarín*, 13 January 2001; J. M. Pasquini Durán, "Panorama Político," *Página/12*, 13 January 2001; Elvira Martorell, "Recuerdos del presente: memoria e identidad (una reflexión en torno a HIJOS)," in *Memorias en presente: Identidad y transmisión en la Argentina posgenocidio*, edited by Sergio J. Guelerman (Buenos Aires: Norma, 2001), 135–43; Benedetta Calandra, "Entre historia 'fría' y testimonios 'calientes': H.I.J.O.S. de los desaparecidos argentinos (1976–1983)," in *Memorias de la violencia en Uruguay y Argentina: golpes, dictaduras, exilios (1973–2006)*, edited by Eduardo Rey Tristán (Santiago de Compostela: Universidad de Santiago de Compostela, 2007), 309–16.

9. Daniel M. Brinks, *The Judicial Response to Police Killings in Latin America: Inequality and the Rule of Law* (Cambridge: Cambridge University Press, 2007), 122; Kent Eaton, "Paradoxes of Police Reform: Federalism, Parties, and Civil Society in Argentina's Public Security Crisis," *Latin American Research Review* 43, no. 3 (2008): 5–32; "Reconstruyen la muerte de una mujer en un edificio de la SIDE," *Clarín*, 18 June 1999.

10. "Ruckauf debe cambiar la Policía," *Clarín*, 22 February 2001.

11. Judith Zur, "The Psychological Effects of Impunity: The Language of Denial," in *Impunity in Latin America*, edited by Rachel Seider (London: Institute of Latin American Studies, 1995), 57–62; Diane M. Nelson, *A Finger in the Wound: Body Politics in Quincentennial Guatemala* (Berkeley, Calif.: University of Los Angeles Press, 1999), 7–12.

12. Hugo Hortiguera, "News, Fiction and Marketing in the Time of Crisis: The Argentine Media and the Yabrán Case," in *Argentinean Cultural Production During the*

Neoliberal Years (1989–2001), edited by Hugo Hortiguera and Carolina Rocha (Lewiston, Me.: Edwin Mellen Press, 2007), 133–54.

13. No. 1599, Jesús Sabra, Director, Economics Division, MRE, to Argentine Ambassador to the UN, 23 July 1992; Sabra, "Informe sobre lo realizado por la Argentina en el último año en material de crecimiento y cooperación en el orden nacional, regional y global," July 1992, 219–1994, AGD; Abel Posse, "La política internacional y los recursos naturales y culturales," in *Siete escenarios para el siglo XXI*, edited by Fernando López-Alves and Daniel Dessein (Buenos Aires: Sudamericana, 2004), 91–94.

14. Guido di Tella, Foreign Minister, "Hacia una realpolitik internacional argentina," 18 June 1991, 331, AGD.

15. Ibid.

16. Daniel Muchnik, *Los últimos cuarenta años: Argentina a la deriva* (Buenos Aires: Capital Intelectual, 2004), 92–95; Corte Suprema de la Nación (Supreme Court), Argentina, "Ekmekdjian, Miguel v. Sofovich" (Case No. 1992–315–1492), 07/07/1992; No. 477/94, Human and Women's Rights Division, MRE, to Legal Counsel, MRE, "Tratados de derechos humanos y Constitución Nacional" 1 July 1994, 62, AGD; Lisl Brunner, "Leaning on International Law to Prosecute the Past: The Arancibia Clavel Decision of the Argentine Supreme Court," *Oregon Review of International Law* 10, no. 1 (2008): 243–83; Francisco Martorell, *Operación Cóndor: El vuelo de la muerte* (Santiago, Chile: LOM Ediciones, 1999), 100–2.

Bibliography

Primary Sources—Argentine Government Documents (AGD)

Armed Forces
Committee on Refugee Eligibility
Ministry of Education and Justice
    Secretariat of Justice
    Sub-Secretariat of Legislative Affairs
Ministry of Foreign Relations (MRE)
    Eastern European Division
    Economics Division
    Foreign Affairs Department
    Foreign Policy, Director General
    General Directorate of International Bodies
    Human Rights Division
    International Relations Secretariat
    Judicial Affairs Division
    Latin American Affairs Division
    Special Social Affairs Division

Ministry of Health and Social Action
Ministry of Social Welfare
Ministry of the Interior
National Commission on Indigenous Policy
National Commission on the Disappeared
Presidency
    Council for the Consolidation of Democracy
State Intelligence Secretariat
Government of the Province of Tucumán

Interviews

Beltramino, Juan Carlos. Interview with David Sheinin. Buenos Aires, 28 July 2003.
Coggi, Juan Martín. Interview with David Sheinin. Buenos Aires, 17 July 2007.
García, Luis. Interview with David Sheinin. Buenos Aires, 5 July 2004.
Kahan, Emmanuel. Interview with David Sheinin. Tempe, Arizona, 13 June 2011.
Levin, Rosita. Interview with David Sheinin. Buenos Aires, 14 July 2004.
Palma, Sergio Victor. Interview with David Sheinin. Buenos Aires, 20 February 2008.
Sempé, Raúl Alconada. Interview with David Sheinin. Buenos Aires, 30 July 2004.

Newspapers and Magazines

Al Hamishar (Jerusalem)
Aurora (Tel Aviv)
Billiken (Buenos Aires)
Boston Globe Magazine
Canada Argentina Bulletin (Toronto)
Clarín (Buenos Aires)
Cronista Comercial (Buenos Aires)
Diario Perfil (Buenos Aires)
El Gráfico (Buenos Aires)
El País (Madrid)
El Periodista (Buenos Aires)
Gente (Buenos Aires)
Globe and Mail (Toronto)
Goles (Buenos Aires)
Goles Match (Buenos Aires)
Horizontes y convergencias (Córdoba)
Hoy (La Plata)
Journal de Genève (Geneva)
La Hora de Guatemala (Guatemala City)
La Mañana Neuquén (Neuquén)
La Nación (Buenos Aires)
La Razón (Buenos Aires)

Le Monde (Paris)
Logos (Rio de Janeiro)
New York Times
Noticias (Buenos Aires)
Página/12 (Buenos Aires)
Prensa Libre (Guatemala City)
Radiolandia 2000 (Buenos Aires)
Revista 10 (Buenos Aires)
Satiricón (Buenos Aires)
Semana (Buenos Aires)
Siete Dias (Buenos Aires)
The Nation (New York)
The National Jewish Monthly (Washington, D.C.)
Time (New York)
Ya (Madrid)

Other Primary Sources

Americas Watch and Centro de Estudios Legales y Sociales. *Police Violence in Argentina: Torture and Police Killings in Buenos Aires*. New York: Human Rights Watch, 1991.

Amnesty International. *Argentina: Further Evidence of Violations of Human Rights since the Military Coup of 24 March 1976*. London: Amnesty International, 1978.

———. *Argentina: The Military Juntas and Human Rights*. London: Amnesty International, 1987.

Amnesty International USA. *Visit Beautiful Argentina, but Remember the Forgotten Prisoners*. New York: Amnesty International, [1978].

Argentina. Congreso de la Nación. *Trámite parlamentario No. 2*. [Buenos Aires]: Imprenta del Congreso de la Nación, 1991.

Camps, Ramón J. A. *Caso Timerman: Punto Final*. Buenos Aires: Tribuna Abierta, 1982.

Comisión Interamericana de Derechos Humanos. *Informe, 1976*. Doc. OEA, Ser. L/V/II 40 doc. 5 del 11 de febrero 1977.

Comisión Nacional Sobre la Desaparición de Personas. *Nunca Más: Informe de la CONADEP*. Buenos Aires: EUDEBA, 1985.

Corte Suprema de la Nación (Supreme Court), Argentina [CSJN]. "Ekmekdjian, Miguel v. Sofovich" (Case No. 1992-315-1492), 07/07/1992.

Inter-American Commission on Human Rights. "Resolution 15/87. Case 9635." OEA/ser. L/V/II.71, Doc. 9, rev 1 (1987).

Mittlebach, Federico. *Informe sobre desaparecedores*. Buenos Aires: Ediciones de Urraca, 1986.

Organization of American States. Inter-American Commission on Human Rights. *Annual Report of the Inter-American Commission on Human Rights, 1979–1980*. OEA/Ser.L/V/II.50, Doc. 13, rev. 1 (2 October 1980). http://www.cidh.org/annualrep/79.80eng/toc.htm.

United Nations Working Group on Forced Disappearances. "Argentina: Information Reviewed and Transmitted to the Government." E/CN.4/1989/18, January 1989.

Secondary Sources

Aboy Carlés, Gerardo. *Las dos fronteras de la democracia argentina: La reformulación de las identidades políticas de Alfonsín a Menem.* Rosario: Homosapiens, 2001.

Aguilar Rubiano, Beira, and Angela Milena Salas Garcia. "Dictadura, transición, y experiencias locales de reparación: el caso argentino." In *El tránsito hacía la paz: de las herramientas nacionales a las locales,* edited by Camila de Gamboa Tapias, 30–65. Bogotá: Editorial Universidad del Rosario, 2010.

Alabarces, Pablo, and Carolina Duek. "Fútbol (argentino) por TV: entre el espectáculo de masas, el monopolio y el estado." *Logos* 17 (2010): 16–28.

Alam, Florencia. "Civilización/barbarie en los manuales de historia secundario." *Nómadas. Revista Crítica de Ciencias Sociales y Juridicas* 16 (2007): 393–401.

Alonso, Juan. *¿Quién mató a Aramburu?* Buenos Aires: Sudamericana, 2005.

Amorín, José. *Montoneros: La buena historia.* Buenos Aires: Catálogos, 2005.

Archetti, Eduardo P. "Estilo y virtudes masculinas en *El Gráfico*: la creación del imaginario del futbol argentino." *Desarrollo Económico,* 35 (1995): 419–42.

Armony, Ariel C. *Argentina, the United States, and the Anti-Communist Crusade in Central America, 1977–1984.* Athens: Ohio University Press, 1997.

———. "Transnationalizing the Dirty War." In *In from the Cold: Latin America's New Encounter with the Cold War,* edited by Gilbert M. Joseph and Daniela Spenser, 134–68. Durham, N.C.: Duke University Press, 2008.

Arnson, Cynthia. "The U.S. Congress and Argentina: Human Rights and Military Aid." In *Argentina-United States Bilateral Relations,* edited by Cynthia J. Arnson, 83–96. Washington, D.C.: Woodrow Wilson International Center for Scholars, 2003.

Arthur, Paige. "How 'Transitions' Reshaped Human Rights: A Conceptual History of Transitional Justice." *Human Rights Quarterly* 31, no. 2 (2009): 334–40.

Aruguete, Eugenia. "Lucha política y conflicto de clases en la posdictadura. Límites a la constitución de alianzas políticas durante la administración Alfonsín." In *Los años de Alfonsín ¿El poder de la democracia o la democracia del poder?* edited by Alfredo Pucciarelli, 413–60. Buenos Aires: Siglo XXI, 2006.

Avelar, Idelber. "Cómo respiran los ausentes: La narrativa de Ricardo Piglia." *MLN* 110, no. 2 (1995): 416–32.

———. *The Untimely Present: Postdictatorial Fiction and the Task of Mourning.* Durham, N.C.: Duke University Press, 1999.

Baisotti, Pablo. "La política de distensión a partir de los años 80 y el resurgimiento de la sociedad civil en Argentina." *Investigaciones Sociales* 10 (2006): 505–22.

Baker, Mark B. "The South American Legal Response to Terrorism." *Boston University International Law Journal* 67 (1985): 67–74.

Barromi, Joel. "Israeli Policies toward Argentina and Argentinian Jewry during the Military Junta, 1977–1983." *Israel Affairs* 5, no. 1 (1998): 27–44.

Basombrío, Cristina. "Estudiantes universitarios y esfera pública: la influencia del grupo de niño en el gobierno de Alfonsín." *Modernidades* 3 (December 2007). http://www.ffyh.unc.edu.ar/archivos/modernidades_a/VII/Revista_e-ModernidadesVII.htm.

Baud, Michiel. *El padre de la novia: Jorge Zorreguieta, la sociedad argentina y el régimen militar.* Buenos Aires: Fondo de Cultura Económica, 2001.

Bazan, Victor. "La problemática indígena y sus mutaciones constitucionales en Argentina." *Revista de Derecho Constitucional Latinoamericano* 8 (2004): 1–29.

Beltrán, Gastón J. "Acción empresaria e ideología. La génesis de las reformas estructurales." In *Los años de Alfonsín ¿El poder de la democracia o la democracia del poder?* edited by Alfredo Pucciarelli, 199–244. Buenos Aires: Siglo XXI, 2006.

Berardi, Mario. *La vida imaginada: vida cotidiana y cine argentino, 1933–1970.* Buenos Aires: Ediciones del Jilguero, 2006.

Bietti, Lucas M. "'Piercing Memories': Empty Spaces in the Histories of Argentinean Families—Personal Reflections." *Memory Studies* 4, no. 1 (January 2011): 83–87.

Blaustein, Eduardo, and Martín Zubieta. *Decíamos ayer. La prensa argentina bajo el proceso.* Buenos Aires: Colihue, 1998.

Bonasso, Miguel. "De los 'desaparecidos' a los 'chicos de la guerra.'" *Nueva Sociedad* 76 (1985): 52–61.

Borreli, Marcelo, and Jorge Saborido. "La prensa del 'Proceso.' El diario *Convicción* durante la dictadura militar argentina (1976–1983)." *Estudios sobre el Mensaje Periodístico* 14 (2008): 49–78.

Bratt, Duane. *The Politics of CANDU Exports.* Toronto: University of Toronto Press, 2006.

Bravo, Nazareno. "El discurso de la dictadura militar argentina (1976–1983). Definición del opositor político y confinamiento-'valorización' del papel de la mujer en el espacio privado." *Utopia y Praxis Latinoamericana* 8 (2003): 107–23.

Brennan, James P. "Industrial Sectors and Union Politics in Latin American Labor Movements: Light and Power Workers in Argentina and Mexico." *Latin American Research Review* 30, no. 1 (1995): 39–68.

Brinks, Daniel M. *The Judicial Response to Police Killings in Latin America: Inequality and the Rule of Law.* Cambridge, Mass.: Cambridge University Press, 2007.

Briones, Claudia. *La alteridad del "Cuarto Mundo": una deconstrucción antropológica de la diferencia.* Buenos Aires: Ediciones del Sol, 1998.

———. "Questioning State Geographies of Inclusion in Argentina: The Cultural Politics of Organizations with Mapuche Leadership and Philosophy." In *Cultural Agency in the Americas,* edited by Doris Sommer, 248–78. Durham, N.C.: Duke University Press, 2005.

Brunner, Lisl. "Leaning on International Law to Prosecute the Past: The Arancibia Clavel Decision of the Argentine Supreme Court." *Oregon Review of International Law* 10 (2008): 243–83.

Bruzonsky, Mark A., and Dale Gavlak. "Israel's War in Lebanon." *Middle East Journal* 38 (Winter 1984): 115–20.

Brysk, Alyson. *The Politics of Human Rights in Argentina: Protest, Change, and Democratization.* Stanford, Calif.: Stanford University Press, 1994.

———. "The Politics of Measurement: The Contested Count of the Disappeared in Argentina." *Human Rights Quarterly* 16, no. 4 (1994): 676–92.

Buffa, Diego. *El Africa subsahariana en la política exterior argentina: Las presidencias de Alfonsín y Menem.* Córdoba: Centro de Estudios Avanzados, Universidad Nacional de Córdoba, 2006.

Cabral, Estevao. "The Indonesian Propaganda War against East Timor." In *The East Timor Question,* edited by Paul Hainsworth and Stephen McCloskey, 69–84. London: I. B. Tauris Publishers, 2000.

Calandra, Benedetta. "Entre historia 'fría' y testimonios 'calientes': H.I.J.O.S. de los desaparecidos argentinos (1976–1983)." In *Memorias de la violencia en Uruguay y Argentina: golpes, dictaduras, exilios (1973–2006),* edited by Eduardo Rey Tristán, 309–16. Santiago de Compostela: Universidad de Santiago de Compostela, 2007.

Calveiro, Pilar. *Poder y desaparición: los campos de concentración en la Argentina.* Buenos Aires: Colihue, 2008.

Canaletti, Ricardo, and Rolando Barbano. *Todos mataron: génesis de la Triple A (el pacto siniestro entre la federal, el gobierno y la muerte).* Buenos Aires: Planeta, 2009.

Carrasco, Morita. *Los derechos de los pueblos indígenas en Argentina.* Buenos Aires: Vinciguerra, 2000.

Carrió, Genaro R. *El caso Timerman: materiales para el estudio de un "habeas corpus."* Buenos Aires: EUDEBA, 1987.

Caviglia, Mariana. *Dictadura, vida cotidiana y clases medias: una sociedad fracturada.* Buenos Aires: Prometeo Libros, 2006.

Ceruti, Leonidas F. *Cultura y dictadura en Rosario: 1976–1983.* Rosario: Ediciones del Castillo, 2010.

Chen, Tina Mai. "Socialism, Aestheticized Bodies, and International Circuits of Gender: Soviet Female Film Stars in the People's Republic of China, 1949–1969." *Journal of the Canadian Historical Association* 18, no. 2 (2007): 53–80.

Chiroleu, Adriana. "La política universitaria de Alfonsín y Menem: Entre la democracia y la equidad." *Revista del Instituto de Investigaciones en Ciencias de la Educación* 15 (1999): 21–32.

Cisneros, Andrés, and Carlos Escudé. *Historia General de las Relaciones Exteriores Argentinas.* Vol. 14. Buenos Aires: Grupo Editor Latinoamericano, 1999.

Clark, Ann Marie. *Diplomacy of Conscience: Amnesty International and Changing Human Rights Norms.* Princeton, N.J.: Princeton University Press, 2001.

"Conversation: Jacobo Timerman and Stanley Diamond." *Dialectical Anthropology* 8 (October 1983): 129–60.

Cook, Richard M. *Alfred Kazin: A Biography.* New Haven, Conn.: Yale University Press, 2008.

Corradi, Juan E. *The Fitful Republic: Economics, Society, and Politics in Argentina.* Boulder, Colo.: Westview Press, 1985.

Corral Talciani, Hernán Felipe. *Desaparición de personas y presunción de muerte en el derecho civil chileno.* Santiago de Chile: Editorial Jurídica de Chile, 2000.

Crawford, Kathryn Lee. "Due Obedience and the Rights of Victims: Argentina's Transition to Democracy." *Human Rights Quarterly* 12, no. 1 (1990): 17–52.

Crenzel, Emilio. "Between the Voices of the State and the Human Rights Movement: Never Again and the Memories of the Disappeared in Argentina." *Journal of Social History* 44 (2011): 1063–1076.

———. *La historia política del Nunca Más. La memoria de las desapariciones en la Argentina*. Buenos Aires: Siglo XXI, 2008.

Crespo, Victoria. "Legalidad y dictadura." In *Argentina, 1976: Estudios en torno al golpe de estado*, edited by Clara E. Lida, Horacio Crespo, and Pablo Yankelevich, 165–86. Buenos Aires: Fondo de Cultura Económica, 2008.

De Gamboa, Camila. "Entrevista a Jaime Malamud." *Semana*, 14–21 August 2005.

De la Torre, Adela, and Julia Mendoza. "Immigration Policy and Immigration Flows: A Comparative Analysis of Immigration Law in the U.S. and Argentina." *The Modern American* 3 (2007): 46–52.

Derby, Lauren. "The Dictator's Seduction: Gender and State Spectacle during the Trujillo Dictatorship." In *Latin American Popular Culture*, edited by William H. Beezley and Linda A. Curcio, 213–39. Wilmington: SR Books, 2000.

Diamint, Rut. "La historia sin fin: el control civil de los militares en Argentina." *Nueva Sociedad* 213 (2008): 95–111.

Donnelly, Jack. "Diplomatic Immunity: Jacobo Timerman's son Héctor says there's no such thing as an anti-Semitic country." *Tablet,* 29 January 2010.

Duhalde, Eduardo Luis. *El estado terrorista argentino. Quince años después, una mirada crítica*. Buenos Aires: EUDEBA, 1999.

Dutrénit Bielous, Silvia. "Represión política y asilo diplomático en el Cono Sur." In *El presente de la dictadura: Estudios y reflexiones a 30 años del golpe de Estado en Uruguay*, edited by Aldo Marchesi, Vania Markarian, Alvaro Rico, and Jaime Yaffé, 109–26. Montevideo: Ediciones Trilce, 2004.

Eaton, Kent. "Paradoxes of Police Reform: Federalism, Parties, and Civil Society in Argentina's Public Security Crisis." *Latin American Research Review* 43 (2008): 5–32.

"El argentino que zafó la pena de muerte." *Hoy*, 17 January 2004.

Elizondo, María Victória. "La construcción/deconstrucción de la memoria nacional a través de la cultura popular: El caso del programa argentino, *Peter Capusotto y sus videos* y del músico apócrifo, *Bombita Rodríguez, el Palito Ortega Montonero*." *452°F. Revista de teoría de la literatura y literatura comparada* 3 (2010): 102–14.

"El trágico ayuno." *La mañana Neuquén*, 31 January 2010.

Endere, María Luz. "The Reburial Issue in Argentina: A Growing Conflict." In *The Dead and Their Possessions: Repatriation in Principle, Policy and Practice*, edited by Cressida Fforde, Jane Hubert, and Paul Turnbull, 266–83. New York: Routledge, 2002.

Escudé, Carlos. *El realismo de los estados débiles*. Buenos Aires: Grupo Editor Latinoamericano, 1995.

———. "From Captive to Failed State: Argentina under Systemic Populism, 1975–2006." *The Fletcher Forum of World Affairs* 30 (Summer 2006): 125–47.

———. *Realismo periférico: Fundamentos para la nueva política exterior argentina*. Buenos Aires: Planeta, 1992.

Esquivada, Gabriela. *El diario noticias: los Montoneros en la prensa argentina*. La Plata, Argentina: Ediciones de Periodismo y Comunicación, 2004.

Fangio, Juan Manuel. *Fangio: My Racing Life*. London: Patrick Stephens, 1990.

Feierstein, Ricardo. *Contraexilio y mestizaje: ser judío en la Argentina*. Buenos Aires: Editorial Milá, 1996.

Feinmann, José Pablo. *López Rega: la cara oscura de Perón*. Buenos Aires: Legasa, 1987.

Feitlowitz, Marguerite. *A Lexicon of Terror: Argentina and the Legacies of Torture*. Oxford: Oxford University Press, 1998.

Felicitas Elías, María. "Derechos humanos, salud y trabajo social." *Anales, Primeras Jornadas Sobre Salud y Trabajo Social*, 1999, Argentina.

Fernández Meijide, Graciela. "¿Valió la pena la CONADEP?, si, volvería a hacerlo." *Derechos humanos: revista de la Asamblea Permanente por los Derechos Humanos* 21 (1989): 10.

Figari, Guillermo Miguel. *De Alfonsín a Menem: Política exterior y globalización*. Buenos Aires: Memphis, 1997.

Filc, Judith. *Entre el parentesco y la política: Familia y dictadura 1976–1983*. Buenos Aires: Biblos, 1997.

Fletcher, Lea. "El sexismo lingüístico y el uso acerca de la mujer." *Feminaria* 1 (1988): 29–32.

Flores, Marta. *La música popular en el Gran Buenos Aires*. Buenos Aires: Centro Editor de América Latina, 1993.

"Ford Falcon, modelo 76." *Página 12*, 26 February 2006.

Fournier, Dominique. "The Alfonsín Administration and the Promotion of Democratic Values in the Southern Cone and the Andes." *Journal of Latin American Studies* 31 (1999): 39–74.

Franco, Marina. "Between Urgency and Strategy: Argentine Exiles in Paris, 1976–1983." *Latin American Perspectives* 34 (2007): 50–67.

Franco, Marina, and Pilar González Bernaldo, "Cuando el sujeto deviene objeto: La construcción del exilio argentino en Francia." In *Represión y destierro: Itinerarios del exilio argentino*, edited by Pablo Yankelevich, 17–48. La Plata: Ediciones Al Margen, 2004.

Gaggiotti, Hugo. "La pampa rioplatense: un espacio degradado en el imaginario hispano-criollo." *Scripta Nova: Revísta electronic de geografía y ciencias sociales* 2 (1998): 14–31.

Galiani, Sebastián, Martín A. Rossi, and Ernesto Schargrodsky. "Conscription and Crime: Evidence from the Argentine Draft Lottery." *Fondazione Eni Enrico Mattei Working Papers*. Working Paper 444 (2010). www.bepress.com/feem/paper444.

Garaño, Santiago, and Werner Pertot. *Detenidos-aparecidos: presas y presos políticos desde Trelew a la dictadura*. Buenos Aires: Biblos, 2007.

Gárate, Manuel. "Tony Manero . . . 'Somos todos de la misma comuna.'" *Nuevo Mundo Mundos Nuevos, Imágenes en movimiento, 2008*. 12 November 2008. http://nuevomundo.revues.org/44173.

García, J. L. et al. *Fuerzas armadas argentinas: el cambio necesario*. Buenos Aires: Galerna, 1987.

"Genera controversias el pasado de un socio y asesor de Zaffaroni." *La Nación*, 9 October 2003.

Gilbert, Abel, and Miguel Vitagliano. *El terror y la gloria: la vida, el fútbol y la política en la Argentina del Mundial 78.* Buenos Aires: Grupo Editorial Norma, 1998.

Gociol, Judith, and Hernán Invernizzi. *Un golpe a los libros: represión a la cultura durante la última dictadura militar.* Buenos Aires: EUDEBA, 2002.

Goldstein, Slavko. *1941: Godina koja se vraća [1941: The Year That Keeps Returning].* Zagreb: Novi Liber, 1965.

Gómez, María Julieta. "El proceso militar de 1976–1983 en el imaginario social de San Luis, Argentina. Un estudio de casos." *Fundamentos en Humanidades* 3 (1998): 89–118.

González Janzen, Ignacio. *La triple-A.* Buenos Aires: Contrapunto, 1986.

Gordillo, Marta, and Víctor Lavagno. *Los hombres de Perón.* Buenos Aires: Puntosur, 1987.

Gringold, Laura. *Memoria, moral y derecho: el caso de Ingeniero Budge (1987–1994).* Mexico, DF: Juan Pablos Editor, S.A., 1997.

Gruber, Rosana. "Las manos de la memoria." *Desarrollo Económico* 36 (1996): 423–42.

Grupo de Estudios en Legislación Indígena. "A Possible Indigenism: The Limits of the Constitutional Amendment in Argentina." In *Decolonizing Indigenous Rights*, edited by Adolfo de Oliveira, 122–31. New York: Routledge, 2009.

Guest, Iain. *Behind the Disappearances: Argentina's Dirty War against Human Rights and the United Nations.* Philadelphia: University of Pennsylvania Press, 1990.

Guglielmucci, Ana. "Visibilidad e invisibilidad de la prisión política en Argentina: La 'cárcel vidriera' de Villa Devoto (1974–1983)." *A contracorriente* 4 (2007): 86–136.

"Guillermo Vilas . . . y él creó el tenis." *Grandes del Deporte Argentino (El Gráfico)*, 1991.

Guitelman, Paula. *La infancia en dictadura: modernidad y conservadurismo en el mundo de Billiken.* Buenos Aires: Prometeo libros, 2006.

Halperín-Donghi, Tulio. *The Peronist Revolution and Its Ambiguous Legacy.* Occasional Papers 17. London: Institute of Latin American Studies, 1998.

Hearn, Kelly. "Ford's Past in Argentina." *The Nation*, 8 May 2006.

Hecht, Ana Carolina. "Pueblos indígenas y escuela. Políticas homogeneizadoras y políticas focalizadas en la educación argentina." *Políticas Educativas* 1 (2007): 183–94.

"Héctor Timerman dirigía un diario que elogiaba a Videla." *Diario Perfil*, 3 November 2007.

Hinton, Mercedes S. "A Distant Reality: Democratic Policing in Argentina and Brazil." *Criminal Justice* 5 (2005): 75–100.

Hortiguera, Hugo. "News, Fiction and Marketing in the Time of Crisis: The Argentine Media and the Yabrán Case." *Argentinean Cultural Production During the Neoliberal Years (1989–2001)*, edited by Hugo Hortiguera and Carolina Rocha, 133–54. Lewiston, Me.: Edwin Mellen Press, 2007.

Howorth, Jolyon. "Consensus of Silence: The French Socialist Party and Defense Policy Under François Mitterand." *International Affairs* 60, no. 4 (1984): 579–600.

Hurtado de Mendoza, Diego. "De átomos para la paz a los reactores de potencia. Tecnología y política nuclear en la Argentina (1955–1976)." *Revista Iberoamericana de Ciencia, Tecnología y Sociedad* 4 (2005): 41–66.

Huyssen, Andreas. "The Mnemonic Art of Marcelo Brodsky." In *Nexo. Un ensayo fotográfico/A Photographic Essay by Marcelo Brodsky*, edited by Marcelo Brodsky, 7–11. Buenos Aires, La Marca Editora, 2001.

Inter-American Commission on Human Rights. *Inter-American Yearbook on Human Rights*. Amsterdam: Martinus Nijhoff, 1997.

Isla, Alejandro. "Terror, Memory and Responsibility in Argentina." *Critique of Anthropology* 18 (1998): 134–56.

Jakubowicz, Eduardo, and Laura Radetich. *La historia argentina a través del cine*. Buenos Aires: La Cruja, 2006.

Jelin, Elizabeth. "La matriz cultural argentina, el peronismo y la cotidianidad." In *Vida cotidiana y control institucional en la Argentina de los '90*, edited by Elizabeth Jelin et al., 25–40. Buenos Aires: Nuevohacer, 1996.

———. *Monumentos, memoriales y marcas territoriales*. Madrid: Siglo XXI, 2003.

———. "The Politics of Memory: The Human Rights Movement and the Construction of Democracy in Argentina." *Latin American Perspectives* 21, no. 2 (1994): 38–58.

Jordán, Alberto R. *El proceso, 1976–1983*. Buenos Aires: Emecé, 1993.

"Juan Manuel Fangio: una leyenda mundial." *Grandes del deporte argentino (El Gráfico)*, 1991.

Klepak, Hal. "The Inter-American Dimension of Future Canadian Security Policy." *Canadian Foreign Policy Journal* 5, no. 2 (1998): 107–28.

Lafourcade, Alejandro. "La revista *Humor* como medio opositor a la dictadura militar." Licenciatura thesis, Universidad El Salvador, Buenos Aires, 2004.

Landrú (Juan Carlos Colombres) and Edgardo Russo. *Landrú por Landrú*. Buenos Aires: El Ateneo, 1993.

Larkins, Christopher. "The Judiciary and Delegative Democracy in Argentina." *Comparative Politics* 30, no. 4 (1998): 423–42.

Larraquy, Marcelo, and Roberto Caballero. *Galimberti: De Perón a Susana, de Montoneros a la CIA*. Buenos Aires: Norma, 2000.

Lattuca, Ada. "La Patria Grande, ¿En la patria chica? Reflexiones sobre política migratoria argentina." *Cartapacio de Derecho* 10 (2006): 1–11.

Laudano, Claudia Nora. *Las mujeres en los discursos militares*. Buenos Aires: Editorial La Página, 1998.

Lelouche, Pierre. "France and the Euromissiles: The Limits of Immunity." *Foreign Affairs*, 62, no. 2 (1983): 318–34.

Lesgart, Cecilia N. "Luchas por los sentidos del pasado y el presente: Notas sobre la reconsideración actual de los años '70 y '80." In *Argentina 1976–2006: Entre la sombra de la dictadura y el futuro de la democracia*, edited by Hugo Quiroga and César Tcach, 167–98. Rosario: Homo Sapiens, 2006.

Levy, Daniel. "Recursive Cosmopolitization: Argentina and the Global Human Rights Regime." *British Journal of Sociology* 61, no. 3 (2010): 579–96.

Lewis, Paul H. *Guerrillas and Generals: The "Dirty War" in Argentina*. Westport: Praeger, 2002.

Lida, Clara. "Enfoques comparativos sobre los exilios en México: España y Argentina en el siglo XX." In *México, país refugio. La experiencia de los exilios en el siglo XX*, edited by Pablo Yankelevich, 205–17. Mexico City: Plaza y Valdes, 2002.

Llairó, María de Monserrat. "La crisis del Estado Benefactor y la Imposición Neoliberal en la Argentina de Alfonsín y Menem." *Aldea Mundo. Revista sobre Fronteras e Integración*, 11 (2006): 57–64.

Lombraña, Andrea N. "Análisis sobre la eficacia de la construcción de inimputabilidad en La Matanza de Lonco Luán: el poder de 'perdonar." *Horizontes y convergencias*, 29 March 2010.

López, Ernesto. *Seguridad nacional y sedición militar.* Buenos Aires: Editorial Legasa, 1987.

Loveman, Brian. "'Protected Democracies' and Military Guardianship: Political Transitions in Latin America, 1978–1983." *Journal of Inter-American Studies and World Affairs* 36, no. 2 (1994): 105–89.

Ludvigsen, Karl. *Juan Manuel Fangio: Motor Racing's Grand Master.* Newbury Park, Calif.: Haynes Publishing, 1999.

Madero, Marcela, and Egie Piedrafita. "La prensa: Los Derechos humanos en noticias." In *Los derechos humanos en la Argentina: Del ocultamiento a la interpelación política*, edited by Norma Fóscolo, 39–89. Buenos Aires: Editorial de la Universidad Nacional de Cuyo, 2000.

Madres de Plaza de Mayo—Línea Fundadora. *¡Presentes! ¡Ahora y Siempre!* Buenos Aires: Colihue, 2007.

Mandler, John P. "Habeas Corpus and the Protection of Human Rights in Argentina." *Yale Journal of International Law* 16 (1991): 3–34.

Marenghi, Patricia, and Laura Pérez López. "Prensa española y dictadura argentina (1976–1983): La imagen del exilio en *ABC, El País,* y *Triunfo." América Latina Hoy* 34 (2003): 49–78.

Martínez, Felipe, Juan S. Montes Cató, Javier M. Real, and Nicolás Wachsmann. "La Revolución Libertadora y el intento por eliminar al peronismo del imaginario de los trabajadores." In *Cine e imaginario social*, edited by Fortunato Mallimacci and Irene Marrone, 265–81. Buenos Aires: Oficina de Publicaciones del CBC, 1997.

Martorell, Elvira. "Recuerdos del presente: memoria e identidad (una reflexión en torno a HIJOS)." In *Memorias en presente: Identidad y transmisión en la Argentina posgenocidio*, edited by Sergio J. Guelerman, 133–70. Buenos Aires: Norma, 2001.

Martorell, Francisco. *Operación Cóndor: El vuelo de la muerte.* Santiago, Chile: LOM Ediciones, 1999.

Masi Rius, Andrés Alberto, and Eduardo Aníbal Pretel Eraso. "Fuerzas armadas y transición democrática argentina, 1983–1989." *Historia Actual Online* 13 (2007): 89–97.

Mazal Nuthes, Roberto. "La libertad religiosa y el derecho migratorio." Presentación en el IX Coloquio Anual del Consorcio Latino Americano de Libertad Religiosa de Septiembre de 2009, Montevideo, Uruguay.

Mazzei, Daniel Horacio. "Primera Plana: modernización y golpismo en los 60." In *Historia de las revistas argentinas*, edited by Asociación Argentina de Editores de Revistas, 13–35. Buenos Aires: Asociación Argentina de Editores de Revistas, 1995.

McSherry, J. Patrice. *Incomplete Transition: Military Power and Democracy in Argentina*. New York: St. Martin's Press, 1997.

Mellibovsky, Matilde. *Circle of Love over Death: Testimonies of the Mothers of the Plaza de Mayo*. Willimantic: Curbstone Press, 1997.

Mendoza, Marcela. "Western Toba Messianism and Resistance to Colonialism, 1915–1918." *Ethnohistory* 51, no. 2 (2004): 293–316.

Mignone, Emilio F. *Iglesia y dictadura: el papel de la Iglesia a la luz de sus relaciones con el régimen militar*. Buenos Aires: Colihue, 2006.

Mochkofsky, Graciela. *Timerman: el periodista que quiso ser parte del poder*. Buenos Aires: Sudamericana, 2003.

Molinari, Aldo Luis. *Aramburu: La verdad sobre su muerte*. Buenos Aires: Talleres Gráficos Valdez, 1993.

Moneta, Carlos J. "El conflicto de las Islas Malvinas en el contexto de la política exterior argentina." In *América Latina y la guerra del Atlántico sur: experiencias y desafíos*, edited by Roberto Russell. Buenos Aires: Editorial de Belgrano, 1984.

Montero, Julio. "Derechos humanos y democracia: Un cambio de paradigma a dos décadas de distancia." In *Pensar la democracia, imaginar la transición (1976/2006)*, edited by Cecilia Macón, 49–62. Buenos Aires: Ladosur, 2006.

Morales Urra, Roberto. "Cultura Mapuche y Represión en Dictadura." *Revista Austral de Ciencias Sociales* 3 (1999): 81–108.

Muchnik, Daniel. *Los últimos cuarenta años: Argentina a la deriva*. Buenos Aires: Capital Intelectual, 2004.

Munck, Gerardo L. *Authoritarianism and Democratization: Soldiers and Workers in Argentina*. Philadelphia: University of Pennsylvania Press, 1998.

Mustapic, Ana M., and Mateo Goretti. "Gobierno y oposición en el Congreso: La práctica de la cohabitación durante la presidencia de Alfonsín (1983–1989)." *Desarrollo Económico*, 32 (1992): 251–69.

Nelson, Diane M. *A Finger in the Wound: Body Politics in Quincentennial Guatemala*. Berkeley: University of Los Angeles Press, 1999.

Nino, Carlos. *Juicio al mal absoluto. Los fundamentos y la historia del juicio a las juntas del proceso*. Buenos Aires: Emecé, 1997.

Norden, Deborah Lee. *Military Rebellion in Argentina: Between Coups and Consolidation*. Lincoln: University of Nebraska Press, 1996.

Novaro, Marcos, and Alejandro Avenburg. "La CIDH en Argentina: Entre la democratización y los derechos humanos." *Desarrollo Económico*, 49 (2009): 61–90.

Novaro, Marcos, and Vicente Palermo. *La dictadura militar (1976–1983): Del golpe de Estado a la restauración democrática*. Buenos Aires: Paidós, 2003.

Nye, Joseph S. "New Approaches to Nuclear Proliferation Policy." *Science* 256, no. 5061 (26 May 1992): 1293–97.

Paoletti, Alipio. *Como los Nazis, como en Vietnam*. Buenos Aires: Contrapunto, 1987.

Paradiso, José. *Debates y trayectoria de la política exterior argentina*. Buenos Aires: Grupo Editor Latinoamericano, 1993.

Partnoy, Alicia. *The Little School: Tales of Disappearance & Survival in Argentina*. Pittsburgh: Cleis Press, 1986.

Payne, Leigh A. "Perpetrators' Confessions: Truth, Reconciliation, and Justice in Argentina." In *What Justice? Whose Justice? Fighting for Fairness in Latin America*, edited by Susan Eva Eckstein and Timothy P. Wickham-Crowley, 158–84. Berkeley: University of California Press, 2003.

Pelacoff, Javier. "La identidad como paradoja, o del remozado sentido de la figura del judío errante." In *La cultura en la Argentina de fin de siglo: Ensayos sobre la dimensión cultural*, edited by Mario Margulis and Marcelo Urresti, 83–94. Buenos Aires: Oficina de Publicaciones del CBC, Universidad de Buenos Aires, 1997.

———. "La oposición obrera a la dictadura (1976–1982)." *Imago Mundi*, 12 February 2008, 1–10

Petrakis, Marina. *The Metaxas Myth: Dictatorship and Propaganda in Greece*. London: Tauris Academic Studies, 2006.

Piglia, Ricardo. *Artificial Respiration*. Translated by Daniel Balderston. Durham, N.C.: Duke University Press, 1994.

———. *Respiración artificial*. Buenos Aires: Editorial Pomaine, 1980.

Pion-Berlin, David. "Between Confrontation and Accommodation: Military and Government Policy in Democratic Argentina." *Journal of Latin American Studies* 23, no. 3 (1991): 543–71.

Plotkin, Mariano Ben. *Freud in the Pampas: The Emergence and Development of a Psychoanalytic Culture in Argentina*. Stanford, Calif.: Stanford University Press, 2001.

Poe, Steven C., Sabine C. Carey, and Tanya C. Vazquez. "How Are These Pictures Different? A Quantitative Comparison of the US State Department and Amnesty International Human Rights Reports, 1976–1995." *Human Rights Quarterly* 23, no. 3 (2001): 650–77.

Portantiero, Juan Carlos, and Germán Bidart Campos. "La cuestión social en la transición a la democracia." In *Política social y democracia*, edited by Raúl Alfonsín et al., 13–24. Quilmes: Universidad Nacional de Quilmes, 1997.

Posse, Able. "La política internacional y los recursos naturales y culturales." In *Siete escenarios para el siglo XXI*, edited by Fernando López-Alves and Daniel Dessein, 80–98. Buenos Aires: Sudamericana, 2004.

Pozzi, Pablo A. *El PRT-ERP: La guerrilla marxista*. Buenos Aires: EUDEBA, 2001.

Quirós, Carlos. *Guia Radical*. Buenos Aires: Editorial Galerna, 1986.

Rabotnikof, Nora. "Memoria y política a treinta años del golpe." In *Argentina, 1976: Estudios en torno al golpe de estado*, edited by Clara E. Lida, Horacio Crespo, and Pablo Yankelevich, 259–84. Buenos Aires: Fondo de Cultura Económica, 2008.

Ranalletti, Mario. "La construcción del relato de la historia argentina en el cine, 1983–1989." *Film-Historia* 9 (1999): 3–15.

Rein, Raanan, and Efraim David. "'Exile of the World': Israeli Perceptions of Jacobo Timerman." *Jewish Social Studies: History, Culture, Society* 16, no. 3 (2010): 1–31.

Rial, Jorge. *El intruso: Todo lo que usted quiere saber sobre la farándula, el deporte y la política*. Buenos Aires: Planeta, 2001.

Riding, Alan. *And the Show Went On: Cultural Life in Nazi-Occupied Paris*. New York: Knopf, 2010.

Rivanera Carles, Federico. *Las escuelas judías comunistas en Argentina*. Buenos Aires: Biblioteca de formación política, 1986.

Robert, Karen. "The Falcon Remembered." *NACLA: Report on the Americas* 38, no. 3 (2005): 12–15.

Roehrig, Terence. *The Prosecution of Former Military Leaders in Newly Democratic Nations*. Jefferson, N.C.: McFarland, 2002.

Rojkind, Inés. "La revista *Controversia*: reflexión y polémica entre los argentinos exiliados en México." In *Represión y destierro: itinerarios del exilio argentino*, edited by Pablo Yankelevich, 223–52. La Plata: Ediciones Al Margen, 2004.

Romero, Luis Alberto. "La democracia y la sombra del *Proceso*." In *Argentina 1976–2006: Entre la sombra de la dictadura y el futuro de la democracia*, edited by Hugo Quiroga and César Tcach, 15–30. Rosario: Homo Sapiens, 2006.

Roniger, Luis, and Mario Sznajder. *The Legacy of Human Rights Violations in the Southern Cone: Argentina, Chile, and Uruguay*. Oxford: Oxford University Press, 1999.

Ruetalo, Victoria. "From Penal Institution to Shopping Mecca: The Economics of Memory and the Case of Punta Carretas." *Cultural Critique* 68 (Winter 2008): 38–65.

Russell, Roberto. "El proceso de toma de decisiones en la política exterior argentina (1976–1989)." In *Política exterior y toma de decisiones en América Latina*, edited by Roberto Russell, 13–59. Buenos Aires: Grupo Editor Latinoamericano, 1990.

Saavedra, Marisol. *La Argentina no alineada: desde la tercera posición justicialista hasta el menemismo (1973–1991)*. Buenos Aires: Biblos, 2004.

Saborido, Jorge. "El antisemitismo en la historia argentina reciente: La revista *Cabildo* y la conspiración judía." *Revista complutense de historia de América*, 30 (2004): 209–23.

Salvatore, Ricardo D. *Imágenes de un imperio: Estados Unidos y las formas de representación de América Latina*. Buenos Aires: Sudamericana, 2006.

Schackt, Jon. "Mayahood through Beauty: Indian Beauty Pageants in Guatemala." *Bulletin of Latin American Research* 24, no. 3 (2005): 269–87.

Schirmer, Jennifer G. "'Those Who Die for Life Cannot be Called Dead': Women and Human Rights Protest in Latin America." *Feminist Review* 32 (1989): 3–29.

Scorer, James. "From la *guerra sucia* to 'A Gentleman's Fight': War, Disappearance and Nation in the 1976–1983 Argentine Dictatorship." *Bulletin of Latin American Research* 27 (2008): 43–60.

Seoane, María. *El burgués maldito*. Buenos Aires: Planeta, 1998.

Sevillano Calero, Francisco. "Cultura, propaganda y opinion en el primer franquismo." In *El primer franquismo (1936–1959)*, edited by Glicerio Sánchez Recio, 147–66. Madrid: Marcial Pons, 1999.

Sheinin, David. *Argentina and the United States: An Alliance Contained*. Athens: University of Georgia Press, 2006.

———. "Nuclear Development and the Shaping of an Independent Argentine Foreign Policy, 1950–1990." *Estudios Interdiciplinarios de América Latina y el Caribe* 16 (December 2005): 37–62.

Sirvén, Pablo. *Quién te ha visto y quién TV*. Buenos Aires: Ediciones de la Flor, 1998.

Snyder, Timothy. *Bloodlands: Europe between Hitler and Stalin*. New York: Basic Books, 2010.

Solingen, Etel. *Industrial Policy, Technology, and International Bargaining: Designing Nuclear Industries in Argentina and Brazil.* Stanford, Calif.: Stanford University Press, 1996.

Sosenski, Susana. "Guardianes de la memoria. La conmemoración del golpe militar entre los exiliados argentinos en México." *Economía, Sociedad y Territorio* 5 (2005): 379–81.

Tal, Tzvi. *Pantallas y revolución: una visión comparativa del cine de liberación y el cínema novo.* Buenos Aires: Ediciones Lumiere, 2005.

Taylor, Diane. *Disappearing Acts: Spectacles of Gender and Nationality in Argentina's "Dirty War."* Durham, N.C.: Duke University Press, 1997.

Timerman, Jacobo. *The Longest War.* London: Chatto and Windus, 1982.

———. *Prisoner without a Name, Cell without a Number.* New York: Alfred A. Knopf, 1981.

Touraine, Marisol. "La représentation de l'adversaire dans la politique extérieure française depuis 1981." *Revue française de science politique* 43 (1993): 807–22.

Ubertalli, Jorge L. et al. *El complot militar: un país en obediencia debida.* Buenos Aires: Ediciones Dialéctica, 1987.

Ulanovsky, Carlos. *Paren las rotativas.* Buenos Aires: Espasa, 1977.

Ulanovsky, Carlos, Silvia Itkin, and Pablo Sirvén. *Estamos en el aire: una historia de la television en la Argentina.* Buenos Aires: Planeta, 1999.

United Nations. Office of the High Commissioner on Human Rights. *Human Rights and Prisons: A Compilation of International Human Rights Instruments Concerning the Administration of Justice.* New York: UN Publications, 2005.

Urrutia, Carolina. "Hacia una política en tránsito. Ficción en el cine chileno (2008–2010)." *Aisthesis* 47 (2010): 33–44.

Van Zyl Smit, Dirk. "Punishment and Human Rights in International Criminal Justice." *Human Rights Law Review* 2, no. 1 (2002): 1–17.

Vargas, Horacio. *Reutemann: el conductor.* Rosario: Homo Sapiens Ediciones, 1997.

Vázquez, Inés. "Aspectos de Memoria y Cultura en la Argentina postdictatorial." In *Un país, 30 años: el pañuelo sigue hacienda historia,* edited by Inés Vázquez and Karina Downie, 201–17. Buenos Aires: Ediciones Madres de Plaza de Mayo, 2006.

Verbitsky, Horacio. *Ezeiza.* Buenos Aires: Contrapunto, 1985.

———. *La última batalla de la tercera guerra mundial.* Buenos Aires: Legasa, 1987.

Vezzetti, Hugo. *Pasado y presente: guerra, dictadura y sociedad en la Argentina.* Buenos Aires: Siglo XXI, 2002.

Viglietti, Daniel. "Reflexiones en torno al exilio desde el ámbito cultural e intelectual." In *Memorias de la violencia en Uruguay y Argentina: golpes, dictaduras, exilios (1973–2006),* edited by Eduardo Rey Tristán, 259–70. Santiago de Compostela: Universidad de Santiago de Compostela, 2007.

Vilanova, Mercedes. "Rememoración y fuentes orales." In *Historia, memoria y fuentes orales,* edited by Vera Carnovale, Federico Lorenz, and Roberto Pittaluga, 91–110. Buenos Aires: Ediciones Memoria Abierta, 2006.

Weissbrodt, David. "Country-Related and Thematic Developments at the 1988 Session of the UN Commission on Human Rights." *Human Rights Quarterly* 10, no. 4 (1988): 544–58.

Wright, Pablo G. "Colonización del espacio, la palabra y el cuerpo en el Chaco argentino." *Horizontes Antropológicos* 9 (2003): 137–52.

Zaffaroni, Eugenio Raúl, and Ricardo Juan Cavallero. *Derecho Penal Militar*. Buenos Aires: Editorial Ariel, 1980.

Zellick, Graham. "Prison Offences." *British Journal of Criminology* 20, no. 4 (2004): 377–84.

Zur, Judith. "The Psychological Effects of Impunity: The Language of Denial." In *Impunity in Latin America*, edited by Rachel Seider, 57–72. London: Institute of Latin American Studies, 1995.

Index

David M. K. Sheinin is professor of history at Trent University (Canada), recipient of the 2013 Arthur P. Whitaker Award for *Consent of the Damned*, and a member of the Argentine National Academy of History, the Martin Institute for Peace Studies and Conflict Resolution (University of Idaho), and Eloisa Cartonera (Argentina). He is the author of *Argentina and the United States: An Alliance Contained* and *El boxeador incrédulo* (The Incredulous Boxer). He is a past president of the Middle Atlantic Council of Latin American Studies, and in 2008 he served as Edward Larocque Tinker Visiting Professor at the University of Wisconsin–Madison.

The University Press of Florida is the scholarly publishing agency for the State University System of Florida, comprising Florida A&M University, Florida Atlantic University, Florida Gulf Coast University, Florida International University, Florida State University, New College of Florida, University of Central Florida, University of Florida, University of North Florida, University of South Florida, and University of West Florida.